LEADERS & LESSER MORTALS

LEADERS & LESSER MORTALS

BACKROOM POLITICS IN CANADA

JOHN LASCHINGER
GEOFFREY STEVENS

KEY PORTER BOOKS

For Carol and Lin

The publisher gratefully acknowledges the assistance of the Canada Council.

Canadian Cataloguing in Publication Data
Laschinger, John
    Leaders and lesser mortals : backroom politics in Canada

Includes index.
ISBN 1-55013-444-2

1. Electioneering – Canada.   2. Campaign management – Canada.   3. Political corruption – Canada.
I. Stevens, Geoffrey, 1942–   . II. Title.

JL193.L38 1992   324.7'0971   C92-094706-9
                      76218

Key Porter Books Limited
70 The Esplanade
Toronto, Ontario
Canada M5E 1R2

Typesetting: Computer Composition of Canada Inc.

Printed and bound in Canada by John Deyell Company Limited.

92 93 94 95 96   6 5 4 3 2 1

Contents

Preface

In the spring of 1973, Geoffrey Stevens, then writing from Ottawa on national political affairs on the editorial page of the Toronto *Globe and Mail*, wrote a column about Robert Stanfield's search for a new national director for the Progressive Conservative Party. Under the headline "Wanted: Masochist," the column began as a mock careers-page advertisement:

> **Wanted:**
> A politically-oriented masochist to take over administration of one of Canada's national political parties. He will be prepared to sacrifice family, work evenings and travel weekends. Ability to fend off his party's creditors a definite asset. Loyalty to the leader essential. Salary: $20,000-$25,000. No pension plan; other fringe benefits negligible. Apply to the Leader of the Opposition, Ottawa.

Stanfield was not besieged with applicants for the national director's position, which in those days ranked among the most thankless in Canadian politics. John Laschinger, a thirty-year-old product manager from IBM Canada, had minimal political experience, having been a volunteer in the Ontario Tories' 1971 election campaign and an advanceman for Stanfield in Atlantic Canada during the 1972 federal election. But Laschinger was invited to apply and he got the job. His appointment was greeted with surprise by experienced political operatives and with suspicion by Stevens, who wrote another column that asked why a supposedly up-and-coming young computer company manager would forsake the income and security of IBM for the "unpredictable, unremunerative and at times unpleasant backrooms of politics." The column ended with a sneering suggestion that there must be something funny going on at IBM — "On the day that Mr. Laschinger quit IBM to become a full-time politician, one of his colleagues also resigned — to open a nudist camp in Quebec."

From that inauspicious beginning grew a friendship based on a shared interest in politics, politicians and the functioning of the political process. Over the years, Laschinger, who left the national director's job in 1978, has run nine election campaigns and eleven leadership campaigns in Ottawa and seven provinces. Today, he is Canada's only full-time professional political campaign manager. Stevens wrote the *Globe*'s Ottawa column until 1981 when he moved into the newspaper's management, serving as managing editor from 1983 to 1989; today, he writes on national affairs for the Montreal *Gazette* and *Toronto Star*.

Leaders and Lesser Mortals combines the perspectives of Laschinger, the political insider, and Stevens, the journalistic voyeur. The book, however, would not have been possible without the assistance and co-operation of a great many individuals from the backrooms and frontrooms of all political parties. Most are identified in the chapter notes at the end of the book. We thank all of them for generously sharing their time and experiences.

We owe particular thanks to Christine Jackson, the director of communications at Elections Canada, who cheerfully dug out all information we requested on election results and party financing; Jean-Marc Hamel, the former Chief Electoral Officer of Canada, who knows more about elections and campaign laws than anyone in the country; Richard Rochefort, communications director of the Royal Commission on Electoral Reform and Party Financing; and F. Leslie Seidle, the royal commission's senior research co-ordinator. Sue Johnston enthusiastically typed the transcripts of our interviews, a task made daunting at times by background noise that tended to drown out interviews taped in the native habitat of backroom politicians: hotel lobbies, cafes and bars.

Jennifer Glossop was a sensitive, constructive editor and a thorough pleasure to work with. Our agent, Jan Whitford of the Lucinda Vardey Agency, was an immense help in organizing our approach to the subject and keeping us on track over the many months it took to research, write and rewrite the book.

Finally, we owe a special debt of gratitude to the late Nancy McLean, a media consultant and widely respected backroom veteran. Although she had one of the best political success records of anyone in her field, McLean was virtually unknown to the public. She believed in keeping her work for her clients confidential. But she agreed to be interviewed, talked to the authors at length and was eagerly anticipating publication of the book. She died of a heart attack on June 12, 1992, at the age of forty-nine. In his eulogy, Senator Norman Atkins, the head of the Tories' Big Blue Machine, described Nancy McLean as "simply the best at what she did."

There are many unsung heroes like Nancy McLean in the backrooms of Canadian politics. They are joined by the bonds that unite insiders. They see a side of politics that the public rarely, if ever, sees. The public, for example, was not there the day in 1974 when Bob Stanfield rejected a proposal to put the federal Tory party into bankruptcy. It was not there in 1979 with Pierre Trudeau as he tried to nurse his wounded pride while fighting an election he could not win — and all anyone cared about was his reaction to the just-published memoirs of his unfaithful young wife. It was not there in Saskatchewan on that memorable day in 1972 when Tory party poohbahs from Toronto, bristling with self-importance, found themselves being welcomed to Regina as leaders of a gay rights movement.

The public was not there in 1969 when Joey Smallwood, fighting desperately to save his job, emptied the hospitals in Newfoundland to pack the meetings that elected delegates to the provincial Liberal leadership convention. It was not there in 1985 when Frank Miller, the last Tory premier of Ontario, made the hard choice and turned down the one strategy that might have extended the Tories' forty-two-year rule at Queen's Park. And the public was not there on that November afternoon in 1988 when Robin Sears, flipping channels on a TV set at NDP campaign headquarters, discovered to his horror what Mulroney's Conservatives were doing on daytime television in Quebec.

Leaders and Lesser Mortals is our invitation to join us on a voyage of discovery through the backrooms of Canadian politics.

JOHN LASCHINGER
GEOFFREY STEVENS

PART ONE

THE BACKROOM

MARCH 2, 1972, WAS A FESTIVE OCCASION AT THE Alberta Legislature in Edmonton. The thirty-six-year reign of the Alberta Social Credit Party had come to an abrupt end late the previous summer. A new Progressive Conservative government under Peter Lougheed had taken office. Now, the galleries were filled with relatives, friends, and well-wishers as the Legislature opened with the Lougheed government's first Speech from the Throne.

As he looked over the dignitaries seated for the opening in rows of chairs on the floor of the chamber, Lougheed was pleased to see that no one recognized a tall, nondescript man who was sitting directly in front of Harry Strom, Socred ex-premier of the province.

Lougheed was also amused. The man was Bob Dinkel, a lawyer from Calgary, who had been the manager of the Tories' triumphant election campaign. Bob Dinkel was the boss of the Lougheed backroom. He was the man nobody knew.

1. THE VIEW FROM THE BACKROOM

"If public life is the noblest of all callings, it is the vilest of all trades."
— Historian Goldwin Smith, 1861

In the fall of 1977, two hired guns from Progressive Conservative headquarters in Ottawa flew to Halifax to lend a hand to the Nova Scotia Tories. John Laschinger was the national director, responsible for the federal party's backroom organization across Canada. Allan Gregg was an obscure researcher, a recent product of Carleton University, who had developed a polling program for the Tories, using borrowed computer time at the university.

Gregg was nervous. He had never met John Buchanan, the affable, decidedly undynamic politician who had been leading the Nova Scotia Conservatives for six unspectacular years. Although some Tories were inclined to write off Buchanan, the three thick black binders in Gregg's lap suggested other possibilities. They contained the results of the first poll Gregg had ever done of political opinion in Nova Scotia, and they showed Buchanan's Tories four percentage points ahead of Premier Gerald Regan's Liberals. They also contained Gregg's analysis of the political situation in Nova Scotia, with detailed advice on everything Buchanan would have to do during the next year if he wanted to be premier.

As the odd couple — Laschinger in his pinstripes and Gregg in his customary scruffy jacket, open shirt, and ponytail — were disembarking from the plane, the pollster stopped. Furtively, he removed a gold earring from his ear. He looked embarrassed when

Laschinger saw him doing it. "I've never met Mr. Buchanan before," Gregg said. "I don't know how he'll take the earring."

Buchanan took the advice Gregg and Laschinger had to offer that day. Among other things, they told him that his recognition level was extremely low. Even though he had been leader of the opposition for six years, Nova Scotians were largely unaware of his existence. Those who had heard of him knew virtually nothing about him beyond the fact that he was a politician; in polling terminology, he lacked "definition." Gregg and Laschinger advised Buchanan to concentrate on making himself known, on getting his picture in the newspapers by participating in public events where photographers would be present. They did not anticipate that Buchanan, in obedience to their instructions, would within two weeks enter a charity bicycle race in which he would run down a child (who, fortunately, was unhurt), fly over his handlebars, and land on his head. But he got his picture on the front pages, albeit bleeding profusely from a gash on his forehead that took twenty-seven stitches to close.

Time cycles on. Despite his misadventures, Buchanan won the Nova Scotia election ten months later. He served as premier for the next twelve years, until, having exhausted the patience of the public and facing certain defeat whenever he chose to call an election, he grabbed a life-preserver thrown by Prime Minister Brian Mulroney. He entered the political twilight zone of the Senate of Canada, there to help secure the passage of the goods and services tax.

Allan Gregg became bigger than Buchanan. He went on to found Decima Research and to establish himself as Canada's first celebrity pollster, a star in the arcane world of "target-voter profiles," "strategic alliances," "conjoint analyses," and "psychographic segments." Today, Gregg, with his leather outfits and gold chains, is in constant demand for speeches and television appearances — a shaggy-headed prophet to an uptight nation in search of its soul. Today, the researcher who grew up to become a guru removes his earring for no politician.

The emergence of political pollsters and party strategists as public figures and media stars — coupled with the publication of reminiscences by such insiders as Keith Davey, Patrick Gossage, and Eddie Goodman — was a phenomenon of the 1980s. It seemed as though the windows of the party backrooms — those legendary smoke-filled dens where deals were cut, cash was dispensed, and favors were sold for votes — were being thrown open.

Despite the illusion of openness, however, the real work of the backrooms is still conducted in secret by men (mostly) and women (a few) who are accountable to no one but the leader and the party they serve.

The backroom is the heart of the political party. It does not matter if the party is large or small; national, regional, or provincial; mainstream or protest; successful or unsuccessful. If it is a political party, it has a backroom. The backroom is the engine that makes the party run. It is where the money is raised and largely where it is spent. It is where the polling is commissioned and the results massaged, where candidates are recruited (or discouraged), where the election platform is packaged, where the campaign plan is conceived and developed, and where the leader's travel is organized. It is where the media strategy is plotted, television debates are rehearsed, and TV commercials are devised and tested.

Politicians tend not to talk about the "backroom." They usually avoid the term because it implies something hidden, clandestine, forbidden, and faintly illicit — like the backrooms of the Prohibition era where something more potent than tea was available, or like gambling dens and betting parlors hidden in the rear of ostensibly respectable businesses. To most North Americans, talk of backroom politics still conjures up visions of New York's Tammany Hall or Chicago's Democratic machine in the heyday of Mayor Richard Daley, Sr.

To many people, backroom politics carries a connotation of sleaziness combined with ruthlessness, characteristics that distinguished the Republican party backroom in the days when it was run by Richard Nixon's most intimate confidant, Charles W. Colson, the strategist-organizer who proudly declared, "I would walk over my grandmother if necessary to help Richard Nixon."

It was the politics of the backroom that gave the "noblest calling" the reputation of being a vile trade, as Goldwin Smith, the nineteenth-century Oxford historian who settled in Toronto, believed. Lester Pearson expressed similar sentiments a century later when he left a dazzling diplomatic career for the rough and tumble of partisan politics. At the Liberal party's famous thinkers' conference in Kingston, Ontario, in 1960, Pearson, then his party's leader, remarked that politics was "the most important of all secular callings; yet it is one in which many men and women of integrity and ability scorn to participate actively. It is considered as a rather unworthy pursuit — like running a confidence game or managing a prize fighter in New York."

The public's low opinion of the political process has not improved in the years since Pearson led the country. That opinion, in fact, has sunk ever lower. From his polling in 1980, Allan Gregg found that 51 per cent of Canadians held a favorable impression of politicians; by 1990, the figure was down to 32 per cent, and falling. In 1980, more than 50 per cent believed that politicians cared about people; by 1990, only 16 per cent still believed it.

Over the past two decades, the most renowned, and efficient, backroom operation in Canada was the Conservatives' Ontario-centred "Big Blue Machine." The label was invented by a journalist and it stuck. Its members, however, never talked about the Big Blue Machine or publicly acknowledged its existence. They preferred to refer to themselves in such banal terms as "just a group of like-minded people trying to help to provide good, moderate government." "They really believed that," said one of the Big Blue Machinists, managing to keep a straight face.

Depending on the party and the circumstances, the backroom may be known by a variety of euphemisms. It may be called the "organization," the "strategy committee," the "election preparedness committee," the "campaign planning committee," the "campaign committee," the "7:00 a.m. committee" or the "breakfast committee" (a campaign committee that meets over breakfast every day during an election), the "functional operations group," the "Sunday afternoon group," or the "leader's advisory committee" (also known as the "kitchen cabinet"). To the troops in the field, the backroom may simply be known by the generic appellation "headquarters" — as in, "Headquarters Says Tour Will Be Advancing the Event for the Boss" (Translation: Get ready. The directors of the national campaign have advised that the managers of the leader's tour will be dispatching advancemen to make the lives of local campaign-committee volunteers miserable as they finalize arrangements for the public meeting that is scheduled during the leader's forthcoming visit to town).

Whatever it is called, the backroom is a room with a view — a unique view of the political process. It is an insider's view of politicians, policy, and strategy, and it is always colored by the imperative of winning the contest at hand.

To those in the backroom, winning is everything. Even such important issues as party policy are tangential to the strategists of the backroom. Similarly, crusades such as the advancement of women in Canadian public life may be of major concern to the public, but they are secondary in the backroom. Given a choice between a male candidate and a female candidate, the backroom organizer will choose the one with the best chance of winning; most times — most backroomers being men — the nod will go to the male.

There is little place for sentiment in political backrooms. The object is to win, and winning means finding candidates who can succeed at the polls. Backroom politicians take a hard, pragmatic view of aspiring frontroom politicians. And in making their choices, they look for that intangible quality: electability. At the local or constituency level, electability begins quite simply with recognition. More important than a prospective candidate's credentials or contribution to the community is how well known he or she is. When Gregg analyses constituency results for the Conservatives, he finds that in almost every instance, barring a powerful national trend, the candidate with the highest level of name recognition wins the election. This finding offers proof of the maxim that it does not matter what the press writes about a politician, as long as it spells his or her name correctly. Only when two or more candidates have the same level of name awareness, Gregg says, do their favorable–unfavorable ratings (admirers versus detractors) come into play. Then the candidate with the highest "net favorable" rating will win. Generally, however, if a well-known but not beloved candidate is running against a less-well-known but better-liked candidate, the former will win virtually every time.

When the public is asked, as it is periodically by pollsters, what attributes it most prizes in politicians, especially leaders, the list is always about the same. Honesty is the most important criterion by far, followed by intelligence, sincerity, education, experience, and so on. But as far as the backroom is concerned, the most prized attribute a national or provincial leader can possess is one that does not appear on any pollster's list of desirable political qualities. It is the ability to be convincing on television.

Nancy McLean was an astute judge of political talent. Virtually unknown outside the world of backroom politics, McLean, who died suddenly in June 1992, was a communications strategist to Conservative and Social Credit politicians, working with such leaders as Robert Stanfield, Joe Clark, and Brian Mulroney in Ottawa; Bill Davis and Michael Harris in Ontario; Bill Bennett in British Columbia; Grant Devine in Saskatchewan; Gary Filmon in Manitoba; and Brian Peckford in Newfoundland. Over the years, she worked with clients in twenty-five election campaigns, seventeen of them successful. That is a 68 per cent "win" rate — exceptionally good in any league. McLean's forte was television. When she saw a politician, one of her own or an opponent, on the screen, she knew what to watch for. In the Ontario election in the summer of 1990, Bob Rae, the New Democratic Party leader, made an immediate, favorable impact on McLean.

"Bob Rae was relaxed," she observed. "Bob Rae was comfortable in his skin. Bob Rae articulated things. He was himself and therefore he lowered the level of fear about his party, and all of that allowed obviously enough people a level of comfort to choose that way to send the message that they wished to send to [Liberal premier David] Peterson and his crowd."

But watching in the months and years since — through an economic recession, catastrophic budget deficits, forced resignations of cabinet ministers, abandoned election promises, and a national-unity crisis — McLean saw a new, unsettled, uncertain Rae. As she said:

> If you look at Bob Rae on television now, you see a totally different person, even though you know he hasn't changed. You see someone who has internal turmoil, who is struggling to find his expression of the [election] mandate. You see someone who is trying to keep the values and principles that he personally has. You see him trying to extend those to a caucus and a cabinet that may or may not share his values. When you are uptight and you're uncool, for whatever reason, it shows on television. Even these little instant sound bites and clips make the people begin to think. The questioning starts — What's bothering him? The concern starts — I feel sorry for him. The uneasiness starts — Boy, this job must be tough. Eventually, it gets to — I don't trust him. The lack of comfort becomes overwhelming.

If McLean was right, unless Rae can rediscover the comfort in his own skin, he is destined to be a one-term premier.

Gabor Apor, a television specialist who has been working with Liberals for two decades, is the media adviser who put David Peterson into red ties. (He did it because no one knew who Peterson was and Apor felt he needed a distinctive trademark.) A politician, Apor says, cannot create a television image by trying to be something today that he was not yesterday. "An image change is like a diet," he says. "It lasts only as long as you're willing to stick to the rules. Just as 99 per cent of diets fail, 99 per cent of image changes fail simply because if you try to assign characteristics to an individual that are untrue or unfamiliar or phony, it is unlikely that he or she will be very comfortable sticking to the rules twenty-four hours a day, seven days a week."

Backroom politicians both value and fear television. TV is relentless. It sees through phoniness and magnifies discomfort. A politician can run from newspapers; he can avoid in-person encounters with the public; but he cannot hide his emotions, his hesitancy and insecurity, from the television camera. To backroom media experts, both Brian Mulroney and Jean Chrétien display a lack of comfort, similar to that which McLean saw emerging in Rae. Mulroney radiates insincerity on camera. The viewer finds his body language at odds with his rhetoric, and is left with an uneasy sense that Mulroney either does not believe what he is saying or has no honest intention of carrying through with his stated objectives. Chrétien, the Liberal leader, seems ill at ease on camera. He projects awkwardness, uncertainty, and an air of superficiality — as though he is not quite sure what he is doing and not entirely convinced that he is up to the task ahead of him.

Backroom politicians also watch for candidates and leaders who are highly motivated. They look for people who know why they want to get into politics and what they hope to accomplish while they are there. Most people who enter politics are attracted to the idea of holding public office, but their drive often stops on election day. Having won, they have no clear idea of what they want to do next.

Patrick Lavelle is an oddity — a seasoned veteran of thirty years in the Liberal backroom who lusts to move into elected office. In the 1984 federal election, John Turner, the newly elected Liberal leader and (briefly) prime minister, asked him to run in Etobicoke, Ontario, against Tory frontbencher and finance minister–designate Michael Wilson. Lavelle had done enough candidate recruitment himself to know he was being invited to be a sacrificial lamb, and he turned Turner down.

In 1992, with another election approaching, the yen to run returned. Lavelle, however, found himself questioning his motivation. Did he, he wondered, have something worthwhile that he wanted to accomplish if he were elected to Parliament, and would he be able to do it? "I would have to have some assurances myself, after having got there, that I would have something to do that would be of interest to me so I would utilize whatever talents I bring. . . . The first rule for anyone who wants to run for office is to prepare yourself in your own situation, and make sure you know why you're getting into it and what you might expect once you get there.''

Just as Lavelle looked into himself to gauge his own motivation, backroom politicians look for candidates who have mental road-maps — ones who know where they want to go and what they hope to accomplish when they get there. A candidate's specific objectives are not of primary importance or interest to backroom organizers, so long as they are not at odds with party policy or strategy. The important thing is the candidate's ability to convey to the electorate the assurance that he or she has a plan or an agenda to accomplish if elected.

Another quality closely related to motivation and also highly prized by backroom politicians is intensity. They look for it in campaign workers and candidates alike. David MacNaughton, the president of Public Affairs International, is a Toronto-based consultant and lobbyist. He has been laboring in Liberal backrooms since his days as a young assistant to Don Jamieson, Newfoundland's representative in Pierre Trudeau's cabinet from 1968 to 1979. MacNaughton campaigned with Jamieson in the 1974 federal election and he remembers the dedication of one of the Jamieson volunteers in the tiny community of North Harbour:

> There were ninety-four eligible voters and this guy said to me at the beginning of the campaign, "I'm going to get them all. I promise you." And I said, "Don't worry about that." But this guy was so keen it was unbelievable. Anyway, we go through the campaign. Election night we're back at Jamieson's home, the party's winning a majority government, everything's fantastic. Jamieson's winning unbelievably. We've elected another member in Newfoundland. Everything's terrific. And this guy is sitting on the couch in the corner in tears. He is just completely devastated. And I went over and said, "What's the problem?" and he said, "I let you down." And I said, "What do you mean, you let me down?" He said, "Those two effing school teachers voted NDP." The results of his poll were ninety-two Liberals, no Conservatives, and two NDP. He was completely devastated.

Larry Grossman, a minister in Bill Davis's Tory cabinet in Ontario, had that intensity. He wanted desperately to be premier, and he brought the same single-mindedness to his career in the Ontario Legislature that Jamieson's worker in Newfoundland brought to his pursuit of the ninety-four votes in North Harbour. Grossman recalls how he felt in 1977 when Davis was shuffling his cabinet and Grossman, still a backbencher, was hoping desperately for a promotion. He knew Davis was leaving in two days for a government business trip to Japan. Grossman sat by the phone all day and all night. Meanwhile, his wife's uncle had died. Carol and Larry Grossman went to the funeral, then to the cemetery and back to the widow's house. Larry Grossman was in a terrible funk. And then:

> I look down at the coffee table and there's a little hand-written message: Urgent call for Larry Grossman. I leap to the phone. "Oh, Mr. Grossman, the premier's been looking for you." My heart's beating a hundred miles an hour. "He'd like to see you this afternoon, but he's leaving for Japan in ten minutes." I said, "No problem, I'll be there." It was raining like a son of a bitch [and] I'm driving on the sidewalks, and going through red lights. I leave the car right in front of the Legislature. I jump out. It's raining hard and my suit's wet. I'm dripping, but I stroll nonchalantly down the hallway to the premier's office. He offers me a cabinet post [minister of consumer and commercial relations]. And I call Carol back at her uncle's house. We weren't to tell anybody about it until the next day. So Carol was unable to tell anybody why she was crying as she and I talked on the phone. They couldn't believe Carol was that close to her deceased uncle.

Intensity like this drives politicians to the top. "Anyone who has been involved in politics, no matter where they are, at some point or another says, 'I'm just as good as the guy who's there. I can do what he's doing,'" says Lavelle. "But it's a very few who have this enormous drive to try to put it into reality."

Intensity is a precious asset to an ambitious politician, as long as he does not let his ambition become too obvious. Backroom organizers look for politicians who have — naturally or through training — an assured manner, an easy style, an ability to move effortlessly and seemingly unconcernedly through stressful daily routines. Tom MacMillan, a Toronto newspaper executive who has worked in many Tory campaigns, considers style to be as important as substance. "Looking like you know what you're doing, arriving at a hall on time, moving through an agenda crisply — little things make a tremendous difference."

Pierre Trudeau had a natural style that contributed to making his public appearances seem effortless. After he became prime minister in 1968, he also got a lot of help from his aides and his organizers. Patrick Gossage, who spent six years as Trudeau's press secretary, was astonished by the manpower that is invested in making a prime minister's day unfold smoothly. "The public would be horrified if it knew how much effort and money go into a simple walk across the street," Gossage says. "It's bizarre. Moving the PM has become a major industry in Ottawa for people who are paid an awful lot of money."

Recognition, TV skills, motivation, intensity, and the ability to project self-assurance and control under stress are all elements of electability — as electability is viewed from the backroom.

Party policy, however, is a different matter. Elected politicians value policy, if only because it serves as a suit of armour, protecting them from opponents' allegations that they have no ideas and no remedies for the problems that afflict the province or nation. To backroom politicians, in contrast, policy is a distraction, even a nuisance, which complicates campaign strategies and confuses tactics. To John Rae, a Power Corporation vice-president (and older brother of Ontario's NDP premier) who ran Jean Chrétien's campaigns for the Liberal leadership in 1984 and 1990, policy is a necessary burden in a leadership race. "If you don't make the effort [to stake out policy positions], you're in trouble, and if you do it badly, you're in trouble, but the attention span on policy in a leadership convention is really not that great," Rae says.

Frontroom politicians insist that their parties have policies on everything from agricultural subsidies to zinc processing, because they believe that the public expects and demands policy. The politicians are right and wrong. They are right to believe that Canadian voters expect political parties to have policies; most voters would think it decidedly odd if a party tried to fight an election without a platform. But they are wrong if they believe that voters decide how to cast their ballot on the basis of which party offers the most agreeable policies.

As backroom politicians are well aware, voters are bored by policy. They simply do not take it in. They are also thoroughly — and understandably — cynical about policy because campaign policy promises have a disconcerting way of disappearing into a black hole when elections are over. In the 1990 Ontario election, Bob Rae's New Democrats published a list of promises called an "Agenda for People." It was an ambitious blueprint for an NDP government in Ontario, and it made everyone in the party feel warm and wonderfully self-righteous to have such a splendid manifesto to offer the electorate. Of course, most Ontarians — including most New Democrats — never read the agenda and did not have the foggiest notion what it contained. Not that it mattered: The NDP won the election, formed a government, ran headlong into the recession, and tossed the agenda into the dustbin, where it will languish unless someone thinks to retrieve it for the next election.

Julie Davis, the president of the Ontario NDP who chaired the party's 1990 election-planning committee, says voters no longer pay much attention to election promises. "I think it's becoming less and less a reason why people vote for you. I don't think that campaign promises make the difference. I would be very surprised if they do, given the level of public cynicism."

David Peterson's Liberals published a party policy on free trade with the United States in their successful 1987 election campaign in Ontario. The only thing that anyone, including the people who wrote it, remembers about Peterson's free-trade policy is that it had six conditions. "We had to find the hook," says Peterson strategist Hershell Ezrin. "We decided that the hook was going to be the number six — six conditions. You didn't have to remember what all the conditions were, you just had to say there were six of them. And that I think was a notable kind of success." Ezrin is right. Peterson's six conditions — whatever they were — helped the Liberals elect a majority government.

The same observation can be made about free trade in the November 1988 federal election. Brian Mulroney's Conservative government had negotiated a free-trade agreement with the United States and signed it in January that year, but the treaty would not come into force until it was formally ratified following the election. In the opinion of most observers and politicians, free trade was *the* issue of the '88 campaign. Yet the government's private polls before the election was called revealed that only 31 per cent of Canadians would admit to knowing anything at all about the Canada–U.S. Free Trade Agreement. And whether they knew anything about it or not, a majority did not like the agreement, according to polls published during the campaign. Yet they re-elected the Tories.

Backroom politicians understand that policy is mainly for show. It is something to put in the window while the real work goes on behind the backroom curtains. What matters to campaign strategists is not policy positions, but issues management. The Conservatives did not win the 1988 federal election because they had brilliant policies that the Canadian people adored. They won because they adroitly managed the major issues. For those worried about national unity, they had the Meech Lake constitutional accord, which had been signed the previous year by Mulroney and the ten provincial premiers. The accord consisted of five points. Four of the points were a mystery to most voters (only the fifth, recognition of Quebec as a "distinct society," had some public awareness). The existence of the accord, not its content, was what mattered. It reassured Canadians that the Tories knew what they were doing when it came to dealing with Quebec and with constitutional issues.

Similarly, the free-trade agreement was presented to the electorate as proof that the Tories could manage Canada's all-important relationship with the powerful neighbor to the south, while the goods and services tax (proposed but not then passed) was cited as evidence that the Conservatives could manage the economy, were not afraid to take hard fiscal decisions, and could be counted on to fight the deficit that they, ironically, had done so much to inflate since taking office in 1984.

The reason the Tories won in 1988 was not free trade, Meech Lake, or the GST. If the country had been voting on those issues, the Conservatives would have been hurled from office. They won because they established themselves in the voters' minds as competent managers with a clear strategy — a road-map — compared to John Turner's Liberals, whom the Conservatives successfully portrayed as confused, incompetent, and untrustworthy.

Senator Finlay MacDonald, a long-service veteran of Conservative backrooms in Nova Scotia and Ottawa, regrets the passing of elections that were won or lost on the strength of policies presented to the voters for approval or rejection. "It strikes me that the old campaigns — this may sound corny — but there was something basic about them. I suppose, truthful. They'd say they were going to increase old age pensions, they were going to do this, they were going to do that. It was more direct. In Nova Scotia politics, of course, the emphasis was on economic development and we put that in the window each time. It was pretty basic."

If the public is cynical — and it is — about the commitment that parties really have to the policies they embrace, much of the blame rests with the backroom strategists who treat policy as issues to be managed rather than as commitments to be honored. Some of the same cynicism greets politicians' professed belief in the importance of opening up the political process to give women the same opportunities for advancement that male politicians enjoy. All parties, including the NDP, have failed to create equal access for women and to attract adequate numbers of capable women to their campaigns. This failure is largely the fault of the insiders who run the party machines. Only in recent years have the backrooms begun to discover that it is worth their while to invest the effort to recruit women candidates in ridings where they actually have a chance of winning.

The obstacles facing women attempting to get into politics can be formidable. Family responsibilities discourage some of them from seeking office until their children are grown, which leaves them years behind their male counterparts in terms of political career development. And because women often have less employment security than men, they run a bigger risk of losing their jobs if they are unsuccessful in their attempt to win office. They are also less likely than men to have developed a network of political patrons and financial supporters. They have more trouble than men do when they try to raise campaign funds, especially at the nomination stage. And, historically, women have found it difficult to persuade backroom bosses that it is in their party's interest to support them for nominations in winnable seats.

Obtaining the nomination of a mainstream party in a riding where they have a realistic chance of being elected is the biggest obstacle to increasing the number of women in public office. It accounts for the discrepancy between the ratio of women nominated to women elected. In the 1980 federal election, for example, women accounted for 8.2 per cent of all candidates nominated, but for only 5.0 per cent of MPs elected. In the next election, in 1984, they accounted for 15.6 per cent of candidates and 9.9 per cent of members elected. In 1988, the figures were 19.4 per cent of candidates and 13.2 per cent of members elected. Although more and more women are running, their odds of getting elected are not improving. The discrepancy between the proportions of women nominated and women elected was 3.2 percentage points in 1980, 5.7 in 1984, and 6.2 in 1988.[1]

The struggle to increase the representation of women in Parliament and provincial legislatures to a level closer to their proportion of the population (51 per cent) continues. Some women's groups are calling for quotas to force parties to nominate more women. The NDP has set an objective of 50 per cent women candidates and

MPs. The Royal Commission on Electoral Reform and Party Financing, in its 1992 report, recommended the adoption of financial incentives to parties to encourage women to seek office. What is needed most, however, is a revolution in the thinking that goes on within political organizations.

Women will not get the encouragement they need until the men who run most of the backrooms believe that their parties' chances of winning will be enhanced, not harmed, by nominating women in crucial constituencies. This realization will not dawn overnight. First, the backrooms need to put their own house in order. In the last national election, no fewer than 72 per cent of campaign managers were men, as were 80 per cent of constituency-association presidents. And it was not until 1987 that the men who dominate Ontario's Big Blue Machine thought to invite their female colleagues in the Conservative backroom to participate in the organization's annual tennis and drinking weekend.

"One of the great debates is how to get women involved," says Hershell Ezrin, a Liberal. "Parties have tried different ways — everything from special fund-raising for them to special grants for child-care funds, anything. Women find it particularly difficult — and not only because they don't have access to the same power organizations that men traditionally have." Women candidates, Ezrin continues, find that their private lives — including their marital situation and the business or professional activities of their spouses — are subject to much greater scrutiny and criticism than those of male candidates. "That's a very serious problem, and a lot of families are not prepared to put up with that," he notes. "To me, it raises one of the most fundamental issues now facing us in the body politic: How are we going to find sufficiently good candidates? People are saying we [political parties] are getting exactly what we deserve."

From the perspective of the Tory backroom, Allan Gregg comes to a similar conclusion about the challenge of improving the calibre of political representation in Canada. He does not think the public is unrealistic in its expectation — "People have decided there are no great men, and are now looking for good men." And women, he should have added.

Despite an illusion of openness and a veneer of candor, the backrooms — the nerve centres of the political parties — still operate in the shadows, out of sight of all but party insiders. The television cameras do not get inside. The public does not see what really takes place in the backrooms, the good or the ill. It does not see the polling that drives the campaign strategy, the fund-raising that oils the gears of the political machine, the thinking behind a leader's election tour, the media strategy that floods the airwaves with negative television commercials, the organizational gaffes that, however hilarious they may seem years later, are anything but funny at the time.

There is more to backroom politics than cynicism and opportunism. The backrooms are people — people who are united by loyalty to an individual, a party, or a cause — and, more important, by loyalty to one another. Most of them are volunteers. Many are foot-soldiers; they knock on doors or man the phones at their candidate's committee rooms. Some put their regular jobs on hold and work full-time at running some aspect of the campaign. Few expect to see any reward for their effort. They do it because they believe in the system and because they love the game.

They are people like Ed Watts, of Kingston, Ontario. Then in his early eighties, Watts was a volunteer who undertook to organize a senior citizens' home to support Keith Norton, the Tory candidate in Kingston and The Islands in the provincial election of 1975. For a year before the election, Watts got to know the two hundred residents of the home, promoting Norton's candidacy at every opportunity. He even made sure that every resident got a card from Norton on his or her birthday.

The day before the election, Norton, who was locked in a desperately close race with the Liberal candidate, came to campaign at the home. He was accompanied by Darcy McKeough, then provincial treasurer in the Tory cabinet. Watts met them and took them around, introducing them to every resident. He had arranged to have the local newspaper, the *Whig-Standard*, send a photographer and, when he arrived, Watts led the group to the second floor to meet the home's oldest resident, a 102-year-old woman who happened to be the great-aunt of Norton's Liberal opponent. Watts performed the introductions and proudly made an announcement: The old lady would be voting for Keith Norton the next day. Naturally, the picture and her quote — "My nephew is a nice young man, but I have been a Conservative all my life" — made the front page of the next day's paper. And that evening Norton became the new member for Kingston and The Islands, defeating the woman's great-nephew by just 203 votes. Ed Watts, the backroom volunteer, deserved some of the credit for the victory.

There are thousands of people like Watts, minor and major players, in the backrooms. Theirs is oral history. It will not be found on television, in the newspapers, or on the reading lists for political science courses. Their story is a vast, uncatalogued collection of memories and anecdotes that are passed from one backroomer to another, often late at night over a bottle of strong refreshment. It is tales of experiences shared, of battles fought and won, of deals and strategies, of dirty tricks and generous gestures, of heels and heroes, of fun and games. It is politics — seen, played, and loved — from the inside.

2. CONFESSIONS OF A CAMPAIGN MANAGER

*"Please don't tell my mother I'm in politics. She thinks I'm
still playing piano in a bordello."*
— Senator Finlay MacDonald,
Tory organizer/fund raiser

Peter Pocklington, a small man with a world-class ego, had three ambitions in life. The first was to be Prime Minister of Canada. The second was to see the National Hockey League team he owned, the Edmonton Oilers, win the Stanley Cup. The third was to live and dine well. Unfortunately for his political career, the second and third ambitions kept colliding with the first. He declared his candidacy for the Progressive Conservative leadership in March 1983. His Oilers made it into the NHL playoffs in April. However serious he may have been about becoming PM, Pocklington, who had a private jet, did not miss a single Oiler playoff game that spring.

His campaign chiefs — co-chairman Ralph Lean, a Toronto lawyer, and manager Errick (Skip) Willis, a consultant with Tory campaign experience in Manitoba — painstakingly organized his political itinerary around the playoff schedule. Knowing that the Oilers were to play the New York Islanders on Long Island on a Tuesday night in early May, Willis, with the help of local Tory MP Jack Ellis, organized a breakfast for the following morning in Belleville, Ontario, to introduce Pocklington to local Conservatives, including convention delegates from four area ridings. They sold five hundred tickets at $25 apiece to party supporters who were undoubtedly attracted, in part, by the chance to have a muffin with the man who employed Wayne Gretzky. Two days before the event, however, Pocklington announced he and his wife would be staying over in New York after the Tuesday-night game to have dinner with friends. The breakfast had to be cancelled, angering Ellis and bruising the feelings of just about every Tory in Belleville. During the leadership convention in Ottawa in June, Pocklington was accosted by the mayor of Belleville, who chewed him out for five minutes. As the mayor stalked off, the candidate looked at his campaign manager and passed the buck. "Skip," asked Pocklington, "just what did you do in Belleville?"

When the convention began, Pat Binns, a Tory member of the Prince Edward Island Legislature (and Pocklington's only caucus supporter on the Island) approached Pocklington's organizers. The provincial caucus members — voting delegates all — would welcome an opportunity to meet Pocklington and hear all about his wonky idea for replacing Canada's existing tax system with a single flat tax, Binns said. It was the sort of invitation a candidate dreams of. A breakfast meeting was quickly arranged. Pocklington, however, neglected to do his homework, to the excruciating embarrassment of his campaign staff. "There were about sixteen of them in a suite in the Château Laurier," Lean recalls. "It was an informal thing where they were listening to Peter talk and answer questions, and one guy asked a good question. Peter answers it and says, 'That was a very good question. What's your name?' The guy says, 'My name's Jim Lee.' Peter says, 'And what do you do down in Prince Edward Island, Jim?' And this guy Lee says, 'I'm the premier.'" While Lean and Willis buried their heads in their hands and wished they were invisible, Pocklington skated. He skated faster than Gretzky. "He got away with it," Lean says. "Peter is the only guy who could have carried it off. He's so charming in some ways."

The worst was yet to come. Each of the major candidates in that 1983 campaign threw a big convention-week party to which all three thousand voting delegates, plus alternates and hangers-on, were invited. These parties were part of the process of courting delegates, but they were also an element in the elaborate mating game that went on all week among the candidates, each seeking second- and third-ballot support from his weaker (he supposed) opponents. A candidate who was interested in an opponent's support would make a point of dropping in to say hello during the opponent's party. Organizers were at pains to make these drop-ins appear to be spontaneous, spur-of-the-moment happenings; in fact, they were negotiated in advance, painstakingly choreographed and scripted, and timed to the minute. (It would never do to have two rivals come face-to-face at a third candidate's party — or for a candidate to arrive after the opponent he was seeking to woo had left the festivities.) In this instance, Mulroney was interested in Pocklington's delegates, and Pocklington, knowing his chances of winning were slim indeed, was interested in being minister of finance in a Mulroney government. The Mulroney organization contacted the Pocklington organization. Would it be convenient, they asked, if Brian were to drop in to greet his good friend Peter during Pocklington's party? Why yes, it would, they were told. The party was scheduled to begin at 9:00 p.m., Pocklington would speak at 9:30, and Mulroney would drop in at precisely 10:10. Not 10:09, not 10:11 — 10:10.

"Mulroney's people were very, very pushy — very pushy," Lean remembers. "They treated us like dirt.... They were very arrogant."

Arrogant, perhaps, but highly organized. Everything had been neatly arranged — only to have Pocklington throw sand in the gears of the organization by announcing he was going to take his wife, Eva, out for (what else?) dinner. This time, Willis, Lean, and the others were prepared. They had an advanceman — a woman — standing by to drive the car. The candidate also had a full-time bodyguard, an ex–RCMP officer, as a result of a kidnapping incident about a year earlier in which Pocklington had been shot in the arm by a man who tried to hold him for ransom. Lean instructed the driver and bodyguard to take the Pocklingtons to the restaurant, to wait for them, and to bring them back without fail by 9:00 p.m. so that the candidate could be briefed on the details of Mulroney's drop-in. Ralph Lean recalls what happened next:

> We're up in the suite and there's a knock at the door at nine o'clock and it's this advance lady and the bodyguard. They said, "Peter's gone!" I said, "What do you mean he's gone? I've got five hundred people waiting downstairs and Mulroney coming over. What do you mean he's gone?" They said he went into a restaurant in Ottawa. They were out front waiting and he looked at the wine list, didn't like it, got Eva up, took the keys from the advance lady and says, "We're going to Hull." He left them standing there. He's off in Hull, I've got five hundred people down at this thing and no goddamn candidate and no one knows where he is. I've got to go downstairs. I got somebody to phone the Mulroney people, saying you may bring Brian over but our guy's not here and we don't

know when he's coming back. It's 10:30 when Peter rolls in, and I'm down there sweating like mad. I'm on stage, saying Peter's going to be there. It wasn't just our supporters. Everyone was there. There was this incredible curiosity because there was speculation — nobody knew — that Wayne Gretzky was going to be there.[1]

Gretzky did not appear. Mulroney's staff held Mulroney in another hotel until Pocklington had reached the Château Laurier and made his speech. Then the soon-to-be prime minister paid his courtesy call on the not-to-be finance minister. They shook hands. Mulroney left — and that was it.[2]

Jean Bazin, a key Quebec Tory, worked for Davie Fulton in the Conservative leadership campaign of 1967, for Joe Clark in his victorious leadership bid in 1976, and for his close friend Mulroney in 1983. "It is an absolute necessity to start building alliances from day one," says Bazin. "All three of those campaigns were decided by alliances. . . . Not enough positive things are said about the hard backroom work involved. A lot of work was done to get second-ballot support in 1983. If Mulroney didn't get [Michael] Wilson and Pocklington, the result would have been different." Mulroney got both of them on the second ballot and won the leadership by defeating Clark on the fourth.

Although old pros like Bazin thrive on it, backroom politics is an unnatural vocation. Campaign managers and their helpers have to be ready to catch the passed buck, to suffer through the embarrassment created by an ill-prepared or gaffe-prone candidate, and to respond to the crises that result when carefully crafted plans go gloriously awry, as they invariably do. Campaign managers' lives are full of contradictions. They get no credit for victories and shoulder a disproportionate share of the blame for losses. They are expected to consult widely, manage by committee, and make all the diverse human elements in a campaign feel that they are an integral and essential part of the effort. Yet campaign managers are also expected to run the campaign with the ruthless efficiency of an iron-heeled martinet. They are supposed to make sure that their candidate is accessible to all potential supporters, yet protect the candidate from distraction and guard him or her against those who would seek favors or waste his or her time. The manager must constantly bolster the candidate's morale without leaving him or her vulnerable to cruel disappointment later by inflating his or her hopes too much. They are supposed to be the candidate's best friend and confidant one moment and his or her most trenchant critic the next. Only one thing is certain in campaign managers' lives — that they will be left in the shadows while their creation dances in the spotlight.

There is no school for backroom managers. There are no videos or training manuals to teach them the tricks of their arcane craft. Yet somehow they have to learn how to build an organization by assembling a group of individuals (anywhere from a hundred to two thousand of them, depending on the campaign) from different backgrounds and regions; co-ordinate their efforts; motivate them without paying most of them; establish clear lines of reporting and communications; assign tasks most of the workers would find beneath their dignity if asked to perform them in their real lives; struggle to control the campaign budget; demand and receive long hours of effort; then dismantle the whole machine just as it reaches the peak of its performance.

Backroom brokers all start the same way: at the bottom. For some, the bottom is answering phones, delivering brochures, erecting lawn signs, driving voters to the polls, or serving as scrutineers on election day. Since the early 1980s, however, the proliferation of computers in political backrooms has created a new kind of entry-level position. There has been an influx of "teckies," people with computer skills, who are needed to operate the computers that massage polling data, generate direct-mail material, group and classify voters on the lists of electors, and identify priority polls for special campaign attention.

Strong drink seems to have played a part in the initiation of many campaign veterans into the world of backroom politics. Douglas Bassett, whose political heroes run an improbable gamut from Robert Kennedy to Brian Mulroney, is president of Baton Broadcasting, the dominant player in the CTV television network, and an active Tory fund raiser. Bassett comes by his passion for politics honestly; his father, John, twice tried to win election to the Commons, and many of the Bassett family friends when young Doug was growing up were active politicians. In 1965, when he was twenty-five, he was a campaign apprentice to one of those friends, David Walker, a Tory senator and a wily veteran of the Diefenbaker cabinet. When the Liberal prime minister of the day, Lester Pearson, called a general election in 1965, Walker and young Bassett set off for Orillia to campaign for another friend of Bassett's father, Dr. Percy Rynard, the longtime (1957–79) MP from Simcoe County. Bassett was to make a speech on behalf of the Young Progressive Conservatives.

"I'm really nervous. I've never made one of these speeches," Bassett told Walker.

> "Dougie boy," he says, "don't you worry about anything. I've got a little something for ya." He pulled out a mickey in the car. He had a driver. We slugged a couple straight. I got up and I was half-cut. The senator said, "You've got to relax. Don't ever forget, Doug, what the Chief [John Diefenbaker] has always said. The Chief never made a speech where he wasn't feeling that worry and, if he didn't have that worry, it wouldn't be a good speech, so you're going to make a great speech. Have another swig." I got up there and I ranted and raved. I talked about "Pinky" Pearson and how his greatest defeat was when the Russians vetoed his appointment at the United Nations and made Dag Hammarskjöld the new secretary general. Well, I had the audience just roaring. Walker, you know, had to follow me. He said, "Well — I trained that young boy."

Tom MacMillan's first job in politics was keeping the ice buckets filled in Allan Lawrence's hospitality suites in the Royal York Hotel during the 1971 Ontario Tory leadership convention in Toronto. Success in tending ice buckets led the young public-relations man to campaign advance work for Bill Davis, the winner of that 1971 convention; then for federal Conservative leader Robert Stanfield; then to a stint as executive assistant to Darcy McKeough, Davis's most powerful minister; then to Brian Mulroney's leadership campaign in 1976 and John Crosbie's in 1983; and on and on. Now vice-president of the *Financial Post*, MacMillan has a theory that backroom politics gave his generation, born too late for the Second World War, a surrogate for more violent activity:

> My theory is that guys our age are a generation denied war. Unlike our fathers, we never had a chance to go and fight in the big one. And leadership campaigns to me are the chance to wage war. No one gets hurt. A few people get laid, but no one gets hurt, and no prisoners are taken. It's a great thing because you're one-upping your friends in leadership campaigns. Screwing around. Trying to figure out how you can break the rules. It's a wonderfully invigorating process, and of course it's great when you take all that energy and turn it against one of the other parties in a general election.

That energy often finds improbable outlets. MacMillan remembers trying to whip up enthusiasm for Stanfield in British Columbia in the months leading up to the 1972 federal election. One of the problems an advanceman, like MacMillan, faces is dealing with the local workers' wildly optimistic crowd expectations. In Vancouver, Tory organizers were predicting that no fewer than five thousand people — an immense crowd for the Conservatives in B.C. in those days — would flock to meet Stanfield in the Hotel Vancouver ballroom (a venue chosen for the strategic reason that sections of the room could be closed off to make it look full when it was not).

MacMillan could see disaster looming. The event's organizers had not done any of the telephoning or taken other promotional steps to build a crowd. He thought they would be extremely lucky to get 1,200 people out. "I told them they were dreaming in technicolor," MacMillan says. "I said, 'If you get more than 1,500, I'll jump in the harbor with my clothes on.' They said, 'Fine,' and they proceeded to go back and hit the membership list, tear up some small local business phone books, and really get at the thing."

The challenge worked. When the big day came, there were 1,800 Tories in the ballroom — and MacMillan went into Vancouver harbor. "They marched me down to the Bayshore Inn," he recalls. "A couple of quick scotches and I went into the water, wearing a blazer, a tie — fully clothed — to their jeers and catcalls. . . . I was taken out fast and we proceeded to kill a bottle of scotch. But I never had any trouble with those people after that. Twenty years later, I bump into people who still remember." As MacMillan sees it, the episode injected some fun into a B.C. Tory organization that had had nothing to laugh about for years (the Conservatives had failed to win a single seat in the province in the federal election of 1968). It generated enthusiasm and convinced the local party that hard work could produce results. The confidence showed in the election in the fall of 1972. The Tories won eight seats in the province. They were well launched on the road back in B.C.

Boyd Simpson got involved in Liberal politics as a student at Wilfrid Laurier University in Waterloo, Ontario, in the late 1960s. He worked on Eric Kierans's campaign for the national Liberal leadership in 1968. After it was over, he got a call inviting him to fly to St. John's to meet John Crosbie, then a disaffected provincial Liberal cabinet minister who was planning to challenge Joey Smallwood's continued leadership of the Newfoundland Liberal party. Barely into his twenties, Simpson did not own a suit; he borrowed one for the trip. "I flew to St. John's and went to the old Hotel

Newfoundland and went upstairs, after going into the liquor store and getting a bottle of that dark rum 'screech' 'cause I'd never had it before," he remembers. "There was a knock on the door and in came this great big bear of a guy with sideburns almost down to his chin and glasses like the bottom of Coke bottles. He walked over — didn't say a word — and just picked up the bottle and poured himself a big shot, with a little splash of water. That was John Crosbie. First introduction."

Crosbie took Simpson to an all-candidates' meeting in Green Harbour, where Smallwood, Crosbie, and other leadership candidates spoke. Simpson did not know he was being inspected:

> The next morning we all met at this fellow's office. We were chatting, having a coffee. About ten minutes later, there's a knock on the door, and the door opened and in came this fellow with a windbreaker on and he walked over and, as he was turning, looked at me and shook his head. I said, "What the hell's going on?" They started laughing and they said, "Oh, it's nothing. We just had Bill here out at Green Harbour last night and he was going to see if he could pick you out of the crowd. But he picked the wrong guy." So Crosbie said I didn't look like a mainlander. "If you want the job, I'll hire you." Their biggest concern was the mainland influence.

Simpson took the job and found himself running the day-to-day operations of the Crosbie leadership campaign. Crosbie failed to unseat Smallwood and soon left the Liberals for the Conservatives, served as a minister in Frank Moores's Tory government in Newfoundland, then moved on to federal politics in 1976.

Crosbie soon became the Tory godfather for Newfoundland. His counterpart on the Liberal side was the silver-voiced ex-broadcaster Donald Jamieson, a federal cabinet minister who later became the provincial Liberal leader, then Canadian high commissioner to Britain. David MacNaughton, now a lobbyist and head of Public Affairs International, was Jamieson's top assistant in the 1970s. He says he still has nightmares about the horrible day on which he thought he had destroyed Jamieson's political career.

MacNaughton was politicking with Jamieson in Newfoundland when they got word that Leonid Brezhnev, the leader of the Soviet Union, was going to stop at Gander on his way back to Moscow after a visit to Cuba and would welcome the opportunity to talk to Jamieson about the United Nations Law of the Sea conference

— a subject of keen concern to Newfoundland, since the province is so dependent on the sea for its livelihood and, with offshore oil, for its future. To Jamieson, Newfoundland's representative in the federal cabinet, an opportunity to be seen discussing the future of the world's oceans with a superpower leader like Brezhnev was manna from political heaven.

MacNaughton read the memo from the External Affairs department with great care and growing excitement. Brezhnev, it said, would be landing at Gander at 1:15 p.m. Jamieson was in Swift Current the night before Brezhnev's arrival and stayed overnight there, a two-hour drive, or more, from Gander. MacNaughton made sure that a fast car was laid on for the next day. Taking no chances, he also arranged to have a helicopter standing by. In the morning, with enough snow falling in Swift Current to ground the helicopter, MacNaughton realized Jamieson would have to leave by road earlier than planned. He phoned the airport manager in Gander. Years later, the distress still rings through in Mac-Naughton's voice:

> I said, "Hi, Jack. How's Brezhnev's plane doing? Is he going to arrive on time?" He said, "David, where the hell are you?" "I'm in Swift Current. Why?" "What the hell are you doing in Swift Current?" I said, "Brezhnev's plane's not arriving until 1:15." But it was 1:15 GMT — Greenwich Mean Time — 9:45 a.m. Newfoundland time. I am like toast. The guy is arriving in three-quarters of an hour and it was a two-hour drive at the best of times. And it's snowing; it's three hours. What a screw up!
>
> I go in. Jamieson's sound asleep. He's in bed snoring and I tap him on the shoulder and I say, "Mr. Jamieson, I've got some good news and some bad news." "What's the good news?" "You don't have to go to Gander." And he said, "That's great. What's the bad news?" I said, "Brezhnev's arriving in a half-hour." He asked for an explanation and so I told him. He rolls over and goes back to sleep. I go out into the living room and pour myself a cup of coffee, and I'm pacing back and forth, back and forth. I think I'm done. He's the head of one of the biggest countries in the world. The phone rings. I had phoned the airport manager and concocted this story that we had set out on the road but the RCMP had turned us back — the road was blocked. I had said this to the airport manager. They had related it to the Russians. Now it's Brezhnev on the phone.

I have to go back and wake Jamieson again, and I said to tell him that we started out and the snow's so bad they had to turn us back. He said, "Comrade, it's so good to talk to you." And he gives him the line. He said it was awful. "I've never seen snow so bad. We're out there and we got blocked off and had to turn around. Yes. I will. I'll catch you next time. I'm sorry. I really wanted to see you. It's just too bad we got turned around by the RCMP and sent back."

He hangs up the phone and looks over at me and says, "Well, you bastard, you owe me one." And goes back to bed. I felt like a complete jerk. He got me back. He told the story at my wedding.

Usually, it is the other way around. Usually, it is the candidate who owes the campaign manager — sometimes for services well beyond the call of duty. After directing operations for John Crosbie in his ill-fated attempt to topple Smallwood in 1969, Boyd Simpson was back in Toronto when a friend called to ask whether he would help out in an ethnic riding in the west end of the city. The Liberals, knowing they had no chance of winning the seat, had looked around for a sacrificial lamb, settling on a young woman of Lithuanian descent, a graduate student at York University. Simpson's friend said he was worried: the woman's father was dead, she lived with her mother, and they had very little money. They could not afford to go into debt to finance the campaign. Simpson agreed to talk to the candidate and soon found himself running her campaign, such as it was. His first act was to go to Liberal campaign headquarters and demand funding for his candidate. He got some and raised a bit more — a total of $6,000 or $7,000. Then he spent it creatively: "We printed one brochure. We painted her house. We fixed up her car. We sent her on a vacation." And when the election was over, they threw a party with the remaining money. Simpson's candidate lost, yet she won. She finished 22,000 votes behind, but not a nickel in debt.

There are occasions, however, when a campaign manager, trying to do the right thing for his candidate, is torn by conflicting choices. John Laschinger was campaign manager for Stuart Douglas Boland "Bud" Smith in the race to succeed William Bennett as leader of the Social Credit Party and as premier of British Columbia in 1986. From polling he had commissioned from Toronto pollster Martin Goldfarb, Laschinger knew two weeks before the convention that Smith could not win, that he would finish third or fourth, and that the new leader and premier was destined to be William Vander Zalm. Smith, using the time to think through his options, had decided before the convention opened to cast his lot at the appropriate time with Vander Zalm. He reasoned that the party desperately needed a fresh face. In addition, Smith knew that the other principal leadership candidates would never go to Vander Zalm, and he wanted, for the sake of party unity, to avoid creating the perception that everyone was ganging up on Vander Zalm. Smith's decision was a tightly held secret. Vander Zalm's people never got a hint of it.

While the votes were being counted following the first ballot at the convention centre in Whistler, a Vander Zalm organizer approached Laschinger and asked him to meet some people. Laschinger was escorted to the basement of the centre, to the chef's office off the kitchen, where he was introduced to two prominent Vander Zalm friends and supporters: Peter Toigo, owner of White Spot restaurants, and Edgar Kaiser, head of the Bank of British Columbia. A chequebook lay on the table in front of them.

They told Laschinger that Vander Zalm was going to win (which Laschinger already knew from Goldfarb's polling). They gave him their prediction of Vander Zalm's first-ballot vote; Laschinger told them they were 20 per cent too high (which they were). In matter-of-fact tones, they asked whether Bud Smith was going to need any help to pay his campaign expenses. Laschinger realized that Smith faced a large deficit. He could have accepted a cheque without in any way altering the outcome of the convention, because Smith was planning to support Vander Zalm anyway. But Laschinger knew it was better that his candidate be broke than be compromised. Politely, he declined the offer. There was no further contact between the two campaigns. Smith was knocked out of the running after the second ballot and threw his support to Vander Zalm. Vander Zalm won on the fourth ballot. Smith left Whistler with $225,000 in campaign debts, which took him many months to pay off.[3]

On other occasions, a campaign manager's desire to do the best he can for his candidate takes him in the opposite direction. He does things in the heat of political combat that he would be ashamed of doing outside politics, things for which he might be roundly censured. For Laschinger, the Ontario Tory leadership convention of January 1985 was one such occasion. William Davis had retired after fourteen years as leader and premier, and four of his cabinet ministers were locked in a desperate struggle to succeed him. The stakes were high: not only the leadership of the party but the premiership of a province that the Tories had ruled for forty-two consecutive years and that they confidently expected to rule for forty-two more. Never before (or since) had so much money — $1 million or more per candidate — been spent in pursuit of the leadership of any provincial party in Canada. On the first ballot, Frank Miller, the right-wing favorite, was in first place, ahead of Dennis Timbrell. Laschinger's candidate, Larry Grossman, lay third, just forty-three votes behind Timbrell. Roy McMurtry, fourth, with three hundred votes, was eliminated. The frantic scramble for McMurtry's delegates began. Laschinger needed to get enough of them to let Grossman vault over Timbrell into second place to establish himself as the centrist challenger to Miller on the third ballot.

In the tumult and confusion of the convention floor, a Grossman delegate appeared at Laschinger's side. "If Larry promises to give an appointment to Bob Nixon," the delegate said, "I can get the local reeve in the area to come to us. This fellow wants to run for us in Brant-Haldimand and he wants Nixon out of the way." Laschinger thought quickly. Robert Nixon, the former leader of the Ontario Liberals, was a fixture in Brant-Haldimand. He and his father, Harry Nixon, who was premier of the province for three months in 1943, had held the seat continuously since 1919. With Bob Nixon there, the Tories would never be able to win the seat, no matter whom they nominated. But with Nixon gone, the seat would be up for grabs.

"Done," said Laschinger. "Tell him it's done."

"But don't you have to talk to Larry?" the delegate asked.

"I'll confirm it with him while you go and bring back the reeve to our box," Laschinger replied.

Laschinger had no intention of mentioning it to Grossman. There would be plenty of time later, if Grossman won, to broach the delicate matter of a promised patronage appointment for an opposition frontbencher. Five minutes later, the reeve, sporting a Grossman scarf and buttons, was proudly seated in the Grossman box. By this time, Laschinger, involved in other last-ditch manoeuvring, had forgotten his commitment. It was not until much, much later that he thought to mention it to Grossman. By then, the question was academic. Grossman did move ahead of Timbrell on the second ballot, but he could not muster enough delegates to stop Miller on the third. Miller became premier, called an election prematurely, waged a disastrous campaign, tried to form a government, and failed. The Liberals took over, and Nixon became minister of everything — House leader, treasurer, minister of economics, and minister of revenue — in David Peterson's administration. Never knowing how close he had come to a grand patronage appointment in 1985, Nixon had to wait until 1991 for the new NDP premier, Bob Rae, to name him Ontario agent general in London.

Finally, there are occasions when deception is a campaign manager's best weapon. David MacNaughton was responsible for recruiting Liberal candidates in Newfoundland for the 1972 federal election. He had a poll that showed the Liberals leading in Gander-Twillingate and trailing in Bonavista-Trinity-Conception. His problem was, he had recruited two prospective candidates, David Rooney and George Baker, both of whom were intent on running in Gander-Twillingate. So MacNaughton lied. "I took the [poll] results and I switched them. I convinced Rooney that I really wanted him as a candidate and I convinced him to run in Bonavista-Trinity-Conception. And he won! It was quite incredible." Ironically, George Baker, who got to run in the more promising riding, Gander-Twillingate, did not win. He lost to a Conservative.

To most backroom politicians, lying about polls is not really lying. "We lied to [Liberal leader] David Peterson all the way through the '87 Ontario election," says MacNaughton. "We didn't tell him how far he was ahead." Not realizing he could have coasted to victory, Peterson campaigned furiously and was rewarded by the election of a majority government.

Peter Pocklington's 1983 campaign for the federal Tory leadership was conspicuous for its absurdly inflated claims of delegate support. On the convention floor, after Pocklington had posted just 102 first-ballot votes, a young reporter from the *Edmonton Journal* collared Peter Regenstreif, Pocklington's pollster/strategist. Why, the reporter demanded, had Regenstreif persisted in predicting that Pocklington would get 250 votes. "I lied," replied Regenstreif, unrepentant. On the other hand, Michael Adams, who had done polling for the Edmonton Oilers owner very early in the leadership race, did not lie, precisely. He invented. Adams's Environics Research Group had done no delegate polling for months, and he did not have the faintest idea about Pocklington's delegate support when the candidate asked him how many votes he could expect. Pollsters are never at a loss for numbers, however, so Adams told Pocklington: "Ninety-nine." What he did not tell him was that he had picked the number from the back of Wayne Gretzky's hockey sweater. And as it turned out, Gretzky's sweater was just three votes out — closer than any of the pollsters.

Jean Pigott still remembers the telephone call she received in May 1976 from Laschinger, then national director of the Conservative party. "We were in Vancouver and the phone rang at 6:30 in the morning and Laschinger said, 'I need you, Pigott.'" He told her that the new leader, Joe Clark, wanted him to arrange a poll to test name recognition of potential candidates in the riding of Ottawa-Carleton, where a byelection was to be held to fill a vacancy created when John Turner, the former Liberal finance minister (and future leader), resigned his seat in Parliament. Pigott, a prominent businesswoman in the capital, was suspicious. She knew the party was eager to find a strong woman candidate, and she was most definitely not interested. Laschinger handed her a tale of woe. Clark wanted the poll done but would not let Laschinger proceed with it because all those listed on the questionnaire were men. "Can we just use your name?" Laschinger wheedled. "I said, 'John, that's not honest because I'm not running. You know I'm not,'" Pigott says. "And he said to me — I knew he had his fingers, toes, and his feet and everything crossed, but he was telling me a lie — he said, 'Look it's just to get the poll done. That's all.' And I guess I was tired; I said yes, and forgot about it. On June 10, I got another call saying, 'Pigott, you topped the poll.'" Then the pressure was applied. Pigott finally agreed to run. She won that 1976 byelection, only to lose the seat to Liberal Jean-Luc Pepin in the 1979 general election.

Crossing swords with his candidate can be a tricky business for a backroomer. In 1991, Laschinger was campaign manager for June Rowlands, a right-wing grandmother running on a law-and-order platform for mayor of Toronto. Rowlands was a Liberal. Liberal colors are red and white. She was also actively (and financially) supported by the Conservative party establishment of Toronto. Tory colors are blue and white. Laschinger and the advertising agency he hired both agreed that red and blue should be Rowlands's campaign colors for her lawn signs, buttons, and brochures. Not only would red and blue emphasize that she was the consensus Liberal-Conservative candidate, they were also the colors of the Metropolitan Toronto police force — a subtle reminder of her popular stance as the candidate who supported the police and who stood for making the streets safer for citizens.

Unfortunately, June Rowlands preferred green. She loved green.

She had used green in all her successful municipal campaigns in the past. It was her lucky color, and she saw no reason to change. She did not care that green was the NDP color or that her NDP opponent, Jack Layton, was using it. Nor did she care that green was the color used by environmentalists, who were definitely not part of her political constituency. She was adamant. At her second meeting with Laschinger, Rowlands gave Laschinger a bag of fifty fluorescent lime-green buttons that she had designed herself. He felt nauseated. The advertising agency was aghast. The green that Rowlands had chosen was not a standard shade and could not be duplicated from printer to printer or application to application.

With time running out to order buttons and signs, Laschinger had a final meeting with his candidate. He proposed that they resolve the dispute by tossing a coin. Heads for red and blue. Tails for green. Warily, Rowlands agreed. Charlie Bartlett, a junior account executive at the ad agency, flipped the coin. "Heads," he declared. Red and blue, it would be. A self-conscious smile flickered on Bartlett's face. Laschinger knew better than to ask to see the coin. If Rowlands had not been halfway across the room, if she had checked the coin, she might — who knows? — have been the fluorescent-lime-green candidate she longed to be.[4]

As a general rule, deceiving the news media or the public is fraught with few perils. The media expect to be lied to. Reporters are too skeptical to believe anything that backroom politicians say during campaigns or to accept more than half of what they say between elections. The public, accustomed to seeing election promises begin to dematerialize within days, if not hours, of the vote tabulation, have become just as cynical. Voters assume that all politicians are essentially the same — they will say one thing and do another, and if the voters do not like it, they can wait four years and elect a new bunch who will be just as duplicitous as the old bunch.

Even New Democrats, who profess a higher virtue than other mortals, are not above creative deception when it serves their purpose. Their negative television commercials in the 1990 Ontario election campaign, which they won, relied more on invention than on fact. The NDP seized on the Liberals' Patti Starr fund-raising scandal (among other transgressions disclosed in the affair was the fact that a senior aide to Premier Peterson had received a free refrigerator and free paint job for his house). But the NDP commercials twisted the facts and got away with it by fudging the Liberal party identification. As Julie Davis, the chairman of the NDP's planning committee in that election, puts it: "Those ads were based on things that had happened. It was hyperbole, but it was hyperbole based on fact. We could have backed it up. For instance, one of [the ads] talked about a series of news clips." The fictitious "clips" alleged that a number of Liberal cabinet ministers had been convicted in court. That was false — but Davis has an explanation, of sorts. It had to do with the first "L" in Liberal:

> It didn't say "Liberal" ministers. It said "Iberal" ministers. And it said "Caribbean holiday" and a "food processor." That was the fridge and the painting of the house — that kind of stuff. So they all had some [basis in fact]. We could tie them back to something. . . . There were a lot of scandals in the administration. It was a calculated risk. We needed to keep hammering home the message, to feed the cynicism of voters towards the Liberals — that they were arrogant, that they weren't listening, and that they weren't what they were pretending to be.

Davis has no apologies. She and her colleagues did what they believed they had to do to win — just as campaign managers in all parties do. If, in the process, they fuel public cynicism about politics and politicians, so be it. The campaign managers' job is to win elections not public esteem. They all bend the rules when they consider it expedient to do so. And, in truth, bending the rules, and getting away with it, gives backroom politicians more fun than anything short of actually winning a convention or an election. For those who play politics seriously, there is a sense of accomplishment that comes, for instance, from successfully packing a delegate-selection meeting by bussing in scores of senior citizens or transients from a skid-row mission. Even greater satisfaction comes from such "achievements" as creating bogus organizations to elect delegates to a leadership convention.

In the 1983 Conservative leadership race, the rules governing the eligibility of delegates were fairly strict. But Laschinger, running John Crosbie's campaign, found a loophole. Each student Conservative club at a recognized post-secondary institution was entitled to send three voting delegates to the convention in Ottawa. Why, Laschinger thought, not create more "recognized post-secondary institutions"? Crosbie organizers got busy. With the complicity of the Tory government of Newfoundland, they identified twenty-one institutions of various sorts — including the Newfoundland

Flying school. The provincial education minister, Lynn Verge, conferred instant post-secondary status on all twenty-one. Crosbie workers set up Tory clubs at these new post-secondary institutions, organized founding meetings, wrote constitutions, and staged delegate-selection meetings. They then delivered the sixty-three applications for delegate status to Conservative headquarters in Ottawa — and held their breath. With much grumbling and not a little suspicion, the party accepted the credentials of eighteen of the twenty-one new institutions, giving Crosbie a windfall of fifty-four delegates. The Newfoundland Flying school, however, was one of the three that crashed on takeoff.

From bending the rules it is a short step to dirty tricks. At the extreme, dirty tricks may involve fraud or other violations of the law. Enough charges of corrupt practices have been laid against politicians and political fixers in recent years to show that, although the vast majority of people in political life are honest, there are some sordid exceptions. But most dirty tricks, while sneaky or underhanded, are not illegal.

In 1971 the leading candidates for the leadership of the governing Tory party in Ontario were William Davis and Allan Lawrence, both provincial cabinet ministers. It was a close race, and with only a few weeks to go before the convention, the Davis organization could feel the momentum shifting to Lawrence. Davis's campaign manager, John Latimer, who owned a summer camp for boys north of Toronto, decided to try to regain momentum by presenting a dazzling evening of entertainment at the convention. He wanted Anne Murray, Canada's most popular singer, to headline the show. Latimer, however, did not know Murray. He approached one of her fellow Maritimers, Tory guru Dalton Camp, to act as intermediary. Camp agreed to help. But there was a complication: Camp's brother-in-law, Norman Atkins, was managing Lawrence's campaign. Latimer swore Camp to secrecy.

As it turned out, Murray was not available to perform at the convention, and Latimer distributed a memo advising key Davis organizers of this fact. The next day, Latimer bumped into Atkins at a meeting. Atkins told him he had been sorry to hear that Murray could not appear. Flabbergasted, Latimer called Camp, who insisted he had not told anyone, especially not Atkins. Three weeks after the leadership convention (won by Davis), Latimer learned what had happened. Atkins told him that, every night during the leadership campaign, he had had two men in uniforms pick up the garbage from Davis headquarters and bring it to Lawrence headquarters for examination. One night, the garbage yielded a copy of Latimer's Anne Murray memo.

Fourteen years later, at the next Ontario Tory leadership convention (in January 1985, in Toronto) campaigners for candidate Larry Grossman came across two pallets of signs belonging to another candidate, Dennis Timbrell, beneath a tarpaulin under the stands of the convention hall. An enterprising Grossman worker took a felt pen and wrote a sign that he placed on top of the tarp — Do Not Move: By Order of Ed Arundell (Arundell was the official in charge of convention arrangements). Canadians (especially Tories) being ever-respectful of authority, the pile sat there unmolested through the convention. Timbrell ran out of signs after the first ballot. But it was not until workmen were cleaning up after the convention was over (and Timbrell and Grossman had both lost) that someone looked under the tarpaulin and discovered 1,400 spanking new — and thoroughly useless — Timbrell signs.

David Smith, a young lawyer in Moncton, N.B., was actively involved in Tory politics in the late 1960s. The 1968 federal election — Pierre Trudeau's first as Liberal leader — was scarcely a vintage election for the Conservatives. Their candidate in Moncton, Charlie Thomas, was given no chance of taking the seat from the Liberals. On the night before the vote, Smith and a group of campaign workers went out to drown their sorrows. After they had closed the last bar in town, they came up with what passed, in their condition, for a bright idea. Maybe they could attract a few sympathy votes, they thought, if they made it appear that Thomas was the victim of a dirty-tricks campaign. So they set out to deface their candidate's lawn signs, scrawling "Vote Liberal" across many of them. Before long, they were picked up by the police. But the story had a happy ending. The police found they could not legally charge Tories with defacing their own signs. And, to everyone's astonishment, Charlie Thomas was elected to Parliament the next day, the unknowing beneficiary of his organization's phony dirty tricks.

3. LEADERS AND LESSER MORTALS

"Leadership involves finding a parade and getting in front of it."
— American futurist John Naisbitt

Robin Sears, the youthful veteran of NDP backrooms, knows pain. Years ago, when he was living in England and working at the Socialist International, he slipped while puttering on the roof of his house. He fell to the ground and smashed his leg horribly. Many operations and untold pain later, Sears still walks with a limp. "If you haven't been through it, it's hard to convey a sense of how totally debilitating the pain is — intellectually and emotionally, as well as physically," Sears says.

Sears felt a stab of real sympathy on the Tuesday night in late October 1988 when the leaders of the three national political parties assembled at a television studio in suburban Ottawa for the English-language TV debate that was to be a pivotal event in the 1988 election campaign. As deputy director of the New Democratic Party campaign, he was at the studio to assist his leader, Ed Broadbent. Sears was hurrying from the studio to Broadbent's trailer in the parking lot when he passed Liberal leader John Turner, who was making his way into the studio for his one-on-one debate with Prime Minister Brian Mulroney. Turner had campaigned valiantly for weeks, despite a serious back problem that caused him unremitting pain in his lower back and leg. "He could barely walk," Sears recalls.

Every step he took he was walking like a drunken sailor, sort of leaning on his good leg and almost falling over with the exertion and the pain. But the moment he got into the studio, he straightened up and walked absolutely calmly across the floor and took his place, standing at the lectern. The worst thing to do in that circumstance is to have to stand for any extended period of time. It really brought a lump to my throat to watch that. It showed such an incredible amount of control and personal discipline in a difficult situation, which nobody else talked about or commented on — and yet it must have been among the biggest things he had to deal with that night: being in the middle of a sentence and being racked by stabbing pain.

Turner put on one of the finest performances of his entire political career that night. He hammered Mulroney as he never had been hammered before over the Tory government's free-trade deal with the United States. The passion in Turner's voice was gripping:

> We are just as Canadian as you are, Mr. Mulroney, but I will tell you this: You mentioned 120 years of history. We built a country east and west and north. We built it on an infrastructure that deliberately resisted the continental pressure of the United States. For 120 years, we have done that. With one signature of a pen, you've reversed that, thrown us into the north-south influence of the United States, and will reduce us, will reduce us I am sure, to a colony of the United States, because when the economic levers go, the political independence is sure to follow.

Taken aback, Mulroney protested that the free-trade deal was just a "commercial document" that was "cancellable on six months' notice." "Cancellable?" Turner snorted. "You're talking about our relationship with the United States."

That exchange became "the clip" of the 1988 leaders' debates. Overnight, the Liberals began to close the gap on the Conservatives. Soon they moved ahead in the polls. It took a desperate strategy by the Tories, including some of the nastiest negative TV commercials the relatively genteel world of Canadian politics had ever produced — plus a massive pro–free trade advertising blitz by big business — to stop the Liberal momentum, revive the Conservative campaign, and save the Mulroney government from ignominious defeat.

Robin Sears agreed with John Turner on free trade, if nothing else. He had no use for the Liberals and would never have dreamed of voting for them. He thought they had given the country appalling government during Pierre Trudeau's fifteen years as prime minister, and he believed Liberal policies under Turner to be, if possible, even more wrong-headed. Yet, as one political warrior to another, Sears sympathized with and respected Turner — a man who had been prime minister for just eighty days in 1984, who was burdened by an undisciplined and largely incompetent caucus, who had to put down an uprising in Liberal ranks during the 1988 campaign, and who fought through adversity and pain to make that election a real contest.

Sears's feelings were not unique. Backroom politicians are a cynical lot. Yet much of the cynicism is a pose, a protective veneer to hide their true emotions from the public and from one another. Most of them are enthusiasts. If they are not political groupies when they first get involved in the backroom, they soon become groupies. They are star-struck by political leaders — by the leaders they serve and even by some with whom they battle. The frontroom politicians who go forth to dance on the electoral stage, staking their futures on the reviews of the public, are heroes to their acolytes in the backroom. Backroomers are the stage managers in the great production. Most lack the stomach to risk public rejection, even humiliation, as their leaders do every day.

And although backroom warriors would be too embarrassed to admit it, they worship their heroes the way any kid who ever laced on a pair of hockey skates worships Rocket Richard, Gordie Howe, Bobby Orr, or Wayne Gretzky. It is impossible to find anyone who served Trudeau who has an unkind memory of him. There is adulation in the tones of battle-scarred veterans like Keith Davey, Jim Coutts, and Martin Goldfarb when they talk about Trudeau; he gave their lives meaning. "Trudeau had such self-confidence in his own ability!" says Goldfarb. "He was a guy who never had second thoughts about anything important. Trudeau was the one man in my life that I know has lived his dream." A note of something akin to love creeps into the voice of Finlay MacDonald and Flora MacDonald when they reminisce about their political hero, Bob Stanfield. To a half-century of Canadian socialists, Tommy Douglas was a saint — period.

Nancy McLean, the Tory strategist and media consultant, could be as hard-bitten and as cynical as any other backroom player when it came to preparing a candidate for the electoral stage or wringing the last drop of partisan advantage out of a television performance. But she turned nostalgic and sentimental when she talked about her hero — Richard Hatfield, the Conservative premier of New Brunswick from 1970 to 1987. Hatfield, who died of brain cancer in 1991, was an inspired eccentric. In many ways, he was his own worst enemy, pursuing a lifestyle that would have been bold in Toronto or Montreal and was bizarre in Fredericton and Moncton. He was also, however, a politician of conviction and uncommon courage. He adored politics and everything about it. He loved his province and his country with an unfashionable passion, and he was never bashful about letting his love show. He said what he believed. He did what he said he would do. He championed un-popular causes. He made the French-speaking Acadians of New Brunswick at home in the Tory party, and he took immense per-sonal and political delight in New Brunswick's status as an officially bilingual province. He endured as premier for seventeen years — a remarkable stretch in an age when television often burns out political leaders in a single term — until, in the end, he destroyed his party by overstaying his welcome with the voters of New Bruns-wick. "Richard Hatfield was a wonderful, wonderful man," McLean remembered, "and a great Canadian, and someone who never, never lost his sense of humor. While he was totally committed to every ideal and idea that he had, he had this childlike curiosity and quality to him that allowed him to participate in normal events in the normal way."

Hatfield's curiosity and sense of adventure carried him to Wood-stock, New York, and some of the other great rock-music festivals of the late 1960s and early 1970s. He was the only Canadian po-litical leader who would have dared to go — much less admit that he had gone — to controversial counter-culture events such as those. To him, they were part of life's voyage of self-discovery. One of Hatfield's greatest political admirers and closest friends was Flora MacDonald, the backroom Tory who successfully made the tran-sition to the frontroom as an MP and federal cabinet minister. "Rich-ard had an innocent curiosity," MacDonald says. "He believed that all people were good and that when they did things together, things would work out well, even if they were people [as at Woodstock] who were not then part of the mainstream of society." Hatfield was excited when he returned from Woodstock in 1969, telling MacDonald he had heard two new singers whom he was sure were going to be great. Their names were Simon and Garfunkel.

A few years later, Hatfield, by then premier of New Brunswick and a firm believer in nuclear energy as a means of stimulating economic growth in the Maritimes, took up with a group of anti-nuclear activists at a rock festival. "Richard was sitting around with all these people, and they were all talking about various issues — anti-nuclear this and anti-nuclear that," said Nancy McLean. "He sat there and he finally said, 'Now, wait a minute. None of you knows what you're talking about. I'm the only one of you that owns a nuclear power plant.' It was so Richard. He was the only one in the whole pack [of contemporary politicians] you could call a great Canadian, who constantly thought of his country, but who could still be so much a part of something like that."

Love does not make backroom players blind. They know close up all the warts on the leaders they serve. They live with their inconsistencies. They overlook their weaknesses — laziness, drinking, and womanizing being three of the most common flaws in the old boys' club that still dominates Canadian politics. Turner often chose the tennis court over the office. Trudeau was contemptuous of lesser mortals (meaning most people). Jean Chrétien would not read the briefing material prepared for him when he was a cabinet minister. The late Don Jamieson refused to read any memo longer than one-half page. And Brian Mulroney possessed a distorted recollection of events, never forgot a slight (real or imagined), and was congenitally incapable of ignoring his press clippings, every sentence of which he scoured for negative nuances. But in the backrooms, daily exposure to a leader's frailties does not produce disenchantment, nor does familiarity breed contempt — especially not when the leader is under attack or buried in the basement of public esteem. If it is not the "Stockholm Syndrome" (the name given to the rapport that sometimes develops between hostages and their captors), it is something close to it.

In 1978, the Trudeau Liberals, having won a majority government four years earlier, were preparing to call another general election. They wanted to hold it in the fall of 1978. There were two impediments, however. The first was the government's finances, which were in a mess. In the spring of 1978, Trudeau sent a warning to all his ministers to impose severe restraints on departmental expenditures. Nothing happened. Michael Pitfield, the clerk of the Privy Council, reported to the prime minister in the summer that the warnings had had no effect.[1]

Trudeau went off to the "Economic Summit" of leaders of the seven leading Western industrial countries in Bonn, where he heard a great deal of breast-beating about the need for governments to control spending. When he got home, he went on national television to beat his own breast and to announce a program of $1.5 billion in federal spending cuts. (That the prime minister announced the cuts without informing his finance minister, Jean Chrétien, spoke volumes about Trudeau's low regard for Chrétien, the future leader of the Liberal party.)

The second impediment was more serious. Trudeau's pollster, Martin Goldfarb, reported that the Liberals could not possibly win an election in the fall of 1978. "The bottom had fallen out of our numbers," as Keith Davey recalled.[2] Just how far the bottom had fallen became apparent on October 16, when the government, unable to delay any longer in calling byelections to fill a record fifteen vacancies in the Commons, lost thirteen of them.

The Prime Minister's Office became more like a bunker than the hub of government. Among those huddled inside the bunker, however, there was nothing but praise for what they, at least, saw as Trudeau's statesmanship and self-denial in eschewing the opportunity to call a general election that fall. As the gospel according to the PMO had it, the decision had nothing to do with discouraging poll results. It had everything to do with taking the high road: Trudeau did not call an election because the country's condition was too fragile to withstand the strains and stresses of a campaign. (Whether this fragility was supposed to be economic or constitutional was never entirely clear.) Trudeau's then press secretary, Patrick Gossage, a true believer, had deep respect for Trudeau's decision. "He had the best reason not to go," Gossage says today. "It would have been divisive for the country. Thank God he didn't call it. And in 1979, when he ran, he didn't have the numbers, but he lost for the right reason and he was able to come back [in 1980]."

Proximity to power colors perceptions. An onlooker from outside the Liberal backroom/bunker would attribute less lofty motives. Trudeau did not call an election in 1978 because he knew he could not win. He did call an election the following year because the Constitution required it. He lost in 1979 because the country was so weary of his jaded, aimless government that it was prepared to vote for anyone else, even Joe Clark. In one of the great political resurrections of all time, Trudeau returned to power in 1980 because the country was so appalled by the infant Clark government that it was willing to hold its nose and to vote for absolutely anyone else, even Trudeau and his discredited Liberals.

Backroomers respect the courage of a leader who chooses his course and sticks to it, even if they think his course is ill-advised or downright stupid. David Lewis, the leader of the NDP from 1971 to 1975, frequently frustrated his organizers by being bloody-minded on policy issues. Party dogma usually caused the NDP more harm than good in its struggle to broaden its public appeal. Lewis, however, did not believe in short cuts. He knew the importance of consistency in a policy-driven party such as the NDP. "David Lewis was always wise about the big negatives that the party was associated with, whether it was public ownership or abortion," says Robin Sears. "He said, 'Look, the worst thing you can do is to deny the policy. The second-worst thing you can do is to try to downplay it in a way that makes you sound nervous or immature. What you do is say, I'm sorry you don't agree with me. Here is what I believe. There are always other things we can agree on. Let's talk about them.'" (NDP candidates did not always share Lewis's forbearance. In the 1972 federal election, Terry Grier, the NDP candidate in Toronto-Lakeshore, became the target of an anti-abortion campaign. Right-to-lifers from as far afield as Detroit poured into Lakeshore to knock on doors and urge voters to reject Grier and the NDP. One day, while Grier was canvassing, a householder tore a strip off him over his support for the NDP's policy of abortion on demand. "Terry defied all the candidate-training instructions," Sears says, with a laugh. "He said he couldn't resist, that it would be good for his blood pressure. He said, 'Quite frankly, sir, I wouldn't want your vote. I'd be embarrassed if you voted for me.'" Grier won that election, upsetting an incumbent Liberal.)

David MacNaughton gained new respect for his boss, Liberal cabinet minister Don Jamieson, while campaigning in Newfoundland in the same election. "A guy came up to Jamieson and said, 'I want to tell you that I applied for my unemployment insurance six weeks ago and I still haven't heard anything. If I don't get it before election time, I'm not voting for you,'" MacNaughton says. "Jamieson told me to please take this guy's name and social insurance number. So I did. There was a whole bunch of fishermen there. Jamieson said, 'Now, let me tell you something. I'm going to ask my assistant to make sure you *don't* get your unemployment insurance before election time, because I'm not going to put up with that B.S.!'" MacNaughton was impressed. "I went to Ottawa thinking I was going to stay for two years. I stayed for six and a half. It was really because of that kind of stuff."

At times leaders cause their backroom handlers to despair because they are not political enough. MacNaughton felt that way when, more than a decade after his experience with Jamieson in Newfoundland, he worked with his friend David Peterson, the Liberal premier of Ontario from 1985 to 1990. MacNaughton respected Peterson for taking the position that none of his political pals should be rewarded with government jobs after the Liberals came to office in 1985. But fine principles often make lousy politics. "I think David went too far," says MacNaughton. "You can't fault a guy for being too much like that, but all your friends think you're a complete jerk." Peterson, in fact, was hurt in two ways. As the insiders saw it, loyal Liberals who, after forty-two years in opposition, did not get their long-anticipated opportunity to feed at the public trough lost their enthusiasm for the Peterson government. Yet the public perception of Peterson was quite different, and the NDP successfully campaigned against him in the 1990 Ontario election as a lackey to vested interests and to his party's financial supporters, especially large real estate developers.

Brian Peckford also had a streak of political righteousness that was disconcerting to the practical people in the backroom. In 1979, when he captured the Conservative leadership in Newfoundland and, a few months later, when he won the provincial election, he was assisted by a Toronto advertising agency, Camp Associates, and its president (now Senator) Norman Atkins. Atkins, who hoped his agency would land the province's tourism advertising, was upset when Peckford declared that the Newfoundland government would deal only with Newfoundland-based agencies. John Laschinger, who had organized Peckford's leadership and election campaigns, wrote a note to Peckford, suggesting, as tactfully as possible, that it would be smart politics to make sure that friends who had proved helpful in the past were kept happy and keen to participate in future battles. The new premier, he suggested, might at least allow mainland ad agencies to submit bids for provincial business, which could be judged for quality and price against bids from Newfoundland agencies. Laschinger's diplomacy was wasted. Peckford turned him down flat, reminding him of his campaign promise to direct provincial government business to Newfoundlanders as a way of encouraging local enterprise and skills. "All of my statements and position papers — that you and your friends helped to polish and publish — were not just election vote-getters," Peckford admonished Laschinger. "The general public are often cynical of politicians because, to be quite truthful, they often say one thing and mean another. I do not intend to give anyone the chance to so think about myself. I had hoped to change politics in Newfoundland. . . . If the world doesn't let my universe so unfold, well, I'll go back to jigging fish in Hall's Bay." (Camp Associates got no Newfoundland government business in the decade that Peckford was premier. Laschinger organized two more successful election campaigns for him, using local advertising agencies and talent.)

Brian Mulroney was more flexible in such matters. He was prepared to be whatever he had to be to get wherever the parade was going. He had that useful political knack of being able to make his followers believe he shared their views, without actually declaring what his own views, if any, were. But Mulroney did have at least one definite opinion when he moved into the leader's office. He did not like Allan Gregg. Mulroney was sure of that. He did not trust Gregg and did not intend to let his Decima Research do the party's polling. His view was shared and applauded by right-wing members of the Tory caucus who were turned off by Gregg's long hair, his earring, and his habit of dressing like an off-duty musician from a back-up rock band — which was just how some of the adolescent children of Tory MPs dressed.

There seemed to be three reasons for Mulroney's antipathy. Gregg had been the Conservative party pollster under Joe Clark, whose leadership Mulroney had worked so assiduously to undermine. Mulroney believed Gregg should have been strictly neutral during the leadership campaign, but he felt he had favored Clark. Second, the caucus believed, although there was no evidence of it, that Gregg had leaked confidential party polling data to journalist Jeffrey Simpson for his 1980 award-winning book, *Discipline of Power*, a critical assessment of the short-lived Clark government. Finally, Mulroney was not going to forgive Gregg for co-authoring (with journalist Patrick Martin and political scientist George Perlin) a book on the 1983 leadership campaign. The book, *Contenders*, was considerably kinder to Clark, the incumbent, than to Mulroney, the usurper.

The Conservatives were preparing for a general election that they expected the governing Liberals to call in 1984. By February that year — eight months after Mulroney beat Clark for the leadership — virtually all of the election organization was in place. Norm Atkins, the head of Ontario's Big Blue Machine, had been installed as national campaign chairman, and Laschinger as operations manager. Together, they had tapped the resources of the Big Blue Machine and the backroom organizations of Mulroney's opponents for the leadership to assemble their campaign team. The money was rolling in, the machine was purring, and there was only one problem: there was no pollster. Mulroney would not accept Gregg, but he had not replaced him.

Mulroney was never comfortable dealing with Atkins, who was the brother-in-law of Tory backroomer Dalton Camp (the founder of Camp Associates). Atkins had built his reputation as a strategist to Bill Davis in Ontario and Bob Stanfield in Ottawa. Waiting until Atkins was on holiday in Aruba, Mulroney phoned Laschinger. He held out an olive branch. He had never seen any of Decima's work, Mulroney said. Perhaps they should ask Gregg to do a poll of Toronto. Seeing the opening, Laschinger said what they really needed, quickly, was a benchmark survey of the entire country, against which the Tories could measure their performance as the election neared. Mulroney agreed. The impasse was broken. Gregg was commissioned to do the survey and has been polling for the Conservative party ever since. When the Mulroney Tories took office in 1984, Decima Research became the preferred supplier of polling research for the entire federal government.

The Gregg episode revealed two things about Mulroney. A virtuoso at handling his caucus, he will play along with the prejudices of his MPs, as he did with their dislike of Gregg, until some more important objective intrudes — in this case, the need to complete the party's election preparedness. Second, he nurses grudges and personal antipathies. He nurses them for a very long time — but not so long nor so deeply as to interfere with his only real goal: getting elected.

To backroom politicians, John Crosbie is more like his fellow Newfoundlander Peckford than he is like Mulroney, the man who defeated him for the leadership in 1983. Laschinger found himself disagreeing with Crosbie but respecting his principles in that leadership campaign, just as he had disagreed with but respected Peckford four years earlier. With Crosbie, the issue was not one of patronage but of policy. Crosbie took the position that Canada needed a new international trade policy and that the cornerstone of the new policy should be free trade with the United States. Although organizers generally defer to their candidates on matters of policy — policy issues being more interesting and important to candidates than to their handlers — Laschinger, as Crosbie's campaign manager, was worried. He feared that convention delegates would be frightened off by Crosbie's advocacy of free trade with the United States, which traditionally had been a Liberal, not a Conservative policy. He observed that other leadership candidates, notably Mulroney, were arguing against Canada–U.S. free trade. Laschinger urged Crosbie to back off, to soft-pedal his free-trade scheme, perhaps to disguise it as "freer" trade, at least until after the leadership convention. Crosbie refused. He believed in free trade and he continued to espouse it. He did not win the leadership. But at least he did not have to reverse course when Mulroney, performing an ideological arabesque, led Canada into a free-trade agreement with the United States in 1988.

Robert Stanfield was not a man for arabesques. Although he may have seemed dull and plodding — and he must have struck many Canadians that way because they declined in three elections to make him prime minister — to backroom Tories he was a leader of genuine conviction. And he stood by his convictions, frequently at considerable political cost. Stanfield believed in bilingualism, in the equality of French and English, and in the right of English- and French-speaking citizens to demand federal services in their mother tongue wherever they happened to be in Canada. His were not hugely popular beliefs in the Tory caucus in those days — the late 1960s and early 1970s — and it was an ongoing struggle for Stanfield to keep his MPs in line.

The issue came to an ugly head early in the 1974 election campaign when Leonard Jones, the mayor of Moncton, N.B., and an aggressively outspoken opponent of bilingualism, decided to seek the Conservative nomination. Recruiting large numbers of "instant Tories," Jones packed the constituency meeting and wrested the nomination away from Charlie Thomas, the sitting MP. The episode caused a media sensation, which became more sensational when Stanfield, exercising his prerogative as leader, refused to sign Jones's nomination, denying him status as a Tory candidate. Soon after, Stanfield flew to Moncton to ask the executive of the local Conservative constituency association to override the membership and endorse Thomas as their candidate again. The executive agreed, with some misgivings. The internal dispute over Jones having cost the Conservatives valuable time and momentum in the opening stages of the campaign, Stanfield hurried to western Canada to try to gain the initiative by attacking Pierre Trudeau and calling for the imposition of wage and price controls (a policy that Trudeau mocked in 1974 and implemented in 1975).

Three weeks later, Stanfield and Laschinger, the party's national director, sat in the front section of the leader's chartered DC-9, heading for Toronto. It was 2:00 a.m. as they reviewed Stanfield's itinerary for the following week. Stanfield asked Laschinger to make sure the schedule was changed so that he could get back to Moncton at some point in the week. A return to Moncton was the last thing the national director wanted. With Leonard Jones running as an independent, Laschinger knew that Charlie Thomas's cause was hopeless. Stanfield's return to the scene of the dispute would simply give Jones more free publicity, revive the bilingualism issue, rekindle passions and divert the Tories' national campaign from more urgent priorities. Laschinger tried to talk Stanfield out of it, only to be stopped dead in his objections. "John," said Stanfield, "I asked Charlie Thomas to run for me. I wouldn't be able to look at myself in the mirror if I didn't go back to campaign for him."

Stanfield went back to Moncton the following week. As expected, Thomas lost to Jones. Stanfield lost his third consecutive election to Trudeau and shortly afterward announced his departure as Tory leader.

Principle often carries a heavy price in politics. One of the heaviest was in Ontario in 1985. Bill Davis had retired after fourteen years as Conservative leader and premier. Although Davis had his troubles, he left with the Tory string unbroken — forty-two uninterrupted years in power. Before he departed, however, he dropped a political time bomb — a promise to extend full provincial funding to Ontario's Roman Catholic separate schools for all the years of secondary school. It was Davis's way of thanking Ontario's Catholics for their support over the years, but the proposed legislation — Bill 30 — offended many Protestants and distressed Ontarians who believed in the separation of state and church.

The Ontario Tories, who in the past had demonstrated a sixth sense when it came to selecting the right leader at the right time — as they had done with Leslie Frost, John Robarts, and Davis himself — chose the wrong successor to Davis in 1985. Instead of going with youth and freshness, they elected a long-time cabinet minister, Frank Miller, who was too conservative, too rural (a car dealer from Muskoka), and too much a part of the Davis political generation to be able to lead the party through the late 1980s and into the 1990s. Miller compounded the party's grave mistake of choosing him by making the fatal error of calling a hasty election.

Partly because of Miller's leadership and partly because of public anger at Davis over separate schools, the 1985 election was a disaster for the Conservatives. They won a plurality of the Legislature's 125 seats — with 52 to the Liberals' 48 and the NDP's 25. But the Tories' days were numbered, and it became a very small number when the other two parties agreed to oust the Miller government.

They negotiated a two-year "accord" under which the Liberals would govern with NDP support. Unsure of the loyalties of the Conservative backroom, Miller summoned three aides whom he knew he could trust not to have any agenda other than his own — Hugh Mackenzie, Sally Barnes, and Tony Brebner — to help him consider his options.

The three had already been worrying. Some Tories smelled blood, and pressure for another leadership convention was beginning to build. The three loyalists felt Miller needed to be given information and advice that was absolutely untainted by the ambitions of other Conservatives. They secretly retained an outsider, Art Finkelstein from Diversified Research Inc. in New York, to conduct a poll of Ontario voters. About a week before the Legislature was due to vote on the Speech from the Throne — which was when the Miller government would be toppled — Finkelstein flew to Toronto with his poll results and was smuggled up to an apartment at the Sutton Place Hotel, near Queen's Park, for a late-night meeting with Miller.

Finkelstein opened the meeting by saying he had to ask one question: What did Miller think of Bill 30 (the separate-school funding legislation)? "Frank looked at him for a minute and he said, 'I think it stinks,'" Hugh Mackenzie recalls. "And Finkelstein said, 'Fine.' He said, 'I'm talking to you as if you're in the holding cell and the electric chair is next door. We all know there are some real problems here and your options are limited. But within the context of those options, I think there are some things we can do.'"

Finkelstein then sketched a scenario that required Miller to break with Davis, renounce the separate-school policy, and move for an immediate election and a second chance at winning the province. His poll, Finkelstein reported, showed that a very high proportion of Ontarians felt Miller deserved a second chance. Mackenzie remembers the pollster's advice:

> My advice to you is that you announce that you have booked time two days before the Throne Speech on all of the networks in Ontario for a six o'clock speech to the province and that it's sufficiently important that you are cancelling all engagements between now and then. You disappear and you let the media guess where you are and what you're doing. You just let the hype go. And two nights before the Throne Speech, you show up and you basically say four things on TV. One: Do a mea culpa and take full and direct responsibility for the

fact that you did not communicate as clearly as you ought to have during the election. Two: Say that while you have the utmost respect for your predecessor [Davis], it is clear to you that people are not prepared to accept full funding for separate schools to Grade 13 . . . and that you are going to reverse that decision and it is not going to happen. Three: Say that while you won the most seats in the election, you are not prepared to interpret that as a mandate to govern, but that nobody gave Bob Rae [the NDP leader] a mandate to determine who the government of Ontario was going to be. And four: Tell them you will be meeting with the lieutenant-governor and requesting that he agree to the calling of an election . . . and say we're making the commitment now of no funding for separate schools.

The meeting over, Finkelstein was, in Mackenzie's words, "put back in the trunk of the car and taken out to the airport again." The group talked all evening. In the middle of the night, they sought legal opinions on whether the lieutenant-governor would accede to a request from Miller to dissolve the Legislature for another election — or whether he would insist on calling on the Liberal opposition leader, David Peterson, to form a government. The advice they got was that, if the request for dissolution were made before the Miller government was defeated in the Legislature, the lieutenant-governor would likely grant it. But if it were made after the government fell, he would feel bound to turn to Peterson, to give the Liberals a chance to govern.

Miller, however, rejected Finkelstein's daring plan for two reasons. The first was his uncertainty about his ability, given the battered state of the party, to mount an effective election campaign. The second, more important reason was one of principle: Miller was not prepared to disown Davis and repudiate the policy of the Davis government, of which he had been an integral part. His loyalty to Davis would not let him adopt the one strategy that might have kept the Tories in power in Ontario. "At the end of the day, Frank Miller could not bring himself to run a campaign that would be singularly criticizing Bill Davis," says Mackenzie. "He'd spent his career being loyal to Bill Davis."

Miller's decision spelled the certain end of Tory Ontario. His government was defeated on a vote in the Legislature the following week; David Peterson became premier (and the separate schools soon got their funding). On the afternoon of that fateful vote, Tom

MacMillan and a group of Tory backroom veterans gathered for a drink in the bar on the roof of the Park Plaza Hotel to watch the sun set on forty-two years of Conservative rule at Queen's Park. They toasted one another. MacMillan has a vivid memory of that moment.

As the glasses were raised and the sun went down, an advertising blimp bearing the name of an American beer floated eerily across the Toronto twilight. The name on the blimp: MILLER.

PART TWO

MANAGING THE CAMPAIGN

THERE ARE SIX ESSENTIAL TOOLS FOR BUILDING A successful election or leadership campaign. First, campaign directors must have good polling; they can no longer win without it. Second, they need a careful strategy that is securely rooted in the polling research. Third, they have to have a strong, highly motivated organization. Fourth, they must be able to exploit the power of television — commercials, leaders' debates, and campaign news coverage. Fifth, they need to control campaign spending, especially now that election-spending limitations have become the norm. Sixth, they require a professional, efficient fund-raising operation to keep the machine running.

With these six tools, competent backroom managers are equipped to win virtually any campaign they take on. If they lack one or more of them, however, they are courting defeat.

4. WHERE'S THE PONY?

"Like any seer or oracle, the pollster plays a role that is viewed with a combination of respect, fear, intrigue, and controversy."
— Liberal pollster Martin Goldfarb

 It was a late July morning in 1990, one of those mornings that warns of scorching heat to come in the concrete canyons of Toronto. The remnants of the Conservatives' Big Blue Machine had gathered in the eighth-floor boardroom of Hill & Knowlton-PAI, specialists in lobbying and masters of manipulating public opinion. These were not the best of times for Big Blue, the organization that had dominated Ontario politics through William Davis's fourteen years as premier. The Tories had lost power in 1985 and were crushed in the election of 1987, finishing third in both seats and popular vote. Davis was gone, replaced by Frank Miller. Miller was gone, replaced by Larry Grossman. Grossman was gone, replaced by Mike Harris, a genial one-time golf pro from North Bay.

The summer of 1990 should have been a time for cottages and vacation trips, not for an election alert. It was only three years since the last election; Ontario elects its governments to five-year terms, and normally they use up at least four of those years before troubling voters with another call to the polls. But these were not normal times. The Meech Lake constitutional accord had collapsed a month earlier, amid national recrimination. Signs of an economic recession were everywhere. Liberal premier David Peterson, the perfect incarnation of the yuppie 'eighties, though criticized for being too enthusiastic in his support of Prime Minister Brian Mulroney and the Meech Lake accord, was still riding high in the polls. The timing would never be better for him to call a snap election. There was not a pundit or a pollster in the province who doubted that Peterson's Liberals would be re-elected with a massive majority in the 130-seat Ontario Legislature.

Allan Gregg did not doubt it. The pollster of choice for Tories everywhere in Canada for more than a decade, Gregg was the reason for the gathering that sweltering July morning. The principal players of the Ontario Conservative backroom were assembled to hear the results of Gregg's latest taking of the Ontario pulse: 1,200 interviews over the previous two weeks. They had steeled themselves for the worst.

Gregg fiddled with the focus of the overhead projector. He shuffled an inch-thick pile of acetates that set out his findings in painful detail. In matter-of-fact tones, he told a small story. Early one Christmas morning, Gregg began, a young boy rose while his parents were still sleeping and slipped downstairs to see what Santa had left. The only thing in his stocking was a heap of horse manure. Far from being upset, the boy was ecstatic. He raced upstairs, burst into his parents' bedroom, and woke them with an excited cry, "Oh, Daddy, Daddy. Where's the pony?"

Glancing at John Laschinger, the Conservative election campaign chairman, Gregg gestured at his stack of research. "John, I want you to understand — there is no pony for you in these numbers. All you'll find here is horseshit. Peterson and the Liberals are going to elect ninety-nine members, and the PC party will elect four."

Gregg was dead wrong, but so was everyone else. One of the most surprised people in Ontario was Bob Rae, the leader of the New Democratic Party, who found himself premier-elect on September 6, 1990. "We took a poll sometime in the middle of '89 before we were doing our pre-election work," Rae observed later. "We were at 23 per cent. And we worked and we sweated and we took our issues across the province. We did campaigns at the door. We did everything we possibly could. And at the end of that we got it up to 24 per cent."[1] The NDP began election preparations in earnest in the fall of 1989, with David Gotthilf, a Winnipeg pollster, doing its polling. NDP strategist David Reville remembers the months leading up to the midsummer election call in 1990. "We would have been gratified if we held on to the official opposition and we had got up over thirty seats," Reville admitted.[2]

The experts — Rae, Reville, Laschinger, Gregg, Gotthilf, Martin Goldfarb, among many, many others — thought they understood the mood of Ontarians that summer. But they failed to anticipate the pent-up dissatisfaction, the hidden anger that would swamp David Peterson and his Liberal government and — to the utter astonishment of just about everyone (including most New Democrats) and to the horror of many (especially the business community) — elect a majority NDP government.

Table 1

How the party pollsters read the parties' popular support in their last province-wide surveys prior to the calling of the 1990 Ontario election

	Gotthilf (NDP) (Feb.)	Goldfarb (L) (May)	Gregg (PC) (July)	Election Results (Sept.6)	Seats Won (Sept. 6)
NDP	27.9%	31%	32%	37.6%	74
Liberal	46.7	48	48	32.4	36
Conservative	22.9	21	19	23.5	20
Others	2.5	—	1	6.5	0

How did it happen? How did cautious Ontario come to abandon its chaste soul to the socialist hordes? How could such a shocking upset possibly happen right under the expert noses of the pollsters and their comrades in the backroom?

The answer to the last question, according to the pollsters, is that it did not happen without their knowledge. Gotthilf, for example, knew the public mood was volatile. He asked the 60 per cent of Ontarians who come within the NDP's "universe" of potential supporters which party and leader they thought would do the best job of handling the important issues of the day, from cleaning up the environment to protecting jobs. Rae and the NDP always came out on top — which indicated serious dissatisfaction with the government's performance. But when he asked the same potential NDP supporters how they intended to vote, they said "Liberal." The dissatisfaction with the government did not seem to be influencing the voting intentions of Gotthilf's respondents. All the pollsters found the Liberals comfortably ahead. All also found Liberal support was the proverbial one mile wide and one inch deep. But they and their clients — especially the Liberals — were slow to grasp the full implications of the shallowness of Peterson's support.

"A pollster's work is an art form, not just a profession," says Goldfarb, an anthropologist by training and today the leading exponent of polling-as-art. As he explains:

> It is the interpretation of results, not the collection of data, that sets a good pollster apart from an ordinary one. There is no magical formula. As any capable cultural anthropologist knows — and a capable pollster is a sophisticated student of cultural behavior — deciphering the nuances of attitudes, opinions and behaviors in a context of cultural complexity is a difficult task. It requires intellectual instinct, intuition and an immense amount of experience. It requires a genuine intimacy with culture and sensitivity to a generation. Cultural artifacts change quickly in our age, and pollsters must be equally quick to anticipate, recognize and analyze these changes.[3]

But if the art of polling involves such sensitivity, instinct, and intuition (not to mention intimacy with culture), how can it be that the country's most expert, most sensitive, and most expensive pollsters were as oblivious as the man on Main Street to the fact that Peterson was making the miscalculation of a lifetime? But that's what he did that July, when he decided to call an election one year earlier than normal and two years earlier than necessary.

The election brought the NDP success beyond its wildest dreams. The Conservatives, confronting annihilation, survived with a measure of dignity. The Liberals blew themselves out of power. All from following — or not following — their pollsters.

"Polling determines everything," says Michael Adams, president of Environics Research Group and (along with Gregg, Goldfarb, and Winnipeg's Angus Reid) one of the stars in the Canadian polling firmament. "Polling determines when the election is held, what the campaign is all about, what the platform is, where the leader shows up, what he wears and what he talks about, whether his spouse is there, what the television commercials say. Every single detail is determined by polling."

It wasn't always thus. In the beginning — in the dark ages before there were pollsters — there was the newspaper reporter. He walked down the residential streets of his town, knocking on doors and asking whoever answered how he or she planned to vote. More enterprising reporters asked a follow-up question: "And do you think your wife (husband) will be voting the same way as you, sir (ma'am)?" It did not occur to the reporter — this being long before polling had become a science, let alone an art — to ask his respondents about such subtleties as whether they were on the voters' list, whether they intended to vote, whether they knew who the candidates were, or whether they had the foggiest notion of what the election was all about. Sometimes, respondents told the reporter honestly how they were going to vote. If it suited them, they lied to him. Often, they slammed the door in his face and yelled that he should get lost before they set the dog on him. (These respondents the reporter conscientiously marked down as "undecided.")

Reporters called this polling. They loved it. It got them away from the drudgery of the newsroom. It gave them a sense of authority, of importance; they knew what was going to happen before the rest of the community did. Or so they thought.

In the old days, the backroom pols also had their own rudimentary form of polling. "You did it yourself," remembers Clare Westcott, a backroom Tory for a half-century and a longtime aide to former Ontario premier Bill Davis. "It was at a very grass-roots level. I'd go into a small town and sit with a voters' list in a room with a few people who knew everybody in town and go down the list and write in how the people were going to vote." In Ontario's Huron County in 1945, the Conservatives nominated a graveyard-monument maker from Seaforth. The Liberals picked a trucking-company proprietor from nearby Exeter. Westcott knew enough about the political history of Huron County to know that the Tories had a chance only if the candidate of the old Co-operative Commonwealth Federation (now the NDP) polled at least 1,200 votes. But just before nomination day, the CCF candidate announced he was withdrawing from the race because he was out of money. Three days later, "Elmer Bell [the boss of the Tory backroom] put $1,000 in an envelope, slid it under [the CCF candidate's] door in Goderich, and ran," Westcott says. The CCFer revived his campaign and siphoned off the requisite 1,200 votes, and the Tory monument maker won the riding.

From the reading of voters' lists in hotel rooms and the slipping of envelopes of cash under opponents' doors, the political process moved ahead. Campaign managers summoned their advertising agencies and asked them to find out what the people were thinking. Ad agencies were a natural choice. They developed campaigns to peddle consumer goods and services to the public, so they must, presumably, know what the public wanted. The agencies obliged by conducting political polling as an offshoot of their market research. In 1953, for example, the federal Tories, under the leadership of George Drew, a former Ontario premier, asked McKim Advertising to conduct a national poll to identify the issues around which a campaign strategy could be devised. To McKim, it was simple. Knowing that the Tories felt comfortable when railing against confiscatory taxation, McKim asked three thousand Canadians whether they agreed that taxes were too high. Sure enough, most of the respondents, thus prompted, said, yes, darn right, come to think about it, taxes were sure too high. Delighted to have their views thus reinforced, the Conservatives made an attack on high taxes the centre-piece of their 1953 election campaign. The creators of this strategy were dumbfounded on election night when Drew's Tories won only 51 seats to 170 for Louis St. Laurent and the Liberals. The Tory poll was not wrong, as far as it went, but it did not go nearly far enough. It found that people did not like high taxes. It did not find out what issues might actually influence their voting behavior.

The modern era in Canadian political polling dates to the early 1960s when political organizers turned to social scientists with expertise in understanding and predicting human behavior. Enter the professional pollster — and, like most innovations in Canadian politics, he entered from the United States.

The undisputed father of Canadian political polling was an American, Lou Harris, the greatest of the early party pollsters in Washington. Harris established his reputation through his work for John Kennedy and the Democratic party in the 1960 presidential election. If the election had not been such a cliff-hanger, if Kennedy had not beaten Richard Nixon, or if Theodore White had not chronicled the campaign in *The Making of the President 1960*, it might never have occurred to Canada's Liberals — in opposition but dreaming technicolor dreams of replicating Kennedy's Camelot on the Rideau — to invite Harris to do for Lester Pearson what he had done for Kennedy.

For Kennedy, Harris established the strategic base for a campaign in which literally every single vote counted. Canvassing Americans on a wide range of issues, he searched for concerns on which the public gave the outgoing Republican administration of Dwight Eisenhower and Nixon, his vice-president, a negative rating. Harris had to go down to the seventh-rated item of concern before he found an issue on which the Republicans were vulnerable. It was a concern (well-founded or not) that U.S. prestige abroad was deteriorating under the Republicans. Armed with Harris's research, Kennedy zeroed in on foreign policy. He even made an election issue of the status and fate of the obscure Chinese islands of Quemoy and Matsu. The issue helped to tip the balance to Kennedy.

The Kennedy campaign strategy and the crucial work that Harris had done for him were much admired by Canadian Liberals. In the summer of 1961, Keith Davey, bright, young (thirty-five), and thoroughly dazzled by Kennedy, arrived in Ottawa to take over as the Liberal party's national director. He was brimming with enthusiasm, and he needed it. He faced the daunting assignment of reviving a Liberal organization that had fallen to pieces since the Conservatives under the charismatic John Diefenbaker had come to power in 1957. Davey knew in 1961 that he had one year, probably no more, before a general election — one year to pump life into a party that in 1958 had suffered the worst defeat in federal election history (a benchmark for humiliation that would survive until 1984 when John Turner led the Liberals into the abyss against Brian Mulroney's Tories).

Polling was not an entirely foreign concept to the Liberal party in 1961. Maurice Sauvé (later to be a federal Liberal cabinet minister and consort to a governor general) had experimented with polling in the 1960 provincial election in Quebec, which was won by the Liberals under Jean Lesage. And shortly after Davey arrived in Ottawa the following year, he was handed a poll, conducted without charge by MacLaren Advertising, a Toronto agency that had already landed the advertising business of the Ontario Liberal party and now had its eye on the federal party account. As Davey recounts in his memoir, *The Rainmaker: A Passion for Politics*, he was skeptical about the ad agency's competence as a polling house. He took the MacLaren poll to his mentor, Walter Gordon, who agreed it was not adequate. "Keith, you'd better get the best in the business," he told Davey. To Davey, that meant just one person — Lou Harris.[4]

"Harris was just outstanding and he was everything we sought in terms of polling. He found out all kinds of stuff for us," Davey recalls. The Liberals employed Harris in both the 1962 election, which produced a minority Conservative government, and the 1963 campaign, which gave Pearson's Liberals a minority government.

Gordon was a leading Canadian nationalist, and the Liberals, embarrassed that they were using an American as their pollster, tried to keep Harris under wraps. He would sneak in and out of Ottawa. Once, before the 1962 election, Harris and Davey were travelling to Ottawa together on a late flight when they were spotted by Frank McGee, a Tory cabinet minister. Thinking fast, Davey introduced Lou Harris to McGee as "my old friend, Harry Lewis." McGee was none the wiser.

In the capital, Harris stayed away from Parliament Hill and from Liberal headquarters. Instead, he would meet his clients at Davey's house, at Gordon's apartment, or, after Pearson was elected, at 24 Sussex Drive, the official residence of the prime minister. "I remember knocking and Pearson would come to the door," Davey says. "There'd be Walter, Lou, and I, and Pearson would inevitably say, 'Oh, Lou. Oh, Lou, how are you? How bad am I this month?' Well, of course, he was always bad. It was so awful. You wanted to ache for the guy."

Gordon, who became Pearson's first finance minister, would listen to Harris intently — then often do the opposite of the pollster's advice, especially when the advice touched on the cause closest to Gordon's heart, Canadian ownership of the Canadian economy. He did heed Harris's advice, however, when the pollster surveyed five Toronto ridings in which Gordon was considering running for Parliament in the 1962 election. Gordon's strong preference was Rosedale, the riding where he lived in quiet affluence and where he was well known. But Harris's research warned Gordon against Rosedale. It identified Davenport, a working-class riding with a large Italian-Canadian population, as his safest bet. (The Italians, like other postwar immigrants from Western Europe, had come to Canada under the auspices of Liberal governments in Ottawa. They tended, consequently, to identify with the Liberal party.) Gordon ran in Davenport, winning handily, while Rosedale went Tory. It was the first time in Canada that polling had been used to match candidate to constituency. Today, it is a commonplace use.

Lester Pearson never liked polls, mainly because they so often brought him depressing news. Friends suspected he wouldn't really accept pollsters until they produced a poll that told him what he wanted to hear — which was that what Canadians cared about above all else was world affairs. A former career diplomat and external affairs minister, Pearson yearned to lead a campaign centred on foreign policy. But it was not to be. "In rank order, foreign affairs would always be zero," Davey remembers. "That would be absolutely the last issue of concern for Canadians. It was always distressing for Pearson. We kept asking a lot of questions on international stuff just to keep him happy. I can't recall any of it ever being used politically."

Although Harris retired from party polling, Davey continued to consult him. He went to see him before the 1979 federal election to ask whether Harris could think of anything that could be done to save Pierre Trudeau and the Liberals from defeat at the hands of Joe Clark's Conservatives.

"Is there something we can do, or is it over?" Davey asked Harris. "Do what Kennedy did in West Virginia," Harris advised. "Take Trudeau into a couple of places where there's a lot of unemployment. Take him to some of those shelters for the homeless — the Scott Mission and those kind of places — and have him spend a day or two just going around and talking to those guys."

Trudeau, however, refused to do it; he thought such gestures would be interpreted as grandstanding, and that he would be accused of taking advantage of the unfortunate. Davey, however, is convinced that it would have worked, that Trudeau's forbidding image could have been softened and humanized enough to let the Liberals hang on to power in the 1979 election.

Yet, in the opinion of Goldfarb, who became the party pollster in 1973, Trudeau handled polls and pollsters better than any other Canadian leader ever has: "He never doubted his ability to understand and to make a choice. He never had second thoughts about the people he selected or . . . about the choice he wanted to make."

Contrary to his public pose of indifference, even contempt, for all polls, Trudeau was secretly fascinated by them. He asked often for the latest numbers. Goldfarb laughs at the memory of one early meeting with Trudeau at the prime minister's residence when the Liberal government was in a serious slump:

> Trudeau and I and Keith [Davey] and [Jean] Marchand met and had lunch at 24 Sussex Drive. The numbers weren't good at all. They were about as bad as they could be. Keith took me aside before the meeting and asked me to open up gently, to ease into it. [But] on the very first page of my report, the numbers said Marchand should quit; he was causing problems for the government everywhere in English Canada. The next page said, keep [Marc] Lalonde out of English Canada because every time he comes here, we lose votes. So I go through page one, page two, and Trudeau says: "After you get rid of Marchand and Lalonde, what about me? Do you want me to quit, too?"
>
> Trudeau was terrific. He laughed. He had a great sense of humor about it. He took it for what it was worth. He never

looked at polls as truth. He looked at the polls as, "Now I know, so what am I going to do about it?" He used it as information to reduce the risk in decision making. That's what it's for. Some guys look at the numbers and say, "Oh, that's crap, I don't want to hear it." I've worked for guys like that.

When Lou Harris stopped doing party polling, he passed the Liberal business on to another American, Oliver Quayle. By the early 1970s, with Quayle well on his way to drinking himself to death, the Liberals decided it was high time they found a Canadian to look after their polling.

Martin Goldfarb, meanwhile, had set up a consulting business to supplement his income as a teacher. He did some market surveys for an advertising agency with Liberal connections. That led to political-polling assignments for a few Liberal candidates, then for a cabinet minister (Paul Hellyer in the 1968 Liberal leadership campaign), and to an introduction to Keith Davey, who hired him to probe public opinion for the Special Senate Committee on the Mass Media (chaired by Davey), which reported in 1970. Ultimately, Davey took the big step — arranging for Goldfarb to meet Trudeau. He could have sold tickets: the meeting was an epic clash of two monster egos.

"In the first meeting we ever had, Trudeau threw me out," says Goldfarb, still sounding surprised two decades after the encounter. The prime minister had not been amused by an article that Goldfarb had written in *Maclean's* magazine in which he had explained how Trudeau could be beaten. And the prime minister was not mollified by what the pollster had to say at their first meeting — "I told him he was contributing to a moral breakdown in our society. And he was."

Although Goldfarb developed an admiration for Trudeau that borders on hero worship, the affection was never reciprocal. Davey and others kept face-to-face meetings between the prime minister and his pollster to a bare minimum. But as the Liberal party became increasingly dependent on Goldfarb's polling, the Trudeau government became an ever-larger client of Goldfarb Consultants. Government polling business is extremely lucrative, most of it is awarded without competitive tenders, and the lion's share in those days went to Goldfarb. (Just as, a decade later, with the Mulroney Conservatives in office, the largest slice by far went to the Tory party pollster, Gregg's Decima Research. Their relationships with the parties in power made Goldfarb Consultants and Decima the powerhouses in Canadian polling, helping them to attract as clients businesses in the private sector and provincial governments.)

As the pollsters cast their seductive spell over politicians and bureaucrats alike, "government by Goldfarb" became the contemptuous description for governments everywhere in Canada that relied on polls to do their thinking, to rationalize their actions, or to excuse their inaction.

It is an expensive business, polling. It costs a minimum of $50,000 for a fifteen-minute national questionnaire with 1,500 respondents, and far more for larger samples and longer or more complex questionnaires. In the period leading up to, and during, the provincial election campaign in Ontario in 1990, Peterson's Liberals spent a breathtaking $594,500 on Goldfarb polls. The New Democrats, by comparison, were relatively frugal, spending $147,700 on polling, but they read their polls intelligently and adjusted their strategy accordingly. The Tories spent $105,000.[5]

For the national political parties, polling is — and yet, is not — one of the costs of doing business. Polling eats up an increasing share of all parties' campaign budgets, but because of a gaping loophole in federal electoral law, money spent on polls has been exempted from the election-expenditure ceilings. Polling is deemed to be research and, as such, to be an "indirect" election expense. The federal spending limits apply only to "direct" election expenses, such as TV commercials, brochures, lawn signs, the leader's tour, and rental of campaign headquarters. The campaign managers who commission polls and the bureaucrats who administer the rules all agree that it is absurd to exempt polling. For a major national party, it is the most important element of election preparedness and strategy.

Backroom men and women know the perils of not polling. They are aware of the folly of polling only on the eve of an election or only during the actual campaign. They have learned, the hard way in some instances, the importance of polling on a regular basis between elections.

One who learned the hard way was Joe Clark. In 1979, Clark became prime minister at the head of a minority Conservative government. Nine months later, his government was history, and Trudeau was back in power with a majority Liberal government. The reason for the Clark government's premature demise was not its unpopular budget (with an eighteen-cent-a-gallon increase in the excise tax on gasoline) or Clark's rash decision to allow the budget to come to a vote in the House of Commons without being sure he had enough support to win the vote. The Tories made the mistake of virtually daring the opposition parties to defeat the budget, and thereby force an election, without understanding what the public thought about their government and their budget. They knew the Liberals were ahead in the Gallup and other published polls, but they took it for granted that this was the result of normal post-election disillusionment. The Tories assumed that the country shared the government's objectives and would welcome an opportunity to give Clark a majority.

They could not have been more wrong. Having commissioned no internal polls in the period between their election victory in May 1979 and the budget that December, they were wildly out of touch with the thinking of the Canadian public. If they had been polling, they would have realized that they had won in May for just one reason: The people wanted to get rid of the Liberals, who had been in power for sixteen years, eleven of them with Trudeau as prime minister. The public was not particularly attracted to Clark or the Conservatives; they were simply the vehicle for dumping the Liberals. In office, the Tories did nothing to endear themselves to the voters. Clark's decision to take the highly symbolic step of moving the Canadian embassy in Israel from Tel Aviv to Jerusalem — and his embarrassing retreat from that ill-considered policy — made the young administration appear both foolhardy and inept. His determination to privatize the national oil company, Petro-Canada, made no sense to Canadians who liked the idea of a public presence in the petroleum sector. The budget further alienated the people because they did not see how raising the gasoline tax would serve any purpose other than to take more money out of their pockets. Finally, Clark's declared insistence on governing as though he had a majority ignored an important reality — the electorate had withheld a majority from the Tories in May because it did not feel entirely comfortable with Clark and his colleagues and was not quite ready to trust them. Instead of turning their attention in the post-election period to increasing the comfort level of the public, the Tories reinforced the discomfort. By the time of that fateful budget vote in December 1979, the Tories — as Gregg reported later — had fallen twenty-one percentage points behind the Liberals in public support. The election was lost before the budget was defeated.

The Liberals, in contrast, were not caught unawares. Goldfarb had been polling regularly since the election, including two national surveys in the month before the budget, and the Liberals were well aware of the erosion of Conservative support. Even though Trudeau had decided to retire — a decision he subsequently reversed — the Liberals knew they could beat the Tories in an early election. They could hardly believe their good fortune when the Crosbie budget gave them an opportunity to force an election.

Goldfarb was in Nevada, skiing with friends at Tahoe, when Liberal House leader Allan MacEachen phoned his home in Toronto and reached the pollster's wife, Joan. When Joan Goldfarb told MacEachen where her husband was, he replied, "He can't be skiing. I've got to know whether or not we should vote against the government on the budget. . . . What am I going to do?" Goldfarb's wife promised to get a message to Marty, and Goldfarb eventually got back to MacEachen. "I told them to go ahead," says Goldfarb. "We were in opposition. What could happen after the election? The worst that could happen was, we'd still be in opposition. 'What've we got to lose?' I said. 'Let's go for it!' Then Judd Buchanan [a former Liberal cabinet minister] called me. He was all upset — 'Oh, Marty, you're going to destroy the party.' No, I wasn't. We had research. We knew exactly where the public was. We knew what the issues were. . . . We had a strategy."

It worked. The Clark government fell on the budget vote, Trudeau came out of retirement, and the Liberals returned with a majority government in the February 1980 election.

But, wait. Where was Goldfarb skiing the day MacEachen called? Prophetically, on a hill called Election.

"The 1980 federal campaign was brutal, just awful," Allan Gregg remembers.

> There was nothing you could do. We'd done no polling in the pre-writ period at all, and I put out a questionnaire. It had 120 questions. The results were just stunning: things like, "If the Liberals get back in would they govern better, the same or worse than they did before?" Seventy per cent said they'd do better. Where the hell did that come from? How do you fight that? Out of 120 questions, there were only two where there was any positive public opinion or foundation to build on. One was, the Tories really hadn't been given a fair chance to demonstrate whether they were going to provide good government. The other was, we're going to have to make some real, fundamental changes to overcome the problems the country is facing. So our campaign slogan became "Real Change Deserves a Real Chance." It was awful. It was worse than

"The Land Is Strong" [the insipid Liberal slogan in their nearly disastrous 1972 federal campaign]. There was nothing else. I tried to joke about it. I said the preferred slogan would have been "Just Kidding — No Election."

To commission the polling that their parties must have to survive and to win, backroom managers have to be prepared to spend, spend, spend. Polling in a federal election will account for 10 to 15 per cent of their spending — or $800,000 to $1.2 million (roughly $20,000 a day) in a typical campaign. So crucial is polling that it is destined to devour an ever-larger share of parties' budgets, even as campaigns grow shorter. Before long, parties, if they want to make a respectable showing in a national election, will have to be prepared to invest $40,000 to $50,000 per day in polling in its various forms — strategic studies, daily tracking, focus groups to test advertising, surveys to monitor the public response to television debates (which, in turn, will influence decisions on advertising strategy), analyses of support and issues in bellwether ridings, and so on. The expense may seem extreme, but it is worse in the United States. There, an individual candidate for the Senate may well find himself or herself spending more on polling than an entire Canadian federal party spends. A presidential candidate can expect a bill from his or her pollster in the neighborhood of $40 million.

All the money spent on polling, however, is money wasted if the campaign directors do not listen to the advice that their pollster provides, or if they do not grant the pollster access to the central decision makers in the campaign. Polling is pointless if the findings are not interpreted intelligently and conveyed directly to campaign managers who have the authority to translate the research into strategy.

Following their defeat in the 1990 Ontario election, the Peterson Liberals looked for a scapegoat. Some settled on Peterson himself (he had promptly resigned as leader). Peterson, they agreed, was too aloof and too arrogant. Others singled out Goldfarb. The pollster, they said, failed to warn the party of the perils of calling an early election. He did not tell the campaign strategists how vulnerable the Liberals were on their left flank to the NDP. He left them believing that all would be well long after it was becoming apparent that all was far from well — or so they argued in their post-mortems.

In fact, Goldfarb did sound a warning. In May 1990, two months before Peterson called the election, the pollster had produced a massive 211-page report that gave the Liberals the good news and the bad news. The good news was the Liberals had a seventeen-point lead and, with 48 per cent of the decided vote, were actually one percentage point higher than they had been in the 1987 election when they elected a majority government. The bad news required closer scrutiny. The New Democrats had climbed to a solid second (with 31 per cent support, to 21 per cent for the Tories). The NDP was the second choice of most prospective Liberal voters. Bob Rae was almost as highly regarded as Peterson. And people had trouble recalling any achievements of the Liberal government in the previous three years. Goldfarb's advice that May was clear: "The party and party leader that the Liberals need to be most concerned about is the NDP and Bob Rae, not the Tories, and the Liberal campaign strategy needs to reflect this. Liberal campaign strategy should virtually ignore the Tories."[6]

But the warning was not heard, not absorbed, or not understood. The problem lay in the strained relationship between the pollster and the strategy chairman to whom he was expected to report. David MacNaughton, a lobbyist and a friend of Peterson's, was irritated by Goldfarb's ego, his anthropological approach, the aura of omniscience with which he liked to cloak his findings, and the "spin" that many felt he put on the interpretation of his numbers. As MacNaughton would put it later: "Marty is basically an activist who has a set of views about how society should work and he uses his numbers to try to persuade people of his view of society."[7]

The tension between MacNaughton and Goldfarb was evident in the fact that Goldfarb was instructed initially not to draft a campaign strategy to accompany his results. Instead, he was to provide the raw numbers and cross-tabulations directly to Mac-Naughton, who would then prepare the strategy document. This document turned out to be a one-and-a-half-page memo, which was promptly rejected by campaign chairman Kathy Robinson, a Toronto lawyer. Asked then to propose a strategy, Goldfarb outlined a two-pronged campaign: a high-road approach for Peterson, and a hard-hitting anti-NDP campaign that would feature senior Liberal ministers but not Peterson himself. But the second prong, the "Red Scare" campaign, was ignored. For virtually the entire campaign, the Liberals concentrated on just one target: the Tories.

Three years earlier, Goldfarb had worked closely with Peterson's top adviser and most capable strategist, Hershell Ezrin, a backroom veteran of twenty Liberal campaigns, federal and provincial, going back to 1963. Goldfarb had the confidence of Ezrin. Ezrin had the confidence of Peterson. The pollster and the strategist met every day and they charted the campaign that brought the Liberals a majority government in the 1987 election. By 1990, however, Ezrin had left Peterson's office for an executive position with the Molson Companies and he played a reduced role in the campaign. The Ezrin–Goldfarb combination gave way to the duo of Robinson and MacNaughton, who had worked closely together over a period of twenty years. Robinson had Peterson's ear, but she lacked Ezrin's sure political instinct and his rapport with, and regard for, Goldfarb. The pollster found himself shut off from the leader, the Liberal caucus, and all the crucial meetings at which strategy decisions were made.

What distinguishes Goldfarb from other pollsters is his utter commitment and complete involvement — professional and personal, intellectual and emotional — with his political clients. All pollsters want their clients to win. To Goldfarb, however, they *must* win, and if they do not, he is devastated. He is incapable of simply collecting his numbers, making his analysis and tendering his advice, then walking away while the campaign chiefs set the strategy. Goldfarb wants to be involved in organization, policy, and strategy. He insists on being at the centre of the action, an integral part of the campaign team.

"The secret of a good pollster is to have an absolutely trusting relationship with his client," says Goldfarb. He continues:

> Trudeau had an absolute trust in his team. He never questioned whether they would get the job done. The reason we didn't function well in the [1990] election in Ontario is that I never met with the leader. Not once. I never met with him before the election was called to discuss the results of the polls. . . . I never met with the premier at any time during the whole election. I've learned something: if you don't have rapport with the leader, you shouldn't even take the assignment. I would never do it again. It was very frustrating.

There is no doubt in Goldfarb's mind that, had he been able to penetrate the wall around the leader, Peterson's zeal for an early election would have been dampened. Read carefully, his polling revealed that Ontarians were concerned about the integrity of the provincial administration. But the concern about integrity did not show up in the poll results as a single issue, one that would have warned Peterson of the perils that lay ahead. Rather, Goldfarb found concern about the Liberals' integrity underlying several issues, including the premier's unwavering support for Prime Minister Mulroney on the Meech Lake constitutional accord, the Patti Starr political finance scandal, and the forced resignations of several Peterson cabinet ministers. "It was clear if you looked at the data," Goldfarb says. "But if you didn't tie it all together, you couldn't explain there were pitfalls there."

Goldfarb's commitment to Liberals and liberalism is both his strength and his weakness. His detractors contend that his partisanship interferes with his objectivity. His insistence on being a participant overwhelms his detachment. And because his sentiments lie with the progressive wing of the party, say other pollsters, he finds it hard to devise strategy for a campaign against left-of-centre opponents. He is in his element when the Tories are the target; he is uncomfortable when the threat comes from the NDP.

Allan Gregg is a different animal. Where Goldfarb is a missionary, Gregg is a mercenary — a hired gun without a personal investment, philosophical or emotional, in the party whose cause he serves. Gregg, who dresses like a member of a rock band and talks like a sociology professor (in fact, he's both a rock musician and a sociologist), has been polling for Conservatives, federal and provincial, since 1976. To him, a party pollster differs from the person who prints the party's campaign posters only in the degree of influence he wields.

In Gregg's view, a political pollster cannot afford to allow his own values to influence his advice to his client. He loses his utility if he loses his detachment. "The pollster role, properly defined, is amoral. Absolutely amoral. You cannot afford to have personal views [on policy or tactics]. You have to give your advice as absolutely impartially as you can. You have to be able to tell your client, for example, that if you go on an anti-bilingualism campaign in eastern Ontario, yes, you can move voters. [You have to say that] regardless of how you feel yourself. It's up to the politician to say, 'Hold on, what kind of province or country will I have if I do that, if I inflame those [racist] views.'"

Where Goldfarb is hot, Gregg is cool. Where Goldfarb is passionate and involved, Gregg is cynical and detached. As Gregg says:

> The guy who takes a poll and finds 51 per cent of the population agrees with an indiscriminate list of policy propositions is doomed to electoral failure. He's working on the assumption that (a) the population knows what it wants and (b) it will

like what it gets when you give it what it asks for. Neither proposition is true. . . . It doesn't happen in all instances, but the pollster has evolved, when used properly, into a kind of chief strategist, a strategic adjunct to the campaign chairman — an angel or, to put it in perspective, a devil on the shoulder who has a say, but no authority, in everything, absolutely everything. He will tell you this is how the [leader's] tour should go, this is what the advertising should look like, this is how the speeches should be, this is how the policy should be. . . . The pollster has to be able to stand completely back from all that stuff and say, "That isn't my choice, my decision." That's why I say I'm involved in everything, responsible for nothing. The campaign chairman's going to have to live with that. The leader's going to have to live with it. I have to give my advice completely and utterly unfettered by any moral notion of what is good, bad, right or wrong.

For all his own cynicism, Gregg is still taken aback at times by the degree of it he finds among voters. The 1990 Ontario election was one of those times. "The [public's] cynicism has three parts," he says. "It says first, 'The longer you're in power, the worse you get, so therefore I have a built-in incentive for throwing the rascals out because the only time I get good government is in the early stages of the new government.' Experience and incumbency are negatives in today's environment. Second, the cynicism says, 'Power corrupts absolutely; the more power I give you, the more you will abuse it.' Therefore, minority government is inherently good; a majority government is inherently bad."

Gregg's polls tracked the Liberals' loss of momentum in the 1990 Ontario election. When the campaign began, 74 per cent of the people (party preferences aside) expected the Liberals to win; that shrank to 56 per cent by the weekend before the election. At the outset, 57 per cent expected a majority government; by the end, only 26 per cent did. "This [expectation of minority government] fuelled the protest vote," says Gregg. "'Hot damn!' the people said. 'We're getting exactly what we want: I'm going to vote NDP to make sure.' The very evidence of the Liberals losing ground spurred on the protest vote. . . . The people ended up voting NDP in order to get a Liberal minority government in Ontario."

The third part of cynicism, says Gregg, is the public belief that all parties are the same and that politicians are all so corruptible that, in power, they will do whatever they have to do to get re-elected. "It's a vicious circle," Gregg says. "The absence of any sense of risk allowed voters [in Ontario in 1990] to turn the voting act into a process of successive elimination of negative alternatives. Who's worst? Who's second-worst? Who's left? And because there were no risks associated with voting for the NDP, that's what they did."

Table 2

Public expectation (%) for the outcome of 1990 Ontario election

Expected to win	Poll 1 July 12–20	Poll 2 Aug. 11–13	Poll 3 Aug. 18–20	Poll 4 Aug. 28–29	Poll 5 Sept. 1–3
Liberal	74	78	75	67	56
NDP	8	7	8	14	26
PC	15	14	17	14	11
Expected government					
Majority	57	52	57	36	26
Minority	40	46	43	62	70

SOURCE: Decima Research for the Ontario PC party

The Liberal and Conservative campaigns both played into the NDP's hands in that provincial election. The only issue the Tories could find that offered any hope at all was one identified by Gregg's polling: taxes. "We knew it was driving people away from the Liberals," Gregg says. "The Tory campaign said, 'If you are thinking of voting Liberal, think again' — with tax as the example. It was a very, very soft question, but we knew what we had to do. . . . All of a sudden, people said, 'Okay, I will [think again].' The Liberal campaign was without question the stupidest campaign I have seen in fifteen years. They came in and said to people, 'If you think we're bad, look, the Tories are even worse.' And the population said, 'Right on that, too.' So they voted NDP. Bob Rae benefited principally from not being a Liberal or a Conservative."

Hershell Ezrin agrees with that assessment. "I don't believe the NDP campaign was that good a campaign," says the former Peterson strategist. "The Liberals lost the campaign. The NDP didn't win it."

What the New Democrats did with great success, however, was to get the two lines on the pollsters' graphs — voter belief (dissatisfaction with the government) and voting intention — to converge. They did it by establishing an "us versus them" campaign. The "them" was the Liberals, whom the NDP portrayed, day after day, speech after speech, as being aligned with special interests — wealthy, powerful interests such as real estate developers — and as being insensitive or uncaring about the concerns of ordinary people. It was simplistic, but effective. The Conservative campaign, based on attacking the Liberals over high taxes, unintentionally played into the strategy, reinforcing the perception of the Liberals as a government that pampered its privileged friends while callously overtaxing the middle class. Like a quarterback who is unexpectedly sacked by two tacklers from different directions, Peterson crumpled.

The bridge that in the end linked the lines of voter belief and voting intention was Bob Rae. The voters knew virtually nothing about other NDP candidates or about the party platform, the "Agenda for People." But they did know Rae; he had been in public life for twelve years, the last eight as provincial NDP leader. They felt comfortable with him. Bill Knight, who ran the NDP campaign in the 1988 federal election, watched the voters' reaction to Rae in Ontario two years later. "Maybe they were more middle class, maybe they were more downtown Toronto urban or university-based, but a significant portion of that 38 per cent that went to the Ontario NDP went because fundamentally they thought Rae was bright and competent, and they wanted to try something new," Knight says. "I'm not saying they'd quite calculated that he'd be premier, but it paid off in that sense."

The election paid off in a different way for the Tories. They had gone into the campaign with warnings of disaster echoing in their ears. Just four seats, Allan Gregg had said. The once-proud party that had governed Ontario from 1943 to 1985 was in danger of atrophying. Ontario might have become a two-party province, as several others are. But the Conservatives survived to fight another day. They started the campaign with a leader nobody knew: Michael Harris. They had a bank debt of $5 million and only a handful of nominated candidates. But they raised their popular vote, from 19 per cent in Gregg's pre-writ poll in July to 23.5 per cent on election day, and they elected twenty MPPs, enough for a viable caucus and a base upon which to revive a party that had seemed at death's door.

The Tories did it by combing through the pile of manure that Allan Gregg had left under their midsummer Christmas tree. They did not find a pony, but they did discover enough ammunition to

fight a tightly focused war. Gregg found that 60 per cent of Ontario
voters did not want an election in 1990; 64 per cent thought Peterson was preparing an early election solely because he thought
he could win; 77 per cent agreed with an undocumented Tory claim
that the Peterson government had introduced or increased thirty-
two different provincial taxes, boosting tax revenues by 133 per
cent.

Those three scraps of data told Laschinger and his campaign team
that the calling of an early election would be an issue, that most
voters would not accept whatever reasons Peterson might give for
calling it, and that Ontarians were receptive to a campaign centred
on the high level of taxation after five years of Liberal administration.

A week earlier, Laschinger had been given some advice by Mike
Murphy, the Republican communications guru who had been responsible for the aggressive negative television commercials that
had helped George Bush to win the White House by portraying
his Democratic opponent, Michael Dukakis — quite unfairly — as
being soft on crime and violence. Murphy told Laschinger that his
party's liabilities were actually an asset. Because he had an unknown
leader (Mike Harris had become leader only two months earlier),
huge debts, and almost no candidates, he had total freedom to do
whatever he wanted and take whatever chances he felt might help
the party. "You can be truly dangerous," Murphy said.

Ontario election law prohibits any paid political advertising until
the final four weeks of the campaign. But there are no restrictions
on advertising before the issuance of the writ calling the election.
Broke though the party was, Laschinger instructed John Bowen,
president of the Toronto advertising firm of Bowen and Binstock,
and Phil Gillies, a former Tory MPP who had become a free-lance
communications consultant, to produce a cheap newspaper and radio campaign (television was far too costly) to hammer the Liberals
for preparing to call an unnecessary, unwanted election.

The purpose of the ad campaign was twofold: to put the Liberals
on the defensive and to demonstrate to the Tory faithful that, while
the party might be down, it was not out. It showed a fish wrapped
in a newspaper with the headline "Liberals to Call Early Election,"
and a half-dozen lines of text telling readers that, while Ontarians
were off fishing or at their cottages, the Liberals were planning to
spend $40 million to stage an unnecessary early election. The ad
urged voters to ask the Liberals why they were doing it. A companion radio commercial drove home the same message.

Four days before Peterson called the election, Laschinger unveiled the ad campaign at a candidates' briefing, and the ads became a news story, repeated at no cost to the party on newscasts across the province. The Tory candidates took home copies of the newspaper ad and the radio tape, and many placed them in their local media, at the candidates' own expense. Wheedling a bit of money out of Claude Bennett, chairman of the PC Ontario Fund, Laschinger bought a half-page ad in the Toronto *Globe and Mail* for $17,000 and spent another $8,000 on radio spots in five major centres over the weekend.

Peterson was put on the defensive, forced to explain why he was spending $40 million on an election that he had not even called yet. In relative terms, $40 million is peanuts in a province where the government spends $50-plus billion annually, but the symbolism took hold. Forty million dollars spent on an unnecessary election was $40 million wasted. Forty million dollars spent on an election was $40 million not available for more worthwhile purposes — for hospital beds, for example, or classrooms, or the environment, or day-care spaces.

Allan Gregg watched Liberal support leak away. One week into the campaign, he reported that the Liberals had lost eight points, from 48 per cent down to 40. They would be hard-pressed to retain a majority government, assuming the slide could be arrested. But the slide continued.

Meanwhile, the Conservatives worked to exploit the public perception, as revealed by Gregg, that the Liberals were a party of high taxes. It did not matter whether the perception was accurate. Nor did it matter whether the Peterson government had actually increased the tax burden by 133 per cent by creating or raising thirty-two taxes. Election campaigns are not designed for establishing the truth or determining the accuracy of perceptions. For a party in opposition, they are a time for driving home allegations and reinforcing negative stereotypes of the party in power. The Tories' media campaign reinforced the message. Their most dramatic ad depicted an exploding piggy bank.

Journalists found the Tory campaign repetitious, banal, and negative. But journalists were not the target audience, and the media's opinion of the Tory campaign was irrelevant to the backroom managers. Gregg's polling made it clear that taxation was the only issue on which the Conservatives could inflict any real damage on the Liberals — although it was equally clear from Gregg's data that any damage suffered by the Liberals would benefit the NDP most.

Late in the campaign the NDP joined the chorus with a call for "fair taxes." Four weeks into the campaign, Liberal support had dwindled to 31 per cent, Decima reported, and the Tories knew the Liberals were finished. Gregg had the NDP at 43 per cent — enough for a substantial majority.

The Liberals, who had been worrying about the Conservatives' anti-tax campaign when they should have been protecting themselves against the New Democrats on their other flank, suddenly woke up. In the dying days of the campaign, they made a desperate attempt to scare voters away from the NDP. The tactic worked, to a point. As Gregg watched over Labour Day, the final weekend of the campaign, NDP support slipped four percentage points. But the Liberals' own support climbed by only one point. It was too little, far too late.

Polling — and the strategic decisions based on it — played a crucial role in the defeat of Peterson's Liberals and the election of Rae's New Democrats. Although none of the party pollsters had foreseen the outcome of the election when they did their pre-campaign polls, those early surveys revealed the strengths and weaknesses that were exploited on the campaign trail. Gregg tracked the demise of David Peterson and the seemingly invincible Liberal government (as illustrated in Table 3). Respondents were asked to say whether they felt the Liberal government deserved another four years or whether they felt it was time for a change. They were also asked what they thought of Peterson himself. "Net approval" (of Peterson) is the sum of "approve" and "strongly approve" minus the sum of "disapprove" and "strongly disapprove." The intensity of feelings — favorable and unfavorable — about Peterson deepened as the campaign progressed and as Liberal supporters moved from "approve" to "strongly approve" and non-supporters from "disapprove" to "strongly disapprove."

In interpreting the results, Gregg followed two rules of thumb. First, in a three-way race, the incumbent will lose when the percentage of people who believe it is time for a change exceeds 65 per cent. The Liberals had hit 60 per cent by the third Decima poll (August 18–20 — two and a half weeks before the election). Gregg did not ask the question in two subsequent polls, but it was clear that the trend line would carry the time-for-a-change percentage well above 65 by election day, September 6.

Second, a net approval rating of at least +30 percentage points is needed to win a leader-oriented campaign like the Liberals'. By the third Gregg poll on August 18–20, the Liberals' decision to run on Peterson's reputation and ability was exposed as a fatal mistake. At +7, he was no longer an asset to his party. It was for this reason, for example, that Ian Scott, Peterson's attorney general, decided to cut his leader's picture out of his campaign brochure.

Table 3

Analysis (%) of 1990 Ontario Campaign

	Poll 1 July 28	Poll 2 Aug. 11–13	Poll 3 Aug. 18–20
Libs deserve 4 more yrs.	48	41	37
Time for change	47	55	60
Approval of Premier Peterson			
Strongly approve	4	15	12
Approve	61	46	41
Total:	65	61	53
Strongly disapprove	8	15	21
Disapprove	26	23	25
Total:	34	38	46
Net Approval Rating	+31	+23	+7

SOURCE: Decima Research

In the backroom warfare of election campaigns, polling is also a useful weapon for destabilizing the enemy. Immediately prior to the election call in Ontario, the Liberals floated a story that they had conducted a poll in Michael Harris's home riding of Nipissing and had found that Stan Lawlor, the popular mayor of North Bay who had been personally recruited as a candidate by Peterson, was running ahead of Harris. The story gained wide distribution and credence in the news media. Furious, Laschinger assigned the Montreal polling firm CROP to do a quick poll in Nipissing. Although it showed the Liberals were ahead of the Conservatives when respondents were asked which party they favored, the picture changed when the names of the candidates — Harris and Lawlor — were mentioned. Then Harris and the Tories took a seven-percentage-point lead.

Three weeks into the campaign, Laschinger found his chance to get even. A Monday-morning caller from London, Ontario, reported that the premier's wife, Shelley Peterson, had been seen in tears after door-to-door canvassing in Peterson's London Centre riding the previous Friday evening. Laschinger called John Mykytyshyn, a young Tory from Dundas, Ontario, who had done polling for him in previous elections and leadership conventions. Mykytyshyn conducted a fast poll in London Centre. Three days later, the results were in. Peterson was at only 32 per cent, sixteen points behind an unknown NDP candidate, Marion Boyd (later to become a minister in the Rae government), with the Tory candidate far back in third place. Laschinger passed the results to Harris, who made them public the next day. The following morning, a Saturday, Peterson was due to campaign in London. But the entire Liberal campaign went into a tailspin when the *Globe and Mail* reported the Mykytyshyn poll on its front page with the headline "Liberal Leader Behind in Own Riding, Harris Says; Conservative Camp Cites But Won't Release Details of Opinion Poll."

Two weeks later, Peterson lost the riding and the election. On election night, Bob Rae, now premier-elect, telephoned home to talk to his children. He related the conversation later. "Daddy," asked one of his daughters, "does this mean you are now David Peterson's boss?" The second had a simpler question: "Dad, what's a majority?"

If, as Martin Goldfarb suggests, pollsters are seers or oracles, the backroom organizers who employ them are a less exotic breed. They are mechanics. Only by following the Ten Commandments for using polling to create strategy can campaign managers convert the art of the pollster into results at the polls.

5. THE TEN COMMANDMENTS
(for Using Polling to Create Strategy)

*Running a political campaign without polling is riskier than
driving across a strange country without a map.*
— A backroom axiom

Successful campaign strategy never happens by accident. It is built with expert care on a research base provided by sophisticated polling on public perceptions and attitudes. This polling goes far beyond the which-party-is-ahead-today variety that titillates the news media and stimulates superficial coverage of campaigns as though they were horse-races or boxing matches. Real political polling is not for laymen or amateurs; it is not meant for the entertainment of curious spectators in the political galleries. Properly used, it is the most valuable strategic tool available to backroom professionals. But campaign managers have to know how to translate the numbers on their pollster's printouts into votes in an election or a leadership convention. If they lack the skill or understanding to make their polling work for them, it will be worse than useless. Good polling badly used can destroy any campaign.

To avoid the pitfalls, there are ten fundamental rules or commandments — culled from the experiences of political strategists across the country — that campaign managers must follow.

The First Commandment
Always Choose a Pollster Who Also Gives Advice

One day, following the 1988 federal election, John Turner, then

Liberal leader, was lunching at his favorite restaurant in Toronto, Winston's, an eatery patronized by the élites of business and politics. Turner had suffered his second defeat at the hands of Brian Mulroney's Conservatives. In the process, he had taken a personal savaging from an eleventh-hour Tory propaganda campaign that attacked his credibility and trustworthiness. Turner was still fuming when he spotted Allan Gregg across the restaurant. He went over to the Conservative pollster and said: "So, it's the man who bombed the bridge!"

"He was blaming me for the end of his political career," Gregg says. "Was I [responsible]? As the architect of that particular strategy, I guess 'yes' is the shortest answer."

It was Gregg who, in the latter stages of the 1988 campaign — after the pivotal leaders' debates on television — discovered a "bridge" between voter belief (dissatisfaction with the Mulroney government, especially over free trade with the United States) and voting intention (to vote Liberal). The bridge was the credibility of the Liberal leader. If the Tories could "bomb the bridge" and explode Turner's credibility, Gregg told his clients in the Conservative backroom, voters who were unhappy with the government would think twice about voting Liberal.[1]

The crisis for the Tories had materialized suddenly in the two days following the English-language TV debate, in which Turner had rocked Mulroney with a direct attack on free trade. Without warning, the momentum shifted to the Liberals; pollsters for all parties tracked the movement as the Liberals pulled even with the Conservatives and began to surge ahead. Free trade shot to the top of the voters' list of concerns. By a two-to-one margin Canadians told pollsters that they believed Turner was genuine in his belief that the free-trade deal would be disastrous for Canada.

"That's the number. That's the number we've got to move," Gregg reported to the Tory campaign managers. "I'll never forget Allan Gregg coming in," says Tory strategist Paul Curley, "and what Allan said was that John Turner, in the short period of forty-eight hours, had sort of built a bridge of trust between himself and the anxieties of the Canadian public (on free trade). And Allan said, 'We've got to blow up the bridge. You've got to go after people's underlying concern about John Turner as a leader.' So they went out and organized a luncheon in Ottawa, and Mike Wilson [then finance minister] called John Turner a liar."

The Wilson speech, cranked out by four frenzied speech writers, was rough stuff. He addressed Turner's contention that free trade would put Canada's social programs, such as medicare, in jeopardy: "Taking this lie into our senior citizens' homes is the cruellest form of campaigning I've seen in ten years in politics," Wilson declared. "When politicians feel that they have to prey upon the fears and emotions of some of the most defenceless people in our society today, I say that is despicable. . . ."

Following Gregg's advice, the Conservatives flooded the airwaves with a tough television commercial that showed the Canada–U.S. border being drawn back on a map (countering, in spades, a Liberal commercial that showed the border being rubbed out by the Tories). There were full-page newspaper ads, brochures, a barrage of "third-party" advertising from business groups in defence of free trade, and even speeches by corporate executives to their employees, warning them none too subtly about how much they stood to lose if free trade did not come to pass. It was dirty. It was nasty. It was expensive. And it was essential — "It was dire, it was black," Gregg told journalist Graham Fraser. "The election was en route to being lost."[2]

The election was not lost. Gregg's advice saved the Conservatives. Within days, the numbers started to turn around. Swing voters who had begun with the Tories, then moved to the Liberals after the debate, moved back to the Conservatives — the first double reversal that pollsters had ever seen in a Canadian campaign. The Tories won their second consecutive majority government, taking 43 per cent of the popular vote, to 32 per cent for the Liberals. Gregg has no regrets. He gave his advice. The advice was taken, and it worked. "I could say [Turner] did it to himself by not establishing a bulwark to stave off the allegation [of lying]," Gregg says.

The Second Commandment
Use the Numbers to Drive the Strategy

Election campaigns are a time for reinforcing public perceptions and attitudes, not for changing them. A backroom professional knows that sweet reason and gentle persuasion will surely fall on deaf ears in the clamor of electoral conflict. Rather than try to change voters' minds on things they do not like about the party or candidate, the campaign director uses polling to identify issues on which the voters feel most positive towards the party or candidate. The campaign director develops a strategy to reinforce those sympathies. At the same time, he or she uses the polling to locate the opponents' weaknesses — the issues on which they are most vulnerable. That is where the director concentrates the attack.

Gregg's bomb-the-bridge strategy in the 1988 federal election is an illustration of how an election can be won by letting the numbers drive the strategy. The other classic example was the Liberals' strategy of "low-bridging" the leader in the 1980 federal election. Joe Clark's infant Tory government had fallen on the budget vote (on an amendment moved by Bob Rae, then the NDP finance critic in Ottawa) in December 1979. An election was called for February 18, 1980, and the Liberals went into the campaign about twenty percentage points ahead of the Conservatives in all the opinion polls. Their concern was to preserve as much of the lead as possible until election day.

Martin Goldfarb's polls, taken just after the election was called, established the four pillars of the Liberal campaign. First, the Tory budget — which, among other things, increased the excise tax on gasoline by eighteen cents a gallon — was widely unpopular; the public did not share the Tories' conviction that the country would benefit from a dose of strong fiscal medicine. Second, Clark himself epitomized many of the government's problems. Canadians found Clark honest but weak, prone to reversing himself on issues and uncertain in his control over his ministers; he was rated poorly on strength of character, decisiveness, and intelligence. Third, a latent animosity towards Liberal leader Pierre Trudeau still existed, but it was not nearly as pronounced as it had been in the May 1979 election when the voters rejected Trudeau's Liberals for Clark's Conservatives. Fourth, the Liberal lead was so large that the Conservatives could not realistically expect to catch up unless the Liberals made a major mistake.

As Jeffrey Simpson observes in *Discipline of Power*, his excellent account of the Clark interregnum, these four considerations prompted the Liberals to run a tightly controlled, antiseptic campaign, following a strategy of keeping the public's attention focused on Clark and the budget and off Trudeau and his record as prime minister between 1968 and 1979.[3] In a tactic that strategist Jerry Grafstein (later appointed to the Senate by a grateful Trudeau) called "low-bridging," the Liberals sought to avoid reminding voters that the Trudeau who was asking for their support in 1980 was the same Trudeau they used to hate. The Liberals could not change Trudeau or reverse the public's negative attitudes about him, but they could keep him out of sight. In a leader-oriented age, Trudeau managed to become virtually invisible. He set a modern record by

going for forty-three consecutive days without holding a press conference — until twenty-nine members of his media entourage finally sent him a petition, begging him to talk to them. And in one
week in mid-campaign, he made only two public appearances. Even
so, Liberal managers worried that voters were starting to recall their
earlier dislike for Trudeau. A month before election day, an insider
confided to *Toronto Star* columnist Richard Gwyn: "No, er, um,
the numbers haven't changed, but, um, er, a certain, er, um, shak-
iness has started to show up."

In the end, Goldfarb's numbers held, and the strategy that the
numbers drove worked very well. The Liberals won a majority
government with 44 per cent of the vote, twelve points more than
the Conservatives.

Using the numbers to drive the strategy is just as important at
the constituency level. Larry Grossman, later Ontario Tory leader,
remembers his first campaign for the provincial legislature in 1975,
a time when the Tory government of Ontario and then premier
William Davis were out of favor with many voters. Grossman,
however, figured he had an advantage because the downtown Toronto riding he was contesting had been held by his father for
twenty years. Grossman's brochures and door-to-door canvassers
made no reference to the party or leader. Less than three weeks
before the election, however, his friend Goldfarb, although normally a Liberal, took a riding poll for Grossman and found he was
running behind both the Liberal and the NDP candidates.

But the poll also revealed something useful: However negatively
voters reacted to Davis, they were more negative about the Liberal
leader, Robert Nixon. Goldfarb advised Grossman to exploit those
numbers. "Go out and tell your people to start referring to it as
the Progressive Conservative campaign. Tell them to say they're
canvassing for Larry Grossman, the Bill Davis candidate." Grossman told him he was nuts, that angry householders would run his
canvassers off the property. Not so, Goldfarb replied. "You've got
to do that, so that people will react and say, 'I'm not voting for
Bill Davis.' Then you tell your canvassers to ask, 'Are you voting
for Bob Nixon?' The people aren't addressing the alternative, but
they like the alternative less than they like Davis. . . . Make them
deal with what's motivating them." With nothing to lose, Grossman took the pollster's advice. The strategy worked. Enough voters
remembered their dislike of Nixon and the Liberals to give Grossman a 429-vote victory in St. Andrew–St. Patrick (as the Tories
barely scraped back in with a minority government).

The Third Commandment
Restrict the Information

Two of the most difficult decisions confronting a campaign manager are who will have access to the leader or candidate, and who will be allowed to see the polling results. Everyone in an organization wants access to the leader; most should not be allowed near him or her. Similarly, campaign insiders fight for access to polling data. Knowledge of the numbers connotes status and influence. But the wider the circle sharing the information, the greater the risks to the campaign. Leaks within the organization can cause complacency (if the numbers are good) or destroy morale (if they are bad). Leaks to outsiders can provide invaluable strategic information to opponents.

Tory consultant Nancy McLean was unequivocal on the subject of keeping strategic data secret. "Eat the paper before you leave the room!" she declared, only half-facetiously. Some politicians can be astonishingly careless with sensitive information. An Ontario Liberal MP approached pollster Michael Marzolini, who runs Insight Canada, for help prior to the 1988 federal election. The MP knew he was in trouble in his riding and wanted to know what to do. Marzolini took a poll that revealed the problem — the MP's constituents believed he had a drinking problem. The pollster prepared a confidential report that outlined a strategy to convince the voters that their MP was not really a drunk. The careless Liberal, however, left the report on a bus, forcing Marzolini to devise a second strategy to control the damage if the report fell into hands of another party. (As it turned out, someone found the report on the bus and returned it anonymously a few days later.)

Longtime Liberal campaign director Senator Keith Davey is adamant — "I would keep our polling information in the campaign very private. I would level with very, very few people indeed. Trudeau was one. I wouldn't deceive anybody, by the way. If something bad was happening, I'd let them know. But I might not let them know how bad."

For the New Democrats, questions involving openness are always tricky. "The NDP has a kind of internal theological stance about democratic access and essential decision making — in opposition to decision making by a leadership élite," says Robin Sears, the NDP's former federal secretary. "This [democratic organization] is probably the least capable type of organization for interpreting, resolving, and testing polling data. By definition, [the data] cannot be widely held, but if it's not widely held, it becomes part of a generalized attack on the palace guard around the leader."[4]

The importance of restricting access to polling data can be seen in the experience of Bud Smith, a forty-year-old lawyer and backroom politician from Kamloops who decided to go for the leadership of the B.C. Social Credit Party when then-premier Bill Bennett retired in 1986.

A man who favored cowboy boots and checked shirts, Smith was smart, tough, and (some said) arrogant. Never having held public office, he was unknown to most British Columbians. His advantage in a multi-candidate campaign was that very newness; he was a fresh face in a field (of eleven) dominated by weary veterans of the tired Bennett government. Smith's challenge was to place well on the first ballot, with sufficient second-ballot strength to become the irresistible compromise choice. It was a strategy that had carried Joe Clark from a third-place finish on the first ballot to victory in the federal Conservative leadership ten years earlier.

Less than three weeks before the convention, Martin Goldfarb, polling for Smith, flew to Vancouver to present the results of a new delegate poll to John Laschinger, Smith's campaign manager. The numbers were terrible. They showed that William Vander Zalm would win on the third or fourth ballot and that Smith would finish a distant fourth. Laschinger reviewed the findings with Goldfarb but told no one else. He knew that if the devastating results got out, they would spread like wildfire, destroy the morale of Smith's workers, cause key supporters to bolt to other candidates, and cost Smith so many delegates that he would be in no position to command a prominent position in the new government.

Laschinger waited a few days for the right moment to break the news to his candidate. He caught Smith alone at home, following a long day of filming and speech preparation. As a backroom veteran himself, Smith took the news with equanimity and used the next two weeks to plan his actions at the convention. Goldfarb's projections were dead on. Smith finished third on the first ballot and dropped to fourth on the second. His decision long since made, he withdrew and — to the surprise of most delegates — crossed the floor to Vander Zalm. With Smith's support, Vander Zalm came within twelve votes of winning on the third ballot and won handily on the fourth. Bud Smith was elected to the Legislature and went on to become Vander Zalm's attorney general.[5]

The Fourth Commandment
Always Poll, Even When Broke

Politicians are spenders, not conservers. Political parties are always broke — it is their natural condition. If they take in twice as much money this year as last, they will simply spend twice as much, and then some. Money left in the bank for a rainy day, as politicians see it, is money that has not been utilized in the unceasing struggle to stave off the arrival of the rainy day. Most campaign organizers commit between 10 and 15 per cent of their budget to polling; some argue that they should be spending twice as much.

Long before former Liberal premier David Peterson made the mistake of calling an election in Ontario in 1990, the NDP realized that, to be competitive, they were going to have to initiate a serious polling program. They spent $33,700 on polling in the lead-up to the election call and another $114,000 during the campaign period, much of it for nightly tracking (something the NDP had never done before). The polling was crucial to everything else they did. "In the past one of the problems with polling was as much a problem of dollars as anything else," says Julie Davis, who was lent to the NDP strategy group by the Ontario Federation of Labour, of which she was secretary-treasurer. "We didn't have the money, we didn't have it to spend. But we were quite successful this time in our fundraising and budgeted a fair chunk of money for polling. We were doing 'rolling polling,' calling every night and doing the accumulation at the end of the week." ("Rolling polling" involves doing a telephone poll each evening and adding the results from day to day. As the campaign progresses, older results are dropped off as new ones are added, enabling the strategists to track the trends.)

By means of nightly tracking, David Gotthilf, the NDP pollster, saw the party flatten out at 32 to 33 per cent by the end of the third week of the five-week campaign. The decision was made to shift gears, to move Rae away from the attack-only mode that he and the party had been in for the first three weeks. The upward movement resumed.

The Tories had no money — not a cent — for polling in that election. They were $5 million in debt, with no prospect of ever being able to pay it off. But it never occurred to leader Michael Harris or Laschinger, his campaign manager, not to commission polls. They did not spend a vast amount — only $105,000 (about one-sixth as much as the Liberals) — but it was essential spending. Their polling drove their strategy — the attack on high taxes that, in the end, helped to undermine the Liberals and to elect Ontario's first NDP government. The NDP's Robin Sears is a firm advocate of spending early on polling: "I've always argued that the polling money should be spent at least a year in advance. That's when it's crucial to refine what you are going to do."

Parties that try to save money by not polling often regret it — as Joe Clark's federal Tories did when they stopped polling after they elected a minority government in 1979. Had they continued polling, they would have realized the depth of their own unpopularity, would never have risked defeat in the Commons, and would not have been pitched into an election they could not win in February 1980. The same commandment applies to candidates. In 1976, Paul Hellyer, a former Liberal (he had tried for the federal leadership of that party in 1968) decided to run for the Tory leadership. It was a triumph of ambition over common sense. Hellyer spent $287,786 on his campaign; he raised $81,957 in contributions — and wrote a personal cheque for the balance. All this for 231 votes on the first ballot. Hellyer could have saved himself the money and the embarrassment if he had invested $25,000 or $30,000 on a poll of party members that would have told him how futile his candidacy would be. Another candidate at that convention, Sinclair Stevens, spent $294,106 and raised only $114,064. A pollster would have told him to save his money. He ran seventh, with 182 votes.

In Alberta, when Peter Lougheed decided to retire in 1985 after fourteen years as premier, one of the popular favorites to succeed him was his education minister, Dave King. But King was smart. Before committing himself, he spent $30,000 to hire Decima Research to conduct a poll among members of the Alberta Conservative party. When Decima reported that King could not expect to finish higher than fourth, he decided not to run. Then he did another smart thing. He recovered his investment by selling the results of the Decima poll to Don Getty, the front-runner and eventual winner.

The Fifth Commandment
Treat a Poll as a Snapshot, Not a Prediction

A common mistake of amateurs, insists veteran Liberal strategist Hershell Ezrin, is to read too much into polls. "A poll tells you how people have reacted to what you have done," he says. "If you try to use polls simply as a prognostication of the future, you get yourself into a hell of a lot of trouble."

When backroom managers look at the computer printouts of poll results, the responses that interest them most are not the replies to the standard voting-intention question: If an election were held today, which party would you be most likely to support? More important are the answers to a series of questions that determine the issues or circumstances that would strengthen a respondent's voting intention, or would cause him or her to alter that intention.

The Ontario Progressive Conservative Party held two leadership conventions in 1985. In the first, delegates chose industry and trade minister Frank Miller, a car dealer from Muskoka, to succeed William Davis, who was retiring after fourteen years as leader and premier. The choice was a ghastly mistake. Miller was too right-wing and too square (he loved tartan sports coats). He called an election, and although the Tories won more seats (fifty-two) than the Liberals (forty-eight) or the NDP (twenty-five), they could not govern. They were defeated in the Legislature, and power shifted, without another election, to David Peterson's Liberals. For the first time in forty-two years, the Tories found themselves in opposition. They needed to rebuild with new people, new policies, a new organization, and a new leader.

Dennis Timbrell, a thirty-eight-year-old veteran of several cabinet portfolios who had contested the first leadership convention earlier in the year, understood the need for renewal. He launched his second leadership campaign by issuing a challenge to the Tory party to reform itself. He urged it to rebuild from the ground up. He demanded that the party brass pay more attention to the wishes of the grass roots. Timbrell was absolutely right; everything he said made sense. Unfortunately for him, he had the right message at the wrong time.

Timbrell's chief opponent was Larry Grossman, the former provincial treasurer and health minister who was also making his second bid for the leadership. Like Timbrell, Grossman knew that the party had to reform and rebuild. Unlike Timbrell, he knew what he had to do to win the leadership.

Both men were hard-pressed to finance a second leadership campaign in the space of ten months. Timbrell, confident that he understood the mood of the party, decided against commissioning any polling. Grossman was more cautious. Before declaring his candidacy, he asked Allan Gregg to poll the delegates who had attended the first convention — most of whom would be back as delegates at the second.

Gregg's poll surprised Grossman and Laschinger, his campaign manager. It showed Grossman leading Timbrell, as expected. But it also showed that the delegates had not come to terms with the party's fall from power. They could not yet accept their status as a mere opposition party. Reform and renewal were the farthest things from their minds. Eighty-five per cent of delegates, Gregg reported, believed that the Conservatives could regain power simply by changing leaders. The delegates conceded that they had made a minor mistake by choosing Miller, but they thought Ontario voters had made a bigger mistake by not electing enough Tories to govern. Heads firmly in the sand, they saw no need for new policies, new people, or new organization.

Grossman knew the delegates were out of touch with reality. But he and his backroomers also knew enough to accept Gregg's poll for what it was — a snapshot of the delegates as they were on the eve of their second leadership battle in less than a year. It was not a projection of how the party would feel in a year's time or at the next provincial election. And it was certainly not a projection of the party's needs for the future.

Grossman used the snapshot. When he announced his candidacy, he did not challenge the party and he did not propose to change it. Instead, he offered reassurance and hope: "I believe we have more imagination than the Liberals. I believe we have more talent in our caucus, in our organization, and at the grass roots. Our party has known adversity before. We have learned that by working together we can win together." As a campaign theme, it was thin gruel, but Grossman stuck with it. While Timbrell preached the need to swallow the bitter medicine of change, Grossman kept repeating his placebo — there is nothing wrong with the party; Conservatives are good people; the future would be theirs. By the time Timbrell recognized the mood of the party and softened his message, it was too late. Grossman beat him by nineteen votes on the second ballot. The pollster's snapshot made the difference.

The Sixth Commandment
Be Honest with the Candidate
(Except When a Lie Is Useful)

The client pays the bills and he or she has a right to know what the polls are revealing. Although painful, the truth can protect the candidate against even greater hurt. A poll enabled Bud Smith to think through his options and to plan when to throw his support to Vander Zalm at the B.C. Socred convention in 1986. In late

1990, Ken Streatch, a veteran cabinet minister in Nova Scotia, commissioned a poll, the results of which persuaded him to stay out of the race for the provincial Conservative leadership. Instead, Streatch threw his support (and contributed his poll) to the candidate who topped that poll, then–attorney general Tom McInnis. (Unfortunately for both men, the poll was a snapshot, not a forecast; McInnis finished third.)

Every now and again, however, a campaign manager decides that deceit is the better part of valor. In 1976, Laschinger, then national director of Tories, helped recruit Jean Pigott, a prominent Ottawa businesswoman, to run in a federal byelection in Ottawa-Carleton. The seat had been vacated when John Turner, on the outs with Prime Minister Trudeau, resigned from Parliament. Pigott's was the first high-tech byelection campaign, with a sophisticated polling program and an American-style phone bank operating from the library of the Conservative national headquarters in downtown Ottawa. Ten days before the election, the numbers showed Pigott with 50 per cent of the vote, to 30 per cent for the Liberal and 20 per cent for the New Democrat.

Laschinger was worried that Pigott, a novice candidate, and her inexperienced workers might ease up in their campaign efforts if they learned of the magnitude of her lead. One Sunday evening, Laschinger sat in Pigott's living room with the candidate and her husband Arthur. Trying to give the impression of concern and confidence at the same time, he told the couple that, while she was ahead of her lightly regarded Liberal opponent, her lead unfortunately was only five or six points. Pigott would, he warned, have to redouble her efforts lest victory slip away from her. Believing him, she did.

On October 16, 1976, Pigott became the seventeenth woman since Confederation to be elected to the House of Commons. The results mirrored the polling, Pigott winning 51 per cent of the popular vote, the Liberals taking 28 per cent, and the NDP 19 per cent.

Laschinger never had the nerve to tell Pigott of his deception.

The Seventh Commandment
Use Focus Groups, Liberally

There was a time, not long ago, when politicians sneered at the concept of focus groups. It was part of the conceit of politicians that because they got elected they had some special understanding of the public psyche. They believed they could learn more about what the people really think by reading their morning mail, by taking calls in their riding office, or by chatting to constituents at community events. Focus groups, they believed, were for hucksters — for the purveyors of breakfast cereals and the pedlars of detergents.

The politicians were right and wrong. Focus groups are for hucksters. But some of the hucksters are political strategists. For them, focus groups are an increasingly potent weapon in the campaign arsenal. The groups enable politicians to see beneath the pollsters' numbers to understand *why* people feel the way they say they do on issues of current concern. Armed with this understanding, campaign managers can develop a strategy to motivate the voters to support their candidate or party. Regular use of focus groups as a campaign progresses gives an organization the internal discipline that it needs and signals when to shift direction or emphasis.

When political researchers assemble focus groups, they generally choose eight to twelve individuals to represent a cross-section (sex, age, income, education, occupation) of the "universe" — the segment of the electorate — that the campaign proposes to target. Participants are paid a fee (usually about $30) and, directed by a professional discussion leader, spend about two hours airing their concerns in detail. The campaign strategists eavesdrop on the session from behind a pane of one-way glass. The groups are too small for their conclusions to have any statistical validity. Their value is that they enable pollsters and their clients to put flesh and emotion on the stark numbers of the polls. Pollsters use focus groups to help politicians choose slogans, to pre-test television commercials, and to put the most advantageous "spin" on the party platform.

Even the New Democrats have learned the value of focus groups. In the 1990 Ontario election, they retained Peter Donegal, a Toronto market researcher whose speciality was advising commercial clients how to sell consumer goods by tapping the public's subconscious thoughts. Donegal organized focus groups for the NDP in Hamilton, Sudbury, and Toronto, using groups of eight drawn from the NDP's "universe" of potential supporters (these included undecided voters and soft supporters of other parties as well as NDP core supporters). The focus groups expressed general satisfaction with Liberal premier David Peterson; if they were unhappy with him or his government, they were not letting on.

Donegal burrowed deeper. Passing out paper and crayons, he

asked the participants to draw simple pictures that expressed their feelings about the Liberals and the NDP. "The results yielded some heavy symbolism," wrote Georgette Gagnon and Dan Rath in *Not Without Cause*, their chronicle of the 1990 campaign. "One pair of sketches showed Peterson as a devil brandishing a pitchfork on top of a hill, with Rae represented as a farmer in a valley by a clear stream. Another effort showed a large hairy arm wielding a mallet over a tiny stick figure, under the heading of 'Liberal'; the NDP was represented by a giant question mark."[6] Beneath their surface complacency, Donegal reported, people were pessimistic, angry, and resentful. The NDP successfully exploited these negative feelings about the Liberals in their "them versus us" campaign strategy.

For the Conservatives in the same election, Gregg asked 1,200 respondents in July 1990 a series of questions on specific issues, probing to determine whether they thought each issue had improved or worsened in recent (Liberal) years:

Table 1

Perceptions (%) of Changes to the Province

	Significantly Worse	Somewhat Worse	About the Same	Somewhat Better	Significantly Better
Presence of Drugs & Crime	44	34	13	7	1
Level of Taxes	35	42	18	4	—
Affordable Housing	38	34	13	11	1
Auto Insurance	35	36	18	6	1
Quality of Grade-School Education	14	22	31	23	4
Access to Quality Health Care	8	16	39	29	8

SOURCE: Decima Research

From "quantitative regression analyses" (designed to measure the strength of the cause and effect of various factors), the Conservatives concluded that the level of taxes, although not at the top of the list of public concerns, offered the most advantage in campaigning against Peterson's Liberals. They also thought that the public's top-ranked concern, the presence of crime and drugs, created the potential for a tough law-and-order campaign in which the Liberals could be portrayed as being soft on crime, unconcerned about the illicit drug trade, and uncaring about the safety and personal security of ten million Ontarians. The Tories tested their assumptions with focus groups, repeating the exercise with two sessions every Wednesday evening throughout the campaign.

The groups were asked for their comments on two sets of hard-hitting television scripts — one attacking the Liberals on taxes, the other hammering them for allowing crime and drug trafficking to run rampant. The law-and-order attack fired a blank. The focus groups' reactions to the scripts written by communications strategist Nancy McLean and her associate Mitch Patten went like this: Yes, the problem of crime and drugs was getting worse; but, no, it was not Peterson's fault; surely, it was an international problem; General Noriega of Panama had to be blamed more than Peterson; no one could expect the premier to solve this international problem by himself; and so on.

The crime/drugs scripts went in the trash can. The Tories fought the election on the single issue of taxes. It was the only issue that would work for them. The focus groups had made that clear.

The Eighth Commandment
Know When to Leak a Poll
(and When to Invent One)

The proliferation of polls commissioned by the news media — twenty-six national polls were published or broadcast in the 1988 federal election — has drastically changed the way the press covers elections. Coverage, which was never distinguished by great depth or insight, has grown even more shallow. An election is reduced to a horse-race — who is ahead, who is behind, and by how much; who "won" the leaders' debate; who is gaining in the latest polls. Editors and reporters are easily bored by issues. Their eyes go glassy at the mention of white papers, green plans, prosperity initiatives, industrial strategies, equalization arrangements, or constitutional amending formulas. Polls are so much simpler, so much easier to understand — and, in truth, so much more fun. They give journalists an excuse to ignore the issues and cover an election the way they think it ought to be covered — like a sporting event.

Campaign strategists do not complain when their team is judged to be winning. They become aggrieved about the superficiality of press coverage when the media publish polls that suggest that their party or candidate is in trouble. Backroom politicians have ways of fighting back. One recourse is to leak to the press their own internal polls, if they are more favorable than the public polls. If they are not, another recourse is to fib about (or quote selectively from) the findings of the internal polls. A favorite device is to leak results from polling in selected or target ridings and to claim it is a national or, in a provincial campaign, province-wide sample. When all else fails, the final recourse is simply to make it up, to invent a poll. There isn't a campaign manager alive who hasn't done a little creative leaking, fibbing, or inventing in his time.

One of the most blatant instances in recent years of a fabricated poll occurred in Newfoundland in the 1989 provincial election — the election in which the Liberals under Clyde Wells defeated the Tories led by Tom Rideout, who had recently replaced Brian Peckford, the premier for the previous ten years. Knowing that voters are often inclined to go with a front-runner, the Liberals were unhappy with published polls that showed Rideout's Conservatives leading by 6 to 11 percentage points. So the Liberal strategists invented their own poll that put their party 3.5 points ahead and leaked it to the unsuspecting (and unsuspicious) St. John's *Evening Telegram* four days before the election (which Wells won).[7]

Back in the 1968 federal election, when Toronto lawyer Edwin (Fast Eddie) Goodman was running the Conservative campaign, he tried good-humoredly to challenge the press's assumption that the Liberals and their new leader, Pierre Trudeau, had the election in the bag. Having no internal poll worth leaking, he made one up. "We decided that we would publish our own poll based upon some rather superficial inquiries that Gene Rheaume [a Tory organizer] would make across the country in the most optimistic areas," Goodman recalled in his memoir, *Life of the Party*. "It would be published by Confederation Publishing, which was a wholly Tory Party–owned company. The Rheaume-Goodman poll showed the Tories with a comfortable lead out west, a small lead in the Maritimes, within striking distance in Ontario, and doing better than usual in Quebec. This added up to the Tories making considerable gains since the last published Gallup poll."

Next, Goodman called a press conference. About sixty reporters showed up. Goodman started by declaring that he had two important announcements to make, the first being confidential and the second for publication:

> I informed the breathless press gallery that I had it on absolutely impeccable authority that Pierre Trudeau was a lousy lay and that [Tory leader] Bob Stanfield went home every day for a nooner. The gallery took that in the good-natured way that it was meant and waited for the momentous announcement. I then distributed the poll to gasps of disbelief and, in some cases, open derision. . . . I countered [the] criticism by saying we knew more about polls at headquarters than any pollsters did, which was probably true. The main purpose of the exercise, apart from giving Rheaume and me a few laughs, was to slow down the media's reporting of polls and perhaps make them question their accuracy.[8]

Goodman got his laughs, but his adventure in poll making did not slow the media's reporting of polls.

Martin Goldfarb laughs as he recalls the 1984 federal Liberal leadership campaign, the one in which John Turner defeated Jean Chrétien. Goldfarb was not polling for either candidate, but he had been hired by real estate developer Robert Campeau — who, as it turned out, was trying to support Turner and Chrétien simultaneously. Goldfarb conducted a poll that showed the Liberals would do better against Brian Mulroney's Tories if Chrétien was leader than they would if Turner was. He delivered the poll to Campeau who, as the leadership convention began, gave it to Chrétien. Chrétien's chief aide, Eddie Goldenberg, had huge placards printed with Goldfarb's numbers on them, and Chrétien supporters marched around the convention hall with them. Senator Jerry Grafstein, a Turner organizer, was desperate. He grabbed pollster Angus Reid. "At the time Reid was polling for Turner and Grafstein said, 'Give me some numbers,' and he held them up to the press," Goldfarb says. "Jerry made the poll up right there to respond to the poll we had done that said Chrétien would do better against Mulroney than Turner."

The New Democrats used to go to great lengths to rig a different kind of poll in British Columbia. Under B.C. law, the publication of polls was banned during election campaigns. A Vancouver hamburger joint called the Frying Dutchman shrewdly turned the ban into free publicity and increased sales. Every election, it conducted a hamburger poll. Customers were invited to choose burgers named for the party leaders. Running totals were announced and widely reported. Later, a New Westminster spot, Burger Heaven, adopted the same gimmick. "We used to spend so much time and money rigging those goddamned polls that I never wanted to see another hamburger again," Robin Sears says, grimacing at the memory. "Then somebody invented an ice cream poll, which was even more obnoxious."

The Ninth Commandment
Beware of Media Polls — They Can Kill

Michael Adams, the president of Environics Research Group, is one of the few pollsters who still argues that polls do not influence voting behavior. "My paradigm is the fairy tale of the little boy who stood in the parade and said the emperor has no clothes . . .," says Adams. "Polls keep us honest, they correct themselves. The thing we learned in the last election [1988] is the polls do not affect public opinion." Allan Gregg used to agree with Adams, but the 1984 and 1988 federal elections, with their Mulroney landslides in Quebec, changed his mind. "Historically," says Gregg, "the evidence of that [bandwagon] effect was quite small — only 1.5 per cent of the electorate were motivated to change their vote based on who they thought was going to win. But 1984 and 1988 in Quebec threw that conventional wisdom right out the window. There's no question that there's evidence, huge evidence, of bandwagon voting in those two campaigns. They changed their vote to correspond with what they thought was going to be a winning situation. It was strategic voting."

Viewing the same issue from the NDP backroom, Sears agrees with Gregg. "In my perspective, it's complete idiocy to say polls have no impact on the outcome of an election or on the determination of voting behavior. You pick up the Toronto *Globe and Mail* on a Monday morning in the middle of the campaign and you're down six points. You know revenues will be down, volunteers will be down, morale will be down. A negative poll has a very significant impact on a national campaign — and the reverse is equally true."

Backroom managers share a common nightmare. Their campaign is going well; the party is establishing its issues; the workers are gung-ho. Suddenly, a news organization broadcasts or publishes a poll that purports to show that the campaign, far from gaining momentum, is actually slipping in public support. The poll may be wrong. It may be misleading. It may be unscientific or poorly constructed. It may be out of date. None of that matters. The poll is published — and the party is on the defensive. The next few days' schedule goes in the waste basket. There is no use trying to interest the public in the party positions on the environment, health care, or Native rights. The messenger, the press, is interested in only one issue: the poll. (What went wrong? Why is the party slipping? When will the leader hold a press conference to comment?) The poll replaces the campaign as the top item of election news. Speculation about the poll's significance supplants analysis of the issues. And it is not as though there is only one poll per campaign. The twenty-six national polls conducted for news organizations in the 1988 federal election worked out to one almost every second day. The politicians and their campaign managers no longer have time to recover from one negative poll before the next one hits them between the eyes.

Susan Fish knows all about the damage that a negative poll can do. A former Ontario cabinet minister and high-profile Red Tory, she was, she thought, in the thick of the mayoral race in Toronto in the fall of 1991. Until October 10, that is. On that day, the *Toronto Star* published a front-page account of a new Environics poll that showed Fish had succeeded in attracting only 19 per cent of decided voters, leaving her far behind her opponents, June Rowlands and Jack Layton. Although Fish tried to tough it out for another eight days, her funds dried up and her organization collapsed. On October 18, with her debts at $50,000 and rising, she threw in the towel. (It can be argued that the Environics poll did Fish a favor by forcing her out of the race before she could spend even more money that she did not have in a race that she could not win.)

Gary Filmon had a worse experience in the Manitoba provincial election in 1986. Fighting his first general election after taking over the leadership of the Manitoba Conservatives, Filmon was in an uphill struggle against Premier Howard Pawley's New Democrats. Decima Research, polling for Filmon, had the NDP ahead by fifteen percentage points as the campaign began, although an independent poll by the University of Manitoba put the NDP lead at just five points. Decima established a nightly tracking program in twelve swing ridings, and the results showed the Tories gradually closing the gap.

One week before the vote, strategist John Laschinger instructed

Decima to do a full province-wide poll. On the Friday morning before the Tuesday election, Decima delivered the results:

Table 2

Manitoba Election, 1986

PC	44.4%
NDP	40.9
Lib.	11.7
Other	3.0

SOURCE: *Decima Research*

The trend detected in the nightly tracking was obviously province-wide. With a small lead and momentum in their favor, the Tories seemed poised for an upset victory. Then came the moment that campaign organizers dread. At 5:00 p.m. on that final Friday, Laschinger and officials of the other parties were called to the studios of CKND, a Winnipeg television station. The station had commissioned a poll by Winnipeg pollster Angus Reid and the results took Laschinger's breath away. Reid and Decima might have been polling in different provinces. Where Decima had the Conservatives 3.5 points ahead, Reid had them 9 points behind.

Table 3

Manitoba Election, 1986

NDP	45%
PC	36
Lib.	13
Other	6

SOURCE: *Angus Reid Associates*

CKND went on the air with the poll at 6:00 p.m., and Laschinger could hear the air rushing out of the Conservative campaign. The morale of volunteers went into a nosedive. Candidates and senior campaign officers, who had been briefed regularly on Decima's nightly tracking, suspected they had been lied to. Laschinger did not know what to do. Finally, on Sunday, two days before the election, he released the Decima province-wide poll. It got little coverage in the news media. Some journalists did not believe the

Decima numbers. Others thought Laschinger had fabricated the poll. Virtually all considered it an act of desperation from Tories who, in the view of the press, knew they were facing defeat on Tuesday. Then, on Monday, Howard Pawley's father died and Conservative attempts to control the damage of the Reid poll were swept away on a wave of public sympathy for the NDP premier and his family.

On election day 1986, the Tories and NDP finished in a dead heat in the popular vote, with 41 per cent each. But the NDP's 41 per cent, being better distributed, translated into five more seats than the Conservatives' 41 per cent. The 41–41 outcome was within Decima's margin of error. It was outside Reid's margin of error of 3.5 percentage points.

Laschinger was convinced that Reid's was a rogue poll, a "20th poll" (so named because polls claim to be accurate within their margin of error nineteen times out of twenty). The poll and the stories about it robbed the Tories of their momentum and tilted the election to the New Democrats. Howard Pawley continued in power. Gary Filmon had to wait for one more election to become premier. The episode makes a powerful argument for banning the publication of opinion polls, at least in the closing stages of election campaigns.

The Tenth Commandment
Go with the Gut

Polling has done more than any other innovation in recent decades to take the element of chance out of political strategy. Politicians or campaign managers who ignore the advice of their pollster are courting disaster — nineteen times out of twenty. On rare occasions, they may do better by following their instincts instead of their pollster.

John Carnell Crosbie is one who went with his gut. On a January night in 1983, Crosbie sat in a hotel room in Winnipeg, watching the proceedings on television as delegates to the Conservative national meeting in the convention centre nearby voted 1,607 to 795 *not* to hold a leadership convention to replace Joe Clark as leader. Crosbie had at least two reasons to be particularly interested in the outcome of that vote. First, as the finance minister who brought down the budget that precipitated the defeat of the Clark government in December 1979, Crosbie had some direct responsibility for Clark's plight. Second, for the past two years Crosbie had been secretly preparing to run for the leadership as soon as the opportunity presented itself.

As he watched the vote being announced on TV, Crosbie talked on the telephone to John Laschinger, the man who was organizing his leadership campaign. Both agreed that Crosbie's ambitions would have to be put on hold for the foreseeable future, and in preparation for going to the convention centre to show his solidarity with his leader, Crosbie called across the hotel room to his wife, "Jane, see if you can find my 'Joe' button." A moment later, however, the need for the "Joe" button evaporated. Clark stunned his supporters and enemies alike. Moving to the microphones in the convention centre, he announced that, because one-third of the party rank and file did not support him, he was tendering his resignation as leader and calling for a leadership convention to be held at the earliest possible time — a convention at which he would be a candidate.

Only in politics does one-third beat two-thirds. Clark's demonstration of political math baffled people from Burnaby to Buckingham Palace. "What I don't understand is, why was 67 per cent not enough?" asked a puzzled Charles, Prince of Wales.[9]

To some, Clark's decision to put his position on the line at a leadership convention was an act of rare political courage. To others, it was an act of foolish bravado, consistent with the way Clark had thrown away power three years earlier. But Crosbie, that night in Winnipeg, understood. Clark had been fighting the demons within his party ever since the election of February 1980. He believed he needed the support of at least 70 per cent of the delegates — and preferably more — if he was to regain control over the party. But the vote in Winnipeg proved the demons were not going to go away; if anything, his opponents were increasing in numbers and determination. Clark knew he would have to fight them every day for the rest of his time as leader — unless he faced them down in a convention and won a new mandate from the party. Only then, could he hope for peace.

Crosbie understood Clark's dilemma. He also understood that he had just been handed a golden opportunity. Crosbie was one of the wittiest, most sardonic, most engaging politicians ever to come out of Newfoundland. He was also one of the most ambitious.

Although Laschinger was a civil servant at the time (assistant deputy minister of tourism in the Ontario government) and supposedly removed from partisan politics, he had been quietly assembling Crosbie's campaign organization since March 1981, starting with quarterly meetings of Crosbie friends, admirers, and financial backers. Laschinger was in charge of the overall direction of the Crosbie campaign. Two wealthy Newfoundland pals of Crosbie's — businessman Basil Dobbin, and Frank Ryan, who had been Crosbie's campaign manager when he entered federal politics in a 1976 byelection — were in charge of raising the money for the leadership bid. Partly for amusement and partly to preserve secrecy, they developed their own codes. Laschinger, for example, was known as "T.C." (for "Toronto Codfather"); Dobbin and Ryan were the "fishermen" whose "catch" (campaign receipts) was measured in "tons of fish" (thousands of dollars). It was all good fun — a kids' game — until that night in Winnipeg in January 1983.

As Laschinger told Crosbie that night, the preceding two years meant nothing. They had demonstrated that Crosbie had friends and that the friends could raise money. But no one had the faintest idea what chance, if any, Crosbie actually had of winning the leadership. Laschinger recommended that, once everyone got home, he commission a poll of all the delegates who had been in Winnipeg — on the assumption that many of those 2,400-odd voting delegates would also be delegates at an early leadership convention. Laschinger thought a poll would be useful to develop a campaign strategy. Both Crosbie and his manager knew, though, that it would take a ton of sage advice from an army of pollsters to keep Crosbie out of the race.

Table 4

John Crosbie Leadership Poll (Feb. 1983)

First-Ballot Support

Joe Clark	39%
Peter Lougheed*	21
William Davis*	18
Brian Mulroney	11
John Crosbie	3
Others	8

* Did not run.
SOURCE: Canadian Opinion Research, a subsidiary of Market Opinion Research Ltd.

Even so, Laschinger's heart sank two weeks later when he received the results of the poll — done by Detroit-based Market

Opinion Research, headed by Republican pollster Robert Teeter (who in 1992 was campaign director for the re-election of President George Bush). Crosbie had the support of only 3 per cent of Conservative delegates. Respondents had been given a list of prospective candidates — Clark, Crosbie, Brian Mulroney, Alberta premier Peter Lougheed, and Ontario premier William Davis — and asked which one they would vote for on the first ballot.

While Laschinger worried about the poll, Crosbie ignored it. In early March 1983, he hurled himself into the short (three-month) campaign. Although he was arguably the most intelligent of the eight candidates who entered the race, Crosbie's sardonic wit, unrepentant unilingualism, and penchant for saying precisely the wrong thing at the wrong time doomed whatever remote chance he might have had of winning.[10]

Why did he run? It was partly ego, partly stubbornness, partly the love of a good fight, and partly the fact that Crosbie knew he had to run — and run strongly — to consolidate his power base in the party for whatever the future might bring. In fact, he ran astonishingly well. From 3 per cent in February, he pulled himself up to 21 per cent of the delegate vote on the first ballot in June. He lasted three ballots before being knocked off as Mulroney moved ahead of Clark to win on the fourth ballot.[11]

Crosbie lost, yet he won. By ignoring the numbers and going with his gut, Crosbie had secured his position as the "Codfather" of Atlantic Canada in the Tory caucus and cabinet for the next decade.

6. MEET THE MACHINE

"A frequent mistake is to confuse strategy with organization. People need a good reason to vote for you and not for your opponents. That's strategy. If your strategy makes the race close, then your organization will make the difference."
— George Gibault, B.C. Social Credit organizer

They called it the Killer Blimp. It caused pandemonium at the Progressive Conservative leadership convention in Ottawa in 1983. For a few frantic moments, organizers feared it might actually kill a delegate or two — along with the leadership hopes of John Carnell Crosbie.

It seemed like such a good idea when Tom MacMillan first came up with it. MacMillan was one of the original "Dirty Dozen" — the twelve advancemen who worked for Bill Davis in the 1971 Ontario election and who were part of what became known as the Big Blue Machine, the most proficient, and feared, political organization in Canada in the 1970s and 1980s. MacMillan was also one of those backroom politicians who had an unerring instinct for backing a loser. He worked for Allan Lawrence against Davis for the Ontario Tory leadership in 1971, for Brian Mulroney when Joe Clark won the federal Tory leadership in 1976, and for Crosbie against Mulroney and Clark when Mulroney won in 1983. But MacMillan had a creative marketing mind, and John Laschinger asked him to organize the floor demonstration for Crosbie the evening before the convention delegates were to cast their ballots.

When he got to the capital, MacMillan looked around and noticed two large helium-filled blimps with Crosbie's name on the sides floating on a tether outside the Ottawa Civic Centre. Jim Hayhurst, a Toronto advertising executive and Crosbie volunteer, had rented the pair for $2,500 to attract the attention of convention delegates to the Crosbie campaign. A light-bulb flashed on in MacMillan's brain. Candidate demonstrations all tend to be the same: a bunch of psyched-up volunteers march raggedly into the convention hall, waving placards, chanting silly slogans, cheering inanely, and singing campaign songs, off-key. With luck, they are shoved out the opposite door quickly enough to permit the candidate to deliver his painstakingly rehearsed words of inspiration to the delegates before the time allotted for his demonstration and speech expires. (For the Tories in 1983, the limit for demonstration and speech, combined, was a no-nonsense thirty minutes per candidate. Candidates were warned that, at the thirty-minute mark, power to their microphones would be cut off.)

What, MacMillan wondered, if the centre-piece of the Crosbie floor demonstration were one of the twenty-foot-long blimps? He was ecstatic when he learned that the blimps were outfitted with small electric motors — fans, really — and were radio-controlled. They could be made to fly inside the arena.

A good organizer leaves nothing to chance (or so the theory goes). The night before the demonstrations and speeches, Mac-Millan arranged for a secret test flight. A technician with a remote-control unit guided the blimp into the arena, made it sail slowly down to one end, then had it make a stately turn and float slowly back again. The blimp even made a slight dip before leaving the arena, as though saluting the podium where candidate Crosbie would be standing the next evening. It was perfect. It was better than perfect. MacMillan wanted the Crosbie demonstration completed and out of the arena in the space of five minutes to allow Crosbie twenty-five minutes to deliver the most important speech of his political life. The blimp took just three and a half minutes.

One nagging thought picked away at MacMillan's delight. The arena was empty and cool for the test flight. It would be packed and overheated the next night. Would this make the blimp behave differently? The technicians told MacMillan not to worry. If it was hot in the arena, they would simply adjust the amount of helium. Satisfied, MacMillan made no objection when another Crosbie organizer, Ted Aver, went on CBC television with Mike Duffy to tell the nation to watch for something dramatic in the Crosbie demonstration.

With excitement building on the big night, MacMillan stationed himself in the stands to watch. The Crosbie band and the Crosbie demonstrators poured on to the floor. Above their heads — barely above them — floated a sluggish monstrosity: the Crosbie blimp. It was the size of a stretch limousine, and it was barely moving! The memory is still painful to MacMillan:

> The blimp came out very low, extremely low. It looked like a sausage. It was oppressively hot in the Civic Centre, and so it came out and it just sort of stayed there. Then it started to gently rise, but not before it almost landed on a little-old-lady delegate in the first row. It may have been the same little old lady with a sign from one of our competitors who reached up and whacked one of the fans on the side of the blimp. It disabled the fan. So we had a blimp not flying well to begin with now going on one wing. It kind of looked like a whale out of control at this point — and it had a mind of its own. The guy with the radio control was desperately jamming the handle every direction. . . . Not only was it out of control, but as it majestically rose, looking like the blimp from the movie *Black Sunday*, it just headed off and appeared to attack the CBC anchor booth, which was suspended far up in the top end.
>
> At this point my life was flashing before my eyes, because I knew this blimp was part of the demonstration and if the sucker didn't leave within five minutes, we were toast. We were going to be in big trouble. So it went up. It bounced against the window of the CBC anchor booth. It fell back, and then it got a little burst of energy from its one remaining fan and it went over and attacked the CBC French anchor booth. Then it started a long graceful retreat, a slide towards the convention floor. . . . I ran faster than I've ever run in my life down the stairs. I hit the convention floor running, and then it was like the Michael Jordan Coca-Cola commercial where he leaps up to give the kids in the tree house the Coke. The back end of it came down and I am sure to this day I jumped twenty-six feet in the air and I caught one corner of it with my hand. . . . We pulled it down and managed to fit right into the end of the demonstration. We left as if we knew what we were doing — we were under the five-minute time frame.

The Killer Blimp served one useful, if unintended, purpose. It so distracted the crowd that no one noticed when Crosbie, who was following his band across the convention floor, took a wrong turn, missed the stage, and was about to march out of the arena when someone rescued him. He made it back to the stage and delivered his speech, finishing with sixteen seconds to spare.

The episode illustrated the distinction between strategy and organization. Strategy dictated that Crosbie — who entered convention week in third place, needing a boost to put him in a position to seriously challenge Clark and Mulroney — should try to make a splash on speech night. Laschinger would never have considered using a blimp if he had been managing Mulroney's campaign. Mulroney had hurt himself badly by running a far too ostentatious campaign for the leadership in 1976; the last thing he needed was to go out of his way to make a splash in 1983. But the blimp made strategic sense for the Crosbie campaign. It would make his demonstration and speech the talk of the convention. The Crosbie organization, however, failed to make certain that the blimp would perform properly under actual convention conditions. And Crosbie's handlers should never have let the candidate go out on the convention floor, surrounded by ten thousand screaming partisans, without having someone at his side to guide him to the stairs to the stage.

There is nothing mysterious about a political machine. The machine is organization. Organization is making the big things achievable by getting the small things right. There are three keys to successful political organization. The first is attention to detail. The second is attention to detail. And the third is attention to detail. The party or candidate that is best at managing the little things almost always emerges the winner. Former Alberta premier Peter Lougheed traces his political success to an organizational triumph one evening in a church in Edmonton during the 1967 provincial election, his first as leader of the moribund Alberta Tories. Ernest Manning had been the Social Credit premier for twenty-four years, and in 1963 the Socreds had won sixty of the Legislature's sixty-three seats while the Conservatives failed to elect a single member. As the 1967 campaign began, Manning was anxious to avoid a debate with his opponents. He reasoned that sharing a debate platform with Lougheed and the Liberal and NDP leaders would create the impression in the public's mind that he accepted the other three as his political equals. But pressure from the news media and other groups eventually forced Manning to agree to a debate. Conservative organizers were ready. They packed the church where the debate was held with Lougheed supporters, making sure to select the most vibrant young Tories they could find to cheer on their thirty-eight-year-old neophyte leader. Although there was not much to choose among the leaders' performances, the partisan crowd's response was enthusiastically in Lougheed's favor. From then on, the media coverage played up the youth and vitality of the Lougheed campaign. In Lougheed's view, his momentum began that night. He and five other Conservatives won seats, the vanguard of forty-nine who would be elected as the Tories swept to power four years later. "Organization greatly reflects on the individual," says Gabor Apor, the Toronto-based communications consultant who, among other things, advised former Ontario Liberal leader David Peterson to adopt the red ties that became his trademark. "The characteristics of good or bad organization . . . communicate something about the candidate before the candidate opens his mouth. Nothing that you have done to the candidate will make any sense if he arrives late, if the microphone doesn't work, or if the room is half-empty. These are all characteristics of bad organization."

Another characteristic of bad organization is attracting public or press attention. Backrooms are meant to be invisible. To the extent that backroom managers, strategists, and organizers draw attention to themselves, they detract attention from the politicians in the frontroom. The more a campaign's strategy and tactics make news, the harder it is for leaders and candidates to get their messages through to the voters. It was significant that no one knew who Bob Dinkel, Peter Lougheed's provincial campaign manager, was when he attended the opening of the Alberta Legislature in 1972, a few months after the election that had brought the Tories to power. Despite the emergence of pollsters as public figures, anonymity remains one of the hallmarks of effective organization. Lougheed understood that, and he was careful to keep his highly efficient machine under wraps during his fourteen years in power in Edmonton.

Good organization cannot elect a bad candidate, but bad organization can certainly defeat a good candidate. It is the little things that create the image, positive or negative, that makes or breaks a candidate or a leader. Joe Clark never got over losing his luggage on the round-the-world tour he made after his 1976 election as Conservative leader. Clark's organization, in fact, did not lose his luggage at all. An airline was unable to transfer the Clark retinue's suitcases quickly enough to make a tight connection and sent the bags along later. But the press contingent, unwilling to give Clark the benefit of any doubt, reported the "loss" — a trivial occurrence even if true — to Clark's great detriment. The news media inflated the incident out of all proportion, but Clark's organization was partly responsible. It failed to explain to everyone on the tour that the luggage was delayed, not lost, and that the problem rested with the airline, not with the Tories. Clark's organizers also did not move to limit the damage when the first stories about the "lost" luggage were filed by reporters on the tour. When Clark won the election of 1979 and formed a minority government, only to see its wheels fall off in a matter of months, the country was not surprised. How could a leader who was unable to keep track of his own luggage be expected to be competent to govern Canada?

Poor organization and inattention to detail hurt the Ontario NDP in 1985 when Frank Miller, the car dealer who had replaced Bill Davis as Conservative leader and premier, called a quick election. The Liberal machine was ready; the NDP's was not. The New Democrats were hoping to move ahead of the Peterson Liberals, form the official opposition, and be in position to knock the Tories off the next time. But it was not to be. "The first day, Peterson dashed off," recalls former NDP researcher Graham Murray. "He was off on his bus. The next morning, he was out early at the subways, glad-handing people. The poor old NDP campaign was still getting gassed up, ready to start." It was like that all campaign. The NDP never caught up. The party won just twenty-five seats to the Liberals' forty-eight and the Conservatives' fifty-two. When the Miller government fell, it was Liberals who formed a government with the support of the NDP, not the other way around. The New Democrats had to wait another five years to seize power in Ontario.

Everything a political organization does is important — from recruiting and training candidates to preparing the leader to debate on national televison. The one part of an election campaign, however, that is most visible to the public and most vulnerable to sloppy organization is the leader's tour. It is a time-honored ritual, a durable fraud. After the writ for a national election is issued, each major party leader heads within a day or two to Ottawa International Airport to board a chartered aircraft. For the next six to seven weeks, he or she will fly about the country like a politician possessed, accompanied by a score of aides and a few dozen journalists, following an itinerary written by a group of armchair sadists back in Ottawa who call themselves the "tour committee": Saskatoon and Flin Flon today; Prince George and Lethbridge tomorrow; then on to Sault Ste. Marie and Montreal; Stratford, Barrie, Kingston, and

Trois-Rivières; Charlottetown, Saint John, and St. John's; Halifax and Winnipeg. Then back to the capital for a change of socks and a lecture from the campaign manager, pollster, and tour director about how the fun phase of the campaign is ending and the candidate had better be braced for the real work to come. Then back to airport and the aircraft he or she is beginning to hate — and off to Sudbury, Edmonton, and Yellowknife.

Each day follows the same pattern — a statement to the press on whatever subject the backroom has decreed to be the issue of the day; a photo opportunity at a supermarket, fish plant, pulp mill, or some other facility that has some relevance, however tangential, to the issue of the day; a meeting with prominent local Tories (Liberals, New Democrats); a speech to a "public" meeting of invited party supporters. The speech is the standard campaign script with zip-in, zip-out paragraphs of new material daily in both official languages to accommodate the need of the travelling reporters for fresh "sound bites" and to preserve the fiction that a leader's tour is a news event. Then back to the plane and off to Vancouver and Victoria — or is it Sept-Iles and Sydney?

By any rational yardstick, the leader's tour is a waste of time and money (parties often invest 20 per cent or more of their campaign budget in the tour, and even more in terms of organizational time and effort). The tour is an anomaly, a throwback to the days when the only way a political leader could contact the people was by travelling to their community and inviting them to come to hear him or her speak at the local arena or high school auditorium. Nowadays, a leader could reach far more voters by staying in Ottawa and appearing on CBC Newsworld two or three times a week.

The tour, however, endures because it serves three purposes. It provides interesting visual backdrops for the television newscasts each evening. This is especially important in the early stages of a campaign when parties are not permitted to buy advertising time or space. Second, the tour creates the illusion that the leader cares so much about the views of ordinary Canadians that he or she is prepared to spend fifty days, more or less, consulting with them to find out what they really want from their government. The leader may genuinely care, in fact, about what is on the minds of the people, but he or she is not going to find out in a tightly scheduled, closely scripted, hermetically sealed tour. Finally, the tour will endure because it is the showcase for the parties' organizational skills. A leader's tour is an extremely complex undertaking, logistically and politically — the sum of tens of thousands of tiny details, any one of which, unattended to, can bring the enterprise to an abrupt halt. There is no assurance, of course, that a party that can operate a $2 million leader's tour can run the country. But it is a fair assumption that a party that cannot move its leader around the country for a few weeks may have trouble operating a national administration with a quarter-million employees, an annual budget of $160 billion, and an accumulated debt in excess of $400 billion.

The leader's tour must be professional and it must appear to be effortless. If this seems like a dumb basis on which to choose a party to govern a country, it is. But it is no dumber than choosing a government on the basis of election undertakings made by politicians, too many of whom either do not understand the implications of the promises they make or do not have any honest intention of keeping them.

Liberal strategist Hershell Ezrin believes the leader's tour is the most focused part of a general election campaign — and the least understood:

> The leader's tour has become more and more the creation of, and a requirement for, the kind of media age we live in. It's having the appropriate hamburger [press statement] for the day to be doled out at the right time of day with the right photo opportunity at the right event. And it is probably one of the most difficult and toughest things to do. You have to make sure that it all looks like a seamless effort with the right crowds out, the right signage around, things happening appropriately, and a proper venue in which to deliver your message. Because, if you don't, it's the most obvious place for the media to say, "The leader had a terrible day today." "Nobody showed up." "They got the wrong message out." "The speech was late." And, God forbid, the worst of all things, "They did not meet the timing that we, the media, needed to file [our stories]."

If, in organizational terms, the leader's tour is a microcosm of the whole organizational challenge, the 1968 federal election — the first Trudeau-Stanfield election — offered a vivid illustration of the proposition that, as the tour goes wrong, so goes the campaign. The Conservatives were feeling pleased with themselves as Centennial Year, 1967, drew to a happy close. After four years of internal strife, they had finally succeeded in deposing the Chief, John Diefenbaker, and replacing him with Robert Lorne Stanfield, the premier of Nova Scotia. In Stanfield, they had one of the most successful provincial politicians in recent history; he was, as his leadership campaign signs proclaimed, The Man with the Winning Way. They waited impatiently for the Liberal prime minister of the day, Lester Pearson, to call an election. Stanfield versus Pearson — it would be no contest. The Tories were sure of that. But instead of calling an election, Pearson retired and a leadership convention was set. Had the Liberals elected one of their old-line candidates — Robert Winters, Paul Hellyer, or Paul Martin, Sr. — Stanfield would most likely have been prime minister. The Liberals, however, took the biggest flyer that any Canadian party had ever taken (before or since). They passed over the tried and true, the familiar and the tested, in favor of a fling with the unknown. They chose Pierre Trudeau, the swinging bachelor who had been Pearson's justice minister for less than one year — and a Liberal for less than three.

For the Liberals, the selection of Trudeau was not just an exciting gamble. It was a complete change of political generations. Trudeau was new and dramatic, an arresting personality, especially to younger Canadians. In contrast, Stanfield, scion of a Truro, N.S., family that had made its fortune in the manufacture of underwear, was the sort of politician that the parents of young Canadians felt comfortable with. The contrast could not have been more dramatic in the tours of the two leaders during the election that Trudeau quickly called. The Liberals made the generational leap in aircraft, too. They chartered a jet, a DC-9, for their new leader. It was the first time a Canadian party had used a jet aircraft for its leader's tour, and in those days the DC-9 was state of the art. It was the visible symbol of a newer era than the aging turbo-prop, a DC-7C, that the Conservatives, being conservative, chartered for Stanfield. Dubbed "The Flying Banana," the ancient aircraft lumbered about the country at 300 mph, not much more than half the speed of Trudeau's DC-9.

The symbolism of the aircraft was bad enough (Stanfield organizers, realizing their mistake, frantically tried to locate another DC-9, but were unable to find one), but the tour organization was even worse. It was so bad that it was hard to pick out the worst moment. Was it the day that the leader's plane arrived in Quebec City where local organizers, realizing there were no passenger stairs to fit a DC-7C, ordered a temporary ramp built out of wood? Unfortunately, no one had measured the height of the exit from the ground; the ramp was three feet too high, and passengers had to pull themselves up on it and crawl out of the plane on hands and knees. Was it the day in London, Ontario, on which organizers neglected a local bylaw that forbade political rallies in public parks, and the police cancelled Stanfield's open-air rally? Or was it early on, when the Conservatives assembled all their big guns in Winnipeg for the official kickoff of their election campaign, only to let the preliminary speakers natter on so long that the show had gone off national television before the leader rose to speak?

Meanwhile "Pierre de la Plaza," as the press dubbed him, jetted nonchalantly about the country, kissing every teenaged girl in sight (or so it seemed). If there were glitches in the Liberal organization, no one noticed. The Trudeau and Stanfield tours were in the same country, but in different worlds. And the outcome of the election was never in doubt.

However glamorous a campaign may appear to television audiences, there is nothing remotely glamorous about most of the work of political organizers. A lot of it is tedious, as attention to detail tends to be. When the Ontario Liberal party chose a successor to Peterson in February 1992, the job went to Lyn McLeod, who had been one of Peterson's ministers. McLeod won because her organization did everything, especially the little things, well. It even sent two young volunteers out on the floor of Hamilton's Copps Coliseum following her speech to the convention to pick up pompoms that McLeod supporters had dropped at the end of her postspeech demonstration. They carried the pom-poms off in cardboard boxes, to be reused for between-ballot hoopla the next day. It was a very small thing, but Laschinger and other professionals observing the convention noticed. They had a hunch that McLeod's painstaking approach to organization would pay dividends when the convention voted. Sure enough, McLeod defeated the heavy favorite, Murray Elston. Her margin of victory, after a long day of balloting, was just nine votes. Her organization made the difference.

Some of the work of organizers, as veteran Tory backroomer Paul Curley puts it, is "down and dirty" — doing what needs to be done to win. It takes hard work — plus money, contacts, and influence. It may mean tapping contacts in business to find jobs for backroom workers, jobs that will leave them with ample time to devote to campaign activity. In leadership races, it may mean packing delegate-selection meetings with brand-new party members from ethnic community centres, youth groups, senior citizens' homes or, if necessary, skid-row missions. These new members must be bussed to the meeting — otherwise they might fail to show up or arrive too late to be of use. To keep them there until the voting is complete, organizers will take the precaution of asking the bus driver to give them the keys, lest his passengers seek to leave prematurely. If, as is sometimes the case, the new party members do not speak English or French, or have trouble remembering why they were brought to the meeting, they are handed printed lists of the delegates to vote for.

Elected politicians get exercised from time to time about the ethics of "down and dirty" backroom politics. They will deplore the recruitment of "instant" party members to pack meetings and the common practice by which a candidate pays the expenses of "his" delegates to attend the leadership convention. Others argue, however self-servingly, that such practices have the virtue of opening a party to people who would not otherwise become involved in the political process. Backroom managers are content to leave these ethical debates to the politicians in the frontroom. Their job is not to debate, but to marshall the votes needed to win. As far as they are concerned, the end justifies the means.

Paul Curley says the most proficient backroom manager he ever met was the late Rodrigue Pageau, Mulroney's chief organizer in Quebec. "At the grassroots level he was probably the best," says Curley. "He was very narrow. His role was not one of strategy, his role was not one of the grand picture. . . . He'd get the delegates selected for a meeting for your candidate. Part of it was persuasion, part of it was organization, part of it was money — getting jobs, finding the money to get them there. In 1983, he was the key to Mulroney's leadership."

Good organization leaves nothing to chance. Boyd Simpson ran his first campaign in 1969 in Newfoundland. His candidate was John Crosbie. Crosbie was still a Liberal in those days and he was trying to wrest the provincial leadership (and premiership) from a living legend: Joey Smallwood. Simpson was dazzled by the lengths to which the Smallwood organization went to win delegates and the way it used the weight of the Newfoundland government to make certain that "Canada's only living Father of Confederation," as Smallwood styled himself, was not overthrown by the upstart Crosbie. In rural Newfoundland, each provincial riding was to choose fifteen delegates to the leadership convention. The Smallwood organization routinely assigned cabinet ministers to monitor the delegate-selection meetings. Crosbie would have a slate of fifteen prospective delegates committed to him, and Smallwood would have the same, Simpson recalls:

> There were a few independents, so the slates came to around forty people. There weren't any voting booths, just long tables.

So in would come a Liberal party member and he'd have his little slate in his hand, his Crosbie slate given to him at the door, and he'd pick up the ballot and he'd sit down and he'd start checking off names. Well, there'd be a couple of cabinet ministers in Joe's government walking around behind the table and they'd sort of glance over the guy. They'd see a couple of names he'd checked on Crosbie's slate and they'd say, "Tsk, tsk. The premier won't like that, boy, the premier won't like that." It was very tough because a huge proportion of Newfoundlanders were related to the government in one way or another at that time, and after 1949 when they came in [to Canada] they got the baby bonus and they got a lot of government loans. There was a whole ton of loans for fishing gear and fishing boats and long liners. And the government was Joe Smallwood. I mean he brought all these things in. "The premier won't like that, boy." Not only was he rough in that sense, but once the delegates were selected, he had them all out to Roches Line, which was his house, for dinner. He'd have fifteen Crosbie delegates out there and he was fully aware of each of them — their backgrounds, what loans they had, the whole thing. It got pretty messy.

It got even messier. Before the delegates left the premier's house, they were presented with affidavits to sign stating that they supported Smallwood's re-election as leader. Leaving nothing to chance, Smallwood then had the affidavits published in the delegates' local newspapers. Jane Crosbie, the wife of Smallwood's foe, attempted to get elected as a delegate in her husband's riding in St. John's. "On the evening that we had our delegate-selection meeting," she recalls, "Smallwood and his supporters brought them in from everywhere. They carried them in from the local hospitals. There was one lady we called Blue Lips. We were sure that she died before they got her back to the hospital. It was a very rough campaign." Jane Crosbie lost her bid to be a delegate.[1]

A political organization is built on the same three blocks as a hockey or football team: people, communications, and loyalty (called "team spirit" in sports). To these three must be added, of course, generous amounts of money and the latest tools of the political trade, such as sophisticated public-opinion polling, advanced television techniques, and computerized direct-mail methods. But the three fundamentals are people, communications, and loyalty. (See Appendix A for a typical organizational chart.)

It is not enough for a party simply to recruit competent volunteers and to give them interesting work in the backroom. The uncommon nature of campaign business — short periods of intense activity, followed by longer periods of inactivity — means workers need to be challenged constantly to keep their edge honed and their commitment high. And the party must keep seeking younger, brighter, more enthusiastic people to renew the organization. The health of a political machine can often be judged by the ages of the people in its backrooms. A backroom full of grey heads is a backroom in need of renewal. "The world is full of bright young twenty-five-year-olds who are just as bright as we were," says Tom MacMillan, a twenty-year veteran of Tory backrooms. "They just have to be asked and encouraged. Political parties are very fragile things. You look at how fast the Tory party in Ontario fell apart after Bill Davis left it." The same thing happened to the federal Liberals in the latter years of the Trudeau leadership, to Social Credit in British Columbia under Bill Vander Zalm, and to the Tories in Saskatchewan as Grant Devine's government disintegrated. "It's people relying on people to get things done," says MacMillan. "So the onus is really on the people who are interested to make sure that they are getting new people interested."

An organization is only as good as its communications. All workers, whether paid staffers or volunteers, need to know precisely what their duties are, what they are expected to accomplish, to whom they report and from whom they are to take instructions. These lines of communication are especially important in a political party because organizations expand and shrink, depending on the electoral season, and because they rely on volunteers who are forever being distracted or called away by the demands of their real lives and careers outside politics. The lines must be clear to the very top of the organization, where the boss, usually the campaign director, has the final authority, to be overruled only by the leader of the party — and then only in extraordinary circumstances. Tory fund raiser Ralph Lean remembers the disorganization of Dennis Timbrell's two campaigns for the Ontario Conservative leadership, both in 1985, following Bill Davis's retirement: "There were too many people with equal power. What you need is one person running it. You need a dictator."

Loyalty is the glue that holds the organization together. It can be loyalty to a leader, a candidate, or a cause. For years, the New Democrats maintained a more effective organization than seemed possible from their slender financial resources and limited electoral prospects. "We have a mobile unit," says Bill Knight, who directed the NDP's 1988 federal election campaign. "You'll have to forgive me for talking in military terms, but we really do have an army of paratroopers, a flying squad of about two hundred that moves from coast to coast." The New Democrats have always believed in their cause. They did not need to win elections to keep their faith burning. In fact, as the NDP has discovered in Ontario, Saskatchewan, and British Columbia in the early 1990s, too much success at the polls can strain party loyalties. NDP governments discover that they have no choice but to disappoint the faithful. Once in power they find they cannot afford the progressive (and expensive) programs that their supporters expect to see implemented in return for their loyalty through the lean years in opposition.

The members of the Tory Big Blue Machine were drawn together by a different loyalty. It was not loyalty to an ideological cause or even to a specific leader, although Bill Davis, Ontario's premier from 1971 to 1985, and Bob Stanfield, the national party leader from 1967 to 1976, embodied the leadership characteristics that members of Big Blue prized. Rather, as its members saw it, it was loyalty to an ideal: an ideal of good government — government that was a bit to the right of centre; that was fiscally conservative yet socially progressive; that was, above all, professional. "The Big Blue Machine in Ontario was the beginning of the modern era of politics that spanned the 'seventies and 'eighties," said Big Blue Machine media consultant Nancy McLean. "The hallmark was two things — it was professionalism and it was discipline. And while a lot of [the machine's members] were highly motivated and committed to the Tory party, [their partisanship] never seemed to get in the way of the notion that good government equals good politics equals good government equals good politics."

McLean was alarmed by the trend she saw in Canadian politics today. In her view, the process was being trivialized. "Campaigning has become almost like a zoo. Who is going to have their bus run out of gas? What person is going to be found out to have known somebody that once stole cookies from a cookie jar? Which leader on the tour is going to have a sign fall on his head or have that one lonely person walk up and poke him in the chest?" The Reform Party of Canada, she noted, advocates that citizens be given the right to vote to recall their members of Parliament if they feel they are not representing their constituents' wishes. "I don't think it's just that people are upset with governments having to do tough things," McLean said. "The process has become so tainted that people don't even want to be part of it. . . . The process is going to have to be more relevant to the people. They're going to have to see more than just a zoo."

The Reform Party has successfully exploited the public's perception that politics, as practised by the old parties, is a zoo, that the process is tainted, that the issues have been trivialized. As other protest parties have in the past, Reform shows that the bond that holds a political movement together does not have to be based on positive or constructive impulses. The bond can be negative — shared opposition to established parties or policies. The Reform Party is opposed to politics as it is practised by the Conservatives, Liberals, and New Democrats. It wants to tear down the existing political structures. It is driven by a deep sense of exclusion, of being left out of the central decision-making processes in the country.

This sense of exclusion was deftly expressed in a satirical column by Les MacPherson of the Saskatoon *Star Phoenix* in 1989. Preston Manning, the Reform Party leader, liked the column so much that he quoted it in its entirety in his 1992 book *The New Canada*. MacPherson was commenting on the western Canadian grievance over the Mulroney government's decision to award the maintenance contract for Canada's CF-18 fighter aircraft to Canadair Ltd. of Montreal, despite the fact that Winnipeg's Bristol Aerospace Ltd. had submitted a lower and technically superior bid. An excerpt from MacPherson's column:

> OTTAWA — The federal government today announced it would award the Stanley Cup to Quebec, even though Alberta's Calgary Flames won the competition. The cup will go instead to Quebec's Montreal Canadiens, who were defeated by the Flames four games to two in the best-of-seven series.
>
> Prime Minister Brian Mulroney said the hockey series was "only a guideline," and not binding. He conceded that Calgary might have the best hockey team, "but we have to look at what's best for all Canada." "We have to support Canada's hockey industry, which is centered in Montreal," said the prime minister. "Montreal is in the best position to take full advantage of the Stanley Cup." . . .
>
> Quebec Premier Robert Bourassa was delighted to see the Cup go to Montreal. He said the trophy will be re-engraved with its new name — "la Coupe Stanley" — to comply with Quebec sign laws.[2]

Powerful grievances can drive a protest movement a long distance, but solid organization is required to keep a party like Reform competitive once it begins to achieve electoral success and as its grievances start, inevitably, to lose some of their potency. Manning, a management consultant, has built an organization with the same basic structure as the old-line parties he seeks to topple. His young party achieved signal successes in two electoral contests in Alberta in 1989 — a byelection in the federal riding of Beaver River and, a few months later, a special election to fill an Alberta Senate seat. An anti-Tory protest vote assisted the Reform candidates in both contests, but organizational superiority enabled the Reform Party to exploit the public's disenchantment to the maximum.

Reform did the little things exceedingly well. In the Beaver River byelection, Reform candidate Deborah Grey did not take the evening off on the night that four thousand Conservatives gathered in the town of Glendon for a hotly contested nominating convention. She went to the meeting and worked the crowd, shaking hands between ballots and suggesting to Tories that if they did not like their own party's choice, they might prefer to vote for her. The television crews were fascinated by her ploy. Meanwhile, Reform supporters blitzed the parking lot, putting under the wipers of hundreds of Tory cars flyers saying, "If your candidate didn't win the PC nomination and you are unhappy, perhaps you would consider supporting Deborah Grey." Forty-four days later, Grey won the byelection in a landslide and became the first Reform Party member of Parliament.[3]

All parties have the problem of preserving the morale of their backrooms in the face of defeat, often repeated defeat. The Tories invented something called the Grand Clong award for their advancemen, the men and (in recent years) women who go ahead of the leader to check (and frequently to overrule) arrangements for visits to communities on the tour route. The idea of the Grand Clong was borrowed from Jerry Bruno, who was a Democratic party advanceman for John and Robert Kennedy in the early 1960s. In his book, *The Advance Man*, Bruno described the Grand Clong as "a common political disease, occurring when things get hopelessly loused up and you suddenly feel a rush of shit to the heart."[4] Every week during elections, the Tory advancemen — the "Dirty Dozen" — met to have a few drinks and a few laughs as they presented one of their number with the Grand Clong award for the worst screw-up of the week. There was no doubt about the winner one week in the 1972 federal election campaign, the election in which Bob Stanfield's Tories nearly upset the Trudeau Liberals. The Grand Clong award that week went to the advanceman who had booked Stanfield into an hour-long radio phone-in show in small-town southern Ontario — and nobody phoned. From then on, all advancemen were told to carry a roll of coins and to check out the nearest pay phone, to make sure that in future there would be at least one caller.

Morale is always difficult to regulate on the leader's tour. The mood swings wildly from euphoria to despair, depending on the leader's performance that day. Those who travel in a campaign aircraft for weeks on end feel trapped in an aluminium cocoon. They are aware of what is going on in the outside world because they have access to radio, television, and newspapers. They know what the other leaders are doing, saying, and promising. As the weeks pass, however, they find it increasingly difficult to judge how their opponents are faring in relation to their own leader. Their critical faculties become blurred. Because their own campaign is the only one they can see clearly, everything that happens assumes an exaggerated significance. Small reverses become catastrophes. The leader's entourage sinks into depression. The depression spreads like lightning to the journalists travelling on the aircraft. Soon the gloom is being spread on the airwaves to the voting public.

Most news organizations, recognizing that their reporters lose perspective when they stay too long in one aluminium cocoon, rotate them regularly to other leaders' tours. Those left behind seek ways to keep their spirits up. Robin Sears, a former federal secretary and campaign manager for the NDP, remembers the lengths the Ed Broadbent tour went to buoy spirits in 1979, the election that produced the short-lived Joe Clark government:

> We had a very energetic crew of Radio Canada technicians who had figured out how to wire the plane's sound system into their cassette deck and speakers. On one particularly long haul back from Vancouver, they knocked down all the seats in the plane, pushed the backs down so that there was almost a solid floor of seat backs and cranked the sound system up to an enormous level playing some disco track over and over again. And they were dancing on the seat backs. I thought it was all very good fun.

The press corps loved it. NDP staffers and organizers relaxed. Even

Broadbent was pleased. Sears was delighted that everyone aboard was in such good spirits. Everyone, that is, except for Sears's father, Val Sears, a feature writer for the *Toronto Star*, who was covering the Broadbent tour for Canada's largest newspaper. The elder Sears was not at all amused by the hijinks. The son made his way down the length of the plane to where the father was trying to type amid the tumult. "I am going to comment on this, young man," Val Sears warned. "I thought, oh hell," says Robin Sears. "Indeed he did [comment]. He wrote a very nasty piece."

Under a Nanaimo, B.C., dateline, Val Sears wrote:

> Ed Broadbent, his navy blue blazer off, his grey slacks trim and tailored, sits in the front of his chartered jetliner smoking a cigar and sipping champagne and orange juice.
>
> He looks content.
>
> Beside him sits his flack. Behind him, his speechwriter. Across the aisle is his secretary and his tour director.
>
> They all look content. . . .
>
> Their table grace could be that of their sainted founder, J.S. Woodsworth: "What we desire for ourselves we wish for all."
>
> And if this is not exactly what the Regina Manifesto of 1933 envisaged — the eradication of capitalism — then Canada is hardly a depressed dust bowl either. . . .
>
> There was the occasional revival meeting, but mostly Broadbent was costumed and carried from one television setting to another. . . .
>
> As the election campaign approaches midpoint, there is no sign that Ed Broadbent's handlers are going to let go of the key sticking out of his back.

The Big Blue Machine institutionalized its morale boosting in an annual gathering known as the Robertson's Point Inter-Provincial Tennis Classic and Rough-In (so named because the first gathering in 1974 was held at the summer home of Norman Atkins, the head Machinist, at Robertson's Point, N.B.). It is like a fraternity weekend. Once each summer, between thirty and forty Tory men and (since 1987) women — key backroom players in election campaigns across the country — gather somewhere in Canada to play tennis and golf, swim, play cards, drink, and talk politics. It is the Conservatives' way of networking and nurturing their organization.

"You've got to make politics fun," says Tom MacMillan, who today is advertising vice-president of the *Financial Post* and still an active Tory organizer. "I think politics is a tremendous learning experience. It gave us in our careers far more responsibility out on the road with a leader than we would ever have had in our jobs at that point. We did it because it was fun."

There were times, however, when MacMillan's idea of fun was not shared by the people he was meant to serve. In 1972, he went west to teach a group of Conservative candidates about tour organization at a campaign school that the party organized in Regina. MacMillan got to Regina before three other senior Tory organizers who were also coming out to instruct the candidates. Wondering what he could do to have a little fun, he wandered into the bar in his hotel and struck up a conversation with the bartender. The bartender told him that his brother played in a high school band. That was all MacMillan needed. He hired three youngsters from the band, got the hotel's room service to help him make a big welcoming sign, and headed for the airport to greet his Conservative colleagues from Toronto. MacMillan continues:

> I conned the airport manager into letting us go out on the tarmac. Those were the days long before landing gates, when planes just pulled up. I said I had some friends coming and we wanted to have this little airport reception. "I just have a little band and would that be okay?" He thought that was okay. So we stood at the end of the sidewalk as the DC-9 pulled up full of all these big Tory shooters from Toronto. And so, as the crowd started coming off the plane, they had to file by us to get to the terminal, and the band broke into a little frilly version of "Happy Days Are Here Again." And then the sign came up and I stood there and the sign said: "Welcome Gay Liberation Executive."
>
> Now, this is 1972. It was really on the cutting edge. I welcomed my fellow Tories saying, "We're so pleased that you're here for our conference. You'll make such a difference." Well, there were also some local Tory head honchos there to meet this group from Toronto. The word went back to Ottawa. I got in big trouble. My God, there were calls from Malcolm Wickson [the director of campaign operations]. Stanfield was upset. What business did I have doing this? I said, "I'm a volunteer, and I'm having a little fun."

A good organization often makes the difference between victory and defeat in a political campaign. A good organization always makes room for a little fun.

7. ADVENTURES IN VIDEOLAND

"We are taught as schoolchildren that choosing a national leader is about issues and politics and agendas. But then we are taught a lot of nonsense as schoolchildren. Today, choosing a president seems to have more to do with sex, lies, and videotape. And that last one may be the most important."
— *Baltimore Sun* columnist Roger Simon

The atmosphere was tense in the television studio as the interlocuter, sensing a weakness in Liberal leader John Turner's position on a national day-care program for Canadians, moved in for the kill. "The difference between you and me, Mr. Turner — between the New Democratic Party and the Liberal party — is that *we* don't think children are for profit."

Turner almost choked.

Hershell Ezrin laughs as he tells the story. It was Ezrin, a member of the Turner brains trust, who — playing the role of NDP leader Ed Broadbent — threw the child-care curve at Turner during intensive preparations for the nationally televised leaders' debates in the 1988 federal election campaign. Turner got so involved in the preparations that he forgot the rehearsal was not the real debate. "I got him so mad at that comment that it served the purpose of getting him prepared . . . for those kinds of questions," Ezrin says. "He started spluttering, actually, and I said, 'I think we need a better answer than that.'"

Television is the dominant force in election campaigns today. Politicians, especially at the higher levels, cannot hope to succeed without mastering the medium. Not only is television the primary source of news and information for Canadians, it has replaced newspapers as the most believable and authoritative of the media. And TV has powers of mass persuasion that print never did and never will possess — as every backroom politician is well aware. "People don't read," Ezrin says. "The truth is, the good photograph speaks more than ten thousand words and the good television clip even more than that."

The television debates among the party leaders — usually in French one evening and in English the next — are the most eagerly awaited events in the election campaign, as far as rank-and-file party members and the general public are concerned. To the leaders and their handlers, however, they are cause for great anxiety and gruelling preparation. The minutes and hours of the debates are the most crucial in the campaign. They can destroy an incumbent and turn a challenger into a front-runner, or vice versa. They can change the course of an election overnight, as the English-language debate in 1988 transferred the momentum from Brian Mulroney's Conservatives to Turner's Liberals. And, realistically, the debates may provide the only real exposure to issues that large numbers of voters have before they go to the polls to pass judgment, however poorly informed, on the leaders, parties, candidates, and policies.

Each of the leaders wants to "win" the debates, of course. But winning the debate on the strength of superior argument can be a Pyrrhic victory. A leaders' debate is not a fencing match, to be decided on the basis of points scored. If it were, Richard Nixon would have defeated John F. Kennedy in the 1960 U.S. presidential election, and Ed Broadbent would have been prime minister of Canada, at least twice. A leaders' debate is a brawl, a street fight, in which each combatant strives to knock out his opponent with a "killer line" that will become The Clip, to be shown over and over on newscasts and in party commercials for the remaining weeks of the campaign.

"People who watch a boxing match, the majority of the people, know nothing about boxing," says Liberal TV expert Gabor Apor. "What they want to see is who's going to fall at the end. Okay, that's exactly the same with debates. Ninety-nine percent of the audience does not understand the intellectual part of the discussion. They simply want to see which of the candidates is stronger and will beat the other two. That's what debates are about."

In the 1988 vice-presidential debate in the United States, the "killer line" was administered by Democrat Lloyd Bentsen to the chin of Republican Dan Quayle when the feckless Quayle tried to compare his political experience to the icon Kennedy's. Bentsen was aware that Quayle had drawn a similar comparison on previous occasions and he had been polishing his devastating riposte for several days. "Senator," Bentsen replied, "I served with Jack Kennedy. I knew Jack Kennedy. Jack Kennedy was a friend of mine. Senator, you are no Jack Kennedy." Everyone watching knew a knockout had been registered. City Auditorium in Omaha, Nebraska, where the live telecast of the debate originated, erupted with shouts, applause, and hisses. Quayle was rocked. Finally, he responded weakly: "That was uncalled for, Senator." The Democrats wasted no time exploiting Quayle's vulnerability. Within hours, new buttons, some red, the others blue, appeared on the Democratic campaign. The blue ones simply asked, "President Quayle?" while the red ones showed the blip of an electrocardiograph and the warning, "Quayle — A Heartbeat Away."[1] (The public may have been amused, but it was not persuaded. George Bush and Quayle crushed Michael Dukakis and Bentsen.)

Four years earlier, in the Canadian leaders' debates in the 1984 election — Turner, then prime minister, versus Mulroney and Broadbent — the "killer line" was from Mulroney to Turner. As Quayle was to do in the United States four years later, Turner himself created the opening that made the knockout possible. He raised the issue on which he was most vulnerable: patronage. On July 9, 1984, when Turner, newly elected to the Liberal leadership, called a general election for September 4, he also announced patronage appointments for nineteen former Liberal ministers and MPs — appointments he had promised his predecessor, Pierre Trudeau, he would make.

The French-language debate on July 24 was relatively uneventful. But in the English-language debate the next evening, Turner made the fatal mistake of attacking Mulroney for an indiscreet comment the Tory leader had made earlier in the campaign about how he would gladly give patronage jobs to Liberals, "when there isn't a living, breathing Tory left without a job in this country." Mulroney had already apologized publicly for his indiscretion. He could hardly believe his good fortune when Turner raised the subject of patronage on camera. Turner, he declared in feigned outrage to the audience of 7.5 million Canadians, owed the country an apology for his nineteen pork-barrel appointments.

When Turner insisted he had no option (because of his commitment to Trudeau), Mulroney pounced: "You had an option, sir. You could have said, 'I'm not going to do it. This is wrong for Canada and I'm not going to ask Canadians to pay the price....'" Turner again protested, feebly, that he had no option. Mulroney finished him off: "That is an avowal of failure. That is a confession of non-leadership, and this country needs leadership. You had an option, sir. You could have done better."

It was not as crisp as Bentsen's destruction of Quayle, but it left Turner momentarily speechless. By the next day, it was recognized for the "killer line" that it was. Turner was on the defensive for much of the rest of the campaign.

Debates do not always produce killer lines. Frequently, a winner emerges, not on debating points, but on performance measured against expectation. If the four Nixon–Kennedy debates of 1960 are considered together, Nixon outpointed Kennedy. But expectations, in the press, among political professionals, and among the general public, were much higher for Nixon, who had been vice-president for eight years, than for Kennedy, a junior senator. By not demolishing Kennedy, Nixon lost. Kennedy did more than survive the debates. He looked better, sounded better, and radiated more authority than anyone had expected from him in the one all-important debate — the opening one, where most Americans formed their first firm impressions of his candidacy. The 1960 election was the closest in American history. Kennedy's success in "winning" that first debate made it possible for him to win the White House.

It was similar in the 1979 election debate in Canada. Trudeau won the French-language debate. There was no dispute about that; he was the only one of the three leaders who was comfortable in the language. The English-language debate was a different story. The pundits were divided. Some thought Trudeau had won. An equal number picked Ed Broadbent. It soon became apparent, however, that the real "winner" in the assessment of the audience at home was the young Conservative leader Joe Clark.

Clark did not dazzle, but he survived. He was not blown off the set by Trudeau, as all Liberals and most pundits had expected. He took Trudeau's best shots and was still standing at the end. He showed that he could hold his own against a man who had been prime minister for eleven years. On election day, he was elected prime minister himself, albeit at the head of a short-lived government.

In the 1988 Mulroney–Turner–Broadbent debate, it was Turner who won by exceeding all expectations. He was the only one of the three leaders who prepared as though his political life depended on it (which it did), the only one who actually went to a studio (at an Ottawa cable television station) to rehearse in front of television cameras with aides playing the roles of his opponents and the reporters who would be firing questions at the leaders. Two weeks before the debates, Liberal strategist Senator Michael Kirby set out the challenge in a confidential memo to senior Turner organizers:

> [Our] primary objective is to cause the press to rethink their conclusion that the election is already over. To do this, we must surprise viewers and our opponents with Turner's performance; he must be much better than anticipated. [Our] secondary objectives include rallying our own troops ... and obtaining video clips which we can use in a TV ad. ... No one who is an uncommitted voter will watch the whole debate, so the key output will be the thirty-second clip. ... This means that we must give the leader a set of one-liners which we can fit into his answers.[2]

While Mulroney and Broadbent prepared thoroughly but less intensively, Turner was subjected to the sort of quasi-military preparation that marks presidential debates in the United States. His "debate committee" — Henry Comor, Hershell Ezrin, Patrick Gossage, and Ray Heard — assembled briefing books with outlines of strategies, opening and closing remarks, draft questions and replies, issue analyses, and studio production arrangements. In all, Turner spent thirty-six and a half hours preparing for six hours of debate — three hours in each language. (The debates were structured as a series of rotating one-on-one encounters among the three leaders, meaning each was actually called on to debate for two hours per evening.) To ready Turner for the physical ordeal of standing on the set through the debates, his organizers set aside time each day for physiotherapy on his aching back. His schedule looked like this:

Thursday, October 20	— 4 hours review briefing book
Friday, October 21	— 1 1/2 hours debate strategy session
	6 hours rehearsal and review
	1 hour back therapy
Saturday, October 22	— 8 hours debate preparation
	1 hour back therapy
Sunday, October 23	— 6 hours debate preparation
	1 hour inspect debate set
	1 hour back therapy
Monday, October 24	— 1 hour haircut

	4 ½ hours debate preparation
	1 hour back therapy
	3 hours French debate
Tuesday, October 25	— 5 ½ hours debate preparation
	1 hour back therapy
	3 hours English debate

Bill Knight, who was the NDP's campaign director in 1988, realizes that the NDP should have put Broadbent through a similar heavy drill. Instead, NDP strategists chose to give Broadbent time to relax, to reflect, and to study briefing material that included suggested one-liners for the debate. "I think, on reflection, that Ed had to go through the rigors that Turner went through. That's what he should have done," Knight says. "Whether it would have made a difference, I don't know, but I would feel better for him today than I did when it was over. There's a discipline to this. We need to learn discipline about debates."

The hours of discipline, preparation, and play-acting paid off for Turner. He not only atoned for his woeful performance four years earlier, in the English-language debate he succeeded in putting Mulroney on the spot on the free-trade agreement that the Tory government had signed with the United States. He had the prime minister debating out of both sides of his mouth — proclaiming the agreement as being indispensable to Canada's economic well-being and, simultaneously, protesting that it was merely a "commercial document that's cancellable on six months' notice." Turner did not score a knockout, but he did rock Mulroney. Commentators were stunned by the "new" fighting, confident Turner. Although Mulroney went to bed that night satisfied with his own performance, the television audience did not see it that way.

"Debates have enormously large audiences," says Barry McLoughlin, an Ottawa-based media consultant who specializes in training politicians to perform on television. "A debate is the ultimate performance test, and we see under pressure what these leaders are like. And what you are going after with a debate is the swing voter."

The swing voters began to move after the 1988 debate. Overnight, the Conservatives started to slip in the opinion polls and the Liberals to gain. It took the Tory pollster Allan Gregg's "bomb-the-bridge" strategy (see Chapter 5) of negative advertising and direct attacks on Turner's credibility to undo the damage of the debate and rescue the Tories. As McLoughlin puts it, "It's possible to have a lousy debate and still win the election. It's possible to win the debate and lose the election. Having said that, there is a tide that is out there in the affairs of humankind, and you're either on the tide or you're against it."

For a novice, like Gordon Wilson, the Liberal leader in British Columbia, the leaders' debate put him on the tide in the 1991 provincial election. The tide swept the unknown college instructor, the head of a party with no legislature seats and no apparent prospects, from obscurity to prominence as leader of the official opposition. Wilson was good; he outperformed both Social Credit premier Rita Johnston and NDP leader (and soon-to-be premier) Michael Harcourt in the debate. And he was lucky; he did it at a time when the Socreds were collapsing and many voters were looking for a free-enterprise alternative to the New Democrats. The Liberals' popular support doubled after the debate. Without the TV debate, the Liberals would probably still be a fringe party in British Columbia, as they are in neighboring Alberta and Saskatchewan.

Like polling and computer-generated appeals for votes and funds, television debates came to Canada from the United States. The four Nixon–Kennedy encounters in 1960 intrigued organizers in Canadian backrooms. The first TV debate in Canada was held two years later — in the 1962 provincial election in Quebec, won by the Liberals under Jean Lesage. Although there were federal elections in 1962, 1963, and 1965, it was not until 1968 that the national leaders met in a television studio. A bizarre affair, it began with three leaders — the new Liberal leader, Pierre Trudeau; Tory Robert Stanfield; and the NDP's Tommy Douglas. Halfway through, the format expanded to encompass the leader of the fourth party, Social Credit's Réal Caouette, who arrived on the set looking like a groomsman who got caught in traffic and reached the church as the wedding was ending.

After that beginning, it was eleven years before party leaders agreed to debate again. Trudeau, who understood the impact of television better than any Canadian politician of his generation, chose not to risk debates in the 1972 and 1974 elections. He agreed to debate in 1979 because the Liberals were trailing in the polls and a debate at least offered a chance to expose Clark as the klutz that Trudeau's advisers assured him the Tory leader was. But Clark and the Tories won that election, only to be forced into another election in 1980 after their minority government was defeated in Parliament. This time, the roles were reversed. Trudeau, now the challenger, was far ahead of Clark, and the Liberal strategy called for keeping Trudeau's profile as low as possible. The Liberals stalled the debate negotiations as long as they could, then refused to debate at all.

When the next election was called, in 1984, the Liberals had just elected Turner as their new leader, and the Tories pressed for TV debates to be held early in the campaign in the hope of slowing the Liberals' post-convention momentum. A Conservative negotiator, Jean Bazin, recalls that the television networks wanted the debates very late in the campaign; the networks proposed that the English-language debate take place on August 26, just nine days before the election on September 4. "We said that was totally unacceptable," Bazin says. "We needed to have Mulroney go face to face with [then prime minister] Turner to establish some credibility with the electorate early in the campaign. We also wanted to have the French debate ahead of the English so that Mulroney [whose French was stronger than Turner's] would have an opportunity to do well and build some confidence. . . . We got the major things we went after."

Both the 1984 and 1988 election debates confirmed conventional backroom wisdom that incumbents — Turner in 1984 and Mulroney in 1988 — have far more to lose and much less to gain than their challengers. Simply appearing on the same set as the prime minister and debating him as an equal enhances the status of opposition leaders. The audience at home, seeing the incumbent take the challengers seriously, takes them seriously, too. If the debate is close or inconclusive, a challenger wins.

The big fear among media strategists for leaders, especially those who are in power or who are front-runners in an election, is the One Big Mistake — the dread that the leader, under pressure, will say something so outrageous, so insensitive, or so ridiculous as to cripple his election chances. It nearly happened to George Bush during a television appearance in the 1988 U.S. presidential primary in New Hampshire when he blurted out an inane argument about the environmental advantages of the Alaska oil pipeline: "The caribou love [the pipeline]. They rub up against it and they have babies. There are more caribou in Alaska than you can shake a stick at."

It did happen to John Turner with his patronage gaffe in the 1984 Canadian debate, and Boyd Simpson, a veteran organizer who has run campaigns for both Liberal and Conservative candidates, believes that television debates can be dangerous to the morale of party workers. "You've got a much greater chance of blowing it than you do of really scoring a big win," he says. "What you want to do is to assure your supporters that you really are worth supporting. I think a lot of Liberals felt very sheepish going to their jobs the next day with what Turner did [on patronage] in the 1984 debate. They probably still voted Liberal, but they didn't work very hard."

To Paddy Sampson, a television director who coached Trudeau for the 1979 debate, a leaders' debate is a drama and the leaders are actors in it. "The person who understands the dramatic conventions of that best and who works best within them has an advantage over the other," says former Trudeau press secretary Patrick Gossage, who was working with Sampson. "Sometimes simple things can make a big difference when a guy realizes where his particular physical power may be. . . . In the '79 debate, we invented a move. Trudeau moved in on Clark. He actually came out from around the podium. That was the clip everybody used."

The time, effort, and expensive professional coaching that all parties now put into preparing their leaders reflect the emergence of television debates as the pivotal events in the campaign schedule. According to the 1989–92 Royal Commission on Electoral Reform and Party Financing, leaders' debates have become common features of election campaigns in many industrialized democracies. Yet they remain one of the few unregulated areas of election activity. No country has a legal requirement that broadcasters carry debates or that party leaders take part in them. The state of New Jersey uses a financial carrot to encourage candidates to participate; only candidates who take part in a series of campaign debates are eligible for public subsidization of their campaign costs. Quebec tried to regulate participation by providing in its 1984 Election Act that a televised debate had to include the leaders of all parties in the National Assembly plus the leaders of other parties that received 3 per cent of the popular vote in the most recent provincial election. In 1989, however, the act was amended to leave leaders' debates up to the TV networks and political parties.

Laissez-faire is also the order of the day at the federal level. Although 57 per cent of Canadians polled in 1991 believed that there should be a law to require party leaders to debate, such a law is not imminent. The royal commission recommended in February 1992 against making any legislative provision for televised leaders' debates and said that — as in Quebec — the matter should be left to the good sense of the networks and the parties.[3] The Reform Party of Canada, Bloc Québécois, and a dozen smaller parties have no guarantee that they will be able to debate with the major party leaders, or even among themselves, on national television in the next federal election. It will depend on the will of the networks and the whim of the older parties, which may calculate that they have something, or nothing, to gain by agreeing to let Reform leader Preston Manning or others take part.

Politicians are ambivalent about television. They respect and fear its power. They know it is destined increasingly to dominate Canadian politics. Yet they worry that by shrinking the attention span of its audience — their constituents — it trivializes the political process.

Televising the proceedings of the House of Commons was the worst mistake of the last two decades on Parliament Hill. Instead of engaging the public in issues that come before Parliament, the cameras in the House have simply lowered politicians in the esteem of the electorate. To their own dismay, members of Parliament find themselves playing to the cameras — posing, posturing, feigning enthusiasm, and counterfeiting outrage. They rush to fill the seats behind a frontbencher who is on camera — partly so that the audience at home will see their faces and partly to disguise the reality that the Commons chamber is nearly empty a large part of the time. Most of what goes on there is as irrelevant to MPs as it is to most Canadians. They clamor to ask questions that do not need to be asked on subjects of which they are largely ignorant. Cabinet ministers play their own shabby little game. They put down their questioners with answers that provide no useful information but that serve the ministers' purpose: to create a tight, punchy clip for the evening news. The antics on both sides of the House demean the system and dismay the voters as the image of MPs behaving like unruly children goes out live across the country on the parliamentary channel, then reappears in clips on network newscasts.

MPs are also exposed to the pressure of constant coverage by Newsworld, the CBC's all-news channel. "Whether anybody watches Newsworld, or doesn't, isn't important," says Eddie Goldenberg, longtime friend and assistant to Liberal leader Jean Chrétien. "People [in the country] watch the clips, but the people in the Press Gallery watch Newsworld. And the politician is expected to comment now not only for the six o'clock news but also the one o'clock news in the morning, or at two o'clock in the afternoon, or whenever. Politics has been compressed. [Television] probably increases partisanship and increases public disgust for politics."

Conservative Douglas Bassett, the country's most powerful private broadcaster — as president of Baton Broadcasting, he controls eleven stations in the CTV network and several CBC affiliates — is not alarmed. It pleases him to see politicians adapting to television. "They are adapting to the twenty-second clip," Bassett says. "And wherever politicians go, they turn to the TV personalities [correspondents]. They don't go to the radio or newspaper personalities, like in the old days."

To Gabor Apor, the Liberal media guru, this evolution is inevitable. "We now face a generation of people who were brought up on 'Sesame Street,' and 'Sesame Street' solves every problem in fifteen seconds," he says. "And the assumption is that if 'Sesame Street' can solve every problem in just fifteen seconds, and if I turn on the television night after night and most of my problems as a consumer or as a viewer can be solved in a thirty-second commercial, then politicians should be able to communicate in exactly the same manner. Short, concise, and clear."

Coached by experts like Apor and Barry McLoughlin, Canadian politicians are learning to communicate in ten- and twenty-second clips. They — and television — have come a long way since 1956 when national politics and national television first discovered each other — at the Progressive Conservative leadership convention that picked John Diefenbaker. Clare Westcott was there when a CBC director tried unsuccessfully to position the Chief for an interview. Because the camera lens in those days could not be focused, marks were painted on the floor to show Diefenbaker where to stand so that he would be in focus. "Dief wouldn't stand on the foot marks," Westcott remembers. "You know, if you told him what to do, he wouldn't do it. Nobody told him he was going to be out of focus. That was a bit of fun."

Diefenbaker was a speech and print politician. He made a speech in the evening — usually lambasting the Liberals for some sin, real or imagined — and he read every word written about it in the newspapers the next morning. If he did not consider a particular story to be to his satisfaction, he thought nothing of summoning the reporter for a scorching reprimand. Television was not kind to Diefenbaker, and he did not like the medium. He thought it made him look demonic, with quivering jowls and eyes that blazed in a disconcerting fashion.

Diefenbaker would have been totally out of place in the sort of campaign that Marcel Côté, a Montreal consultant and Tory strategist, described in a memo to two other Conservative organizers, Harry Near and John Tory, early in the 1988 election campaign:

> My reading of the present campaign is that too much emphasis
> is put on formal speeches and on answering journalists' ques-

tions. I would prefer that we identify daily thematic objectives
— say, demonstrating a commitment on cleaning our rivers
— and then build scenarios to achieve them. The focus, in
terms of performance, should be the nightly 45 seconds on TV
news, and the morning headlines, front-page photos and lead-
in paragraph. This is 90 per cent of what reach the PC1 [soft
Tory voters] and PC2s [switchers] and this is what we should
be concerned about. The rest is mostly for political junkies,
who had made their mind [up] anyway.[4]

Whether the Tory "commitment" would actually reduce pollution
in a single river in Canada was not the issue. The only thing that
mattered was whether the daily theme would make a clip on the
evening TV news, a morning headline, and a front-page photo. In
three short decades — from Diefenbaker to Mulroney — politics
went from being hearty, if not always digestible, fare to junk food.
"Television has changed the audience," says Gabor Apor. "Television is very reflective of the kind of society we live in, the kind
of lifestyles we live, and it suggests lifestyles to a great majority of
people. And television has acquired a sense of instant credibility.
It's the number-one place where people look for information, and
the assumption is that it didn't happen unless it was on television."

Politicians, in Apor's view, have no choice. They have to adapt,
or perish. If they cannot communicate on television, they cannot
reach the people:

> Television is the only common language we have. The person
> with a Grade 6 education and the person with a Ph.D. sit in
> front of the television set exactly the same way. Time and time
> again it's been proven that our attitude or response to television
> is the same, regardless of education, basically because one of
> the things that television demands is an emotional response.
> It's an inner emotional experience and, from that point of view,
> they all respond exactly the same.

To survive, the politician has to learn far more than how to dress
and how to compress his message for television. He has to be taught
to feel comfortable in his own skin. "If the person who commu-
nicates does not have an engaging outer wrapper, the audience will
spend so much time figuring out what's wrong that there is no
time left to listen to content," says Apor. "The message starts much

before the first word is uttered, and if those messages, which are much faster than any set of sentences, are not correct, there are very few people who will listen to the content."

McLoughlin agrees. "Sixty per cent of all communication is non-verbal, 37 per cent is para-verbal — the total attitude you convey — and only 3 per cent is verbal. In a television age, they say that if you turn down the volume on the television set and you watch a candidate, he or she should be giving you all of the core messages non-verbally."

In an age where people receive most of their information from television, and believe most of what they see and hear, TV over-shadows every other aspect of an election campaign. Campaign managers would kill for a flattering clip of their leader at the top of the national news. This is not to suggest that they would turn up their nose at a laudatory article in *Maclean's* magazine or a puff piece on the op-ed page of the Toronto *Globe and Mail*. Print stories are useful for the troops in the field. They promote campaign morale, but they are tangential to the real challenge — reaching a generation of television viewers who do not read and who expect every problem to be solved in fifteen seconds, just as on "Sesame Street."

As Marcel Côté's 1988 memo to Near and Tory made clear, the media strategy of political parties is concentrated on television to the virtual exclusion of print journalism (which is "mostly for po-litical junkies"). The overriding reason that campaign directors go to the bother and expense ($1 million to $2 million per party) of mounting leaders' tours in national elections is to serve television. Television without pictures is radio, which is boring. Television demands fresh visuals or backdrops every day: yesterday, the Rock-ies; today, the CN Tower; tomorrow, the Gaspé; the next day, the Atlantic. Leaders do not win significant numbers of converts by hurtling frenetically across the country, visiting a gold mine here and a fish hatchery there, a hospital here and a high school there, and delivering their boiler-plate campaign speeches every evening to interchangeable crowds of followers. By keeping on the move, however, by visiting interesting-looking places and appearing be-fore exuberant crowds waving colorful signs, by giving the con-fident impression that this otherwise aimless activity actually serves some rational (if obscure) purpose, leaders keep getting on televi-sion. And that is what the exercise is all about — generating The Clip, day after day after day. More Canadians will see the leaders in a single evening on CBC's "The National" than will see them in person during the entire campaign — more, perhaps, than will see them in the flesh in their entire careers.

The tour is especially important to the parties in the opening weeks of a campaign because they are not permitted by law to buy commercial time on television until four weeks before a federal election. Unable to purchase their own time to deliver their own message the way they want to say it — unfiltered by reporters, commentators, editors, and headline writers — the parties have to settle for second best: television news coverage of their leaders participating in contrived events, manipulated to resemble real happenings.

Once the advertising period begins, so does the serious strategy and the heavy spending. Campaign commercials are often neither pretty nor pleasant. They are created to shore up a party's support and to knock "soft" votes loose from opposing parties. The most effective commercials, unfortunately, tend to be the most unpleasant.

The Conservatives' "bomb-the-bridge" commercials, attacking Turner's credibility, which flooded the airwaves to counter the Liberal leader's strong performance in the 1988 TV debate, may have been tame stuff compared to some of the vicious ads appearing in the U.S. presidential election that fall. But, by Canadian standards, they were rough and tough. A Liberal commercial attacked the Conservatives' free-trade deal with the United States by showing the Canada–U.S. border being rubbed out on a map of North America. The Tories countered with a commercial that attacked the Liberals and showed the border being drawn back in. They followed that with "streeters" — commercials in which supposedly average citizens, interviewed on the street or at work, explained why they would never trust Turner to run the country. To drive the point home, three backroom Tories wrote and produced a tabloid "newspaper," entitled "The Ten Big Lies," attacking Turner; between 5 million and 6 million copies were shipped out before election day.

And the Conservatives quietly took up all the daytime television time they could buy in Quebec. Robin Sears, deputy director of the 1988 NDP campaign, remembers the sinking feeling he felt in the pit of his stomach one afternoon two weeks after the debate as he was flipping channels on his office television. He discovered what the Tories were doing to Turner on French-language TV:

I stopped at some French-language soap opera and I saw the

first version of that devastating Tory ad they did with the clock ticking and a woman's fingers drumming on an ebony surface in a studio in blackout. The script in French was something like, "This is a man who most of his own party wanted to get rid of a few months ago. This is a man who wants to gamble with the future of Canada." And on and on. "Do you think you can trust the future of your children to this man?" Boom! She stops. Her fingers jump in. The clock clicks off. The spot ends. "Non. Pour la bonne chance," or something like that, "vote Tory."

It was at a point when everyone was saying the Tories were really up against it. . . . They didn't talk to anybody about the fact that they were buying up all the women's programming on daytime Quebec television. They didn't brag about it. They just did it. And it was one of those moments of absolute epiphany and horror and I looked at the television and said: "You bastards." It was obviously going to have a great impact.

There will be more negative commercials in the next election, and the one after it, and the one after that. Not only will there be more of them, they will almost certainly be more aggressively negative in their messages — for one simple reason: negative works.

Negative commercials demean democracy by reinforcing the fears and insecurities of voters. They trivialize important decisions and replace reason with emotion. Politicians who hold elected office, or who aspire to it, dislike negative commercials because they hate having to defend their use. But backroom politicians love them. They love them because they work.

Doug Hurley, a market researcher with Goldfarb Consultants for more than fifteen years, says negative commercials work because the shock effect of negative messages causes the audience to remember them better than positive messages. But negative ads succeed only when the message confirms the fears or concerns that the public already has about the object of the attack. Hurley remembers the commercials that the federal Liberals used successfully against Joe Clark's Tories in the 1980 election: "The ad showed a deck of playing cards being built into a house of cards, with each playing card representing a policy initiative of the Clark government. At the conclusion of the ad, the house of cards collapsed. The commercial basically reinforced the concerns and fears that Canadians had formed about the Clark government in the seven months it had been in power."

Because of its power, television is destined to consume an ever-increasing share of the strategic attention of political backrooms and of their election budgets. About 30 per cent of the campaign spending of the three major parties in the 1988 federal election went for television production and air time, and the proportion is rising sharply, especially with the NDP. As overall party budgets increase, roughly fifty cents of each incremental dollar goes to television.

The following table compares the spending of the Progressive Conservatives, Liberals, and New Democrats in the 1984 and 1988 general elections.

Table 1

Major Party Campaign Spending, 1984 and 1988 Elections

	PC		Lib.		NDP	
	1984	**1988**	**1984**	**1988**	**1984**	**1988**
Advertising						
Print	$ 206,651	721,557	763,482	812,365	153,846	155,872
Radio	1,236,075	1,554,677	1,069,248	1,023,465	494,466	476,998
TV	1,757,944	2,440,503	1,695,186	2,024,456	1,158,150	2,495,316
Other						
expenses	3,188,271	3,205,001	2,765,067	2,979,589	2,924,261	3,932,377
Total:	6,388,941	7,921,738	6,292,983	6,839,875	4,730,723	7,060,563
TV as % of Total	27.5	30.8	26.9	29.6	24.5	35.3

SOURCE: Chief Electoral Officer of Canada.
Note: Figures are for national party campaigns only. "Other expenses" do not include money spent on polling, which is not a reportable election expenditure. Figures do not include spending by candidates at the constituency level. Television time is too costly for most candidates, especially in major urban areas.

Figures for the four-election period from the election of 1979 through the election of 1988 show a steady upward trend in party spending on television commercials. The Tories spent 59 per cent more on television in 1988 than they did in 1979, the Liberals 56 per cent more, and the NDP a whopping 224 per cent more, sug-

gesting that the New Democrats have come of age in a hurry —
the television age, at least.

As the politicians' dependence on television deepens, it is not
unreasonable to anticipate that, by the end of the century, political
parties will be spending one-half of their entire election budgets
on the production and broadcast of television commercials. Their
media strategists will be laboring in the backrooms to perfect the
ever-shorter television clip.

Gabor Apor notes that the average length of television news clips
— the time the candidate is actually talking — in U.S. presidential
campaigns shrank from 14.8 seconds in 1984 to 9.0 seconds in
1988. "People ask me, where will it stop? And I remind them that
George Bush's famous quote, 'Read my lips — no new taxes!' only
took four seconds."

8. MONEY MAKES THE (POLITICAL) WORLD GO ROUND

"Pierre Trudeau was a cheapskate. I went out for lunch with him and he had to borrow twenty-five cents for the tip."
— Retired senator John Godfrey

Jack Godfrey, the grand old bagman of the Liberal party, loves to tell the story about Pierre Trudeau borrowing the money to leave a twenty-five-cent tip. He tells it with respect and affection. Parsimony is a virtue that the people who guard the vaults of the political backrooms come to cherish on the rare occasions when they find it in the gaudy, high-spending world of electoral politics. Politicians, of course, are spenders not conservers. They spend to get elected. Once elected, they spend more to keep themselves in office. They spend today and worry about raising the money tomorrow. They spend on polling and television even when their bank accounts are empty and their lines of credit are stretched to the limit. Their fund raisers often feel they are on a treadmill, running harder and harder to keep from falling farther and farther behind the unquenchable financial demands of the politicians they serve.

"The way money is spent in politics would not be defended in any other institutional setting — with the possible exception of the midway at the fairground," says Robin Sears, a former federal secretary and campaign director of the New Democratic Party. "It would certainly not be tolerated in business. I feel guilty as much as anybody. In an absolutely desperate situation, somebody calls up and says, 'We need another three minutes [of TV time] in Vancouver,' and I say, 'Fine. Do it.' There goes $100,000."

If anything, spending is even more difficult to police in a leadership campaign than in a general election. Senator Finlay MacDonald watched the money pour out the door during Joe Clark's doomed, $1.9 million bid to retain the Tory leadership in 1983. "We never had a budget. What the hell's a budget? There's no such thing. At any given point, if you say the budget's 'X' number of dollars, somebody comes in and says, 'Just add a bit more.' The budget's gone, [but] the money goes."[1]

John Rae, the Montreal business executive who ran Jean Chrétien's campaigns for the national Liberal leadership in 1984 (unsuccessful) and 1990 (successful), says the financial officers of a campaign may think they have spending under control and within budget, only to find at the end that workers have spent more than planned and that unexpected bills come in. "You try to drum it into everyone's head," Rae says. "Most of the people who are involved in campaigns are responsible people in dealing with money. The difficulty in politics is that you don't control everybody. It's impossible to control everybody."

Jack Godfrey, now eighty years old, believes that the person who is responsible for raising money should also control the spending — not the detailed items, but the global amounts. Back in 1957, Lester Pearson, the newly chosen federal leader, asked Godfrey to help the Ontario Liberal party by raising a campaign war chest for provincial leader John Wintermeyer. Godfrey agreed, on the condition that he also controlled the party's expenditures. He prepared a budget for the 1959 Ontario election, only to discover that Wintermeyer had authorized an additional — and unbudgeted — $100,000 for television commercials. Godfrey told him the party did not have the money and, unless Wintermeyer could show him where he proposed to find the $100,000, he was going to inform the advertising agency that it would not be paid.

> I said, "Christ, that's crooked. We haven't got any money. You're going to put the thing in debt." I phoned the advertising agency and told them we didn't have the money but I wasn't going to cancel the advertising — they should just do what they thought was right. Of course, they cancelled the advertising and that got in the paper, and there was a crisis [in the party]. According to Wintermeyer, I lost the election for him because [then Tory premier Leslie] Frost said, "If the Liberals can't run their own finances, how can they run the province's finances?" It was a good point.

The feud between Godfrey, the bagman, and Wintermeyer, the leader, spilled over into the next Ontario election in 1963. The Liberals lost again and, when it was over, Wintermeyer threw a party in his hometown Kitchener and sent the bill — for $10,000 — to Godfrey. "He wanted me to pay that bill. I said, 'Piss on you. You lost, it's your party, you pay for it.'"

Godfrey found himself in a similar confrontation with campaign director Keith Davey following the 1974 federal election, when the Liberals under Trudeau regained a majority government. There is still a note of incredulity in Godfrey's voice, nearly twenty years later — "Keith Davey ordered a poll to find out why we had won the election. Why we'd won! You usually order them before [an election]. This poll was done by [Martin] Goldfarb — for $80,000. The bill came and I sent it back and said, 'Keith, it's nothing to do with me, it's nothing to do with the party. You ordered it, you pay it.' I just refused to pay it. Goldfarb didn't get paid for four or five years on that one."

Terry Yates, a General Motors dealer in Hamilton, Ontario, became comptroller of the federal Tories following the 1972 election, in which Robert Stanfield's Conservatives had come within two seats (107–109) of upsetting Trudeau's Liberals. Tory party finances were in rough shape, Yates knew that much. He did not know how rough. Having spent far more than they raised in a frantic campaign in a desperately close election, the Conservatives were in dire straits. They were $2 million in debt — a staggering amount for a party to owe in the early '70s — and when another election came along in the spring of 1974, they could not afford to buy any television time. Yates and Patrick Vernon, the party's chief fund raiser, personally guaranteed a $1.5 million note for the media buy. With aggressive fund-raising and tight spending controls, the Conservative party managed to regain some financial ground during the 1974 campaign, emerging from the election "only" $1 million in the red. But, crushed by the Liberals in that election, the Tories had no prospect of being able to pay off the debt in the foreseeable future.

Vernon decided the party had no alternative but to declare bankruptcy, and he and Yates secretly flew to Halifax to break Vernon's bad news to Stanfield. "We went to lunch, and Stanfield was quite affable. Then we went back to his house and sat in the backyard to talk about the future of the party and what was going to happen," Yates says. "Patrick lays the bombshell on him that the party has to declare bankruptcy. . . . The leader, after he dropped his teeth, said surely there must be another solution. We talked about it and how much the debt was and what could be done. . . . The decision was to make no decision, to just carry on. We felt it would not be the right thing to do, to declare bankruptcy."

What ultimately saved the Tories from bankruptcy was the Election Expenses Act, which came into effect later in 1974. The act did four principal things. It put limits on spending by parties and candidates in general elections and byelections. It provided for the partial reimbursement from the public purse of election expenses incurred by candidates and parties. It required public disclosure of the sources of individual and corporate donations of more than $100 to parties and candidates. And it encouraged contributions by establishing a system of tax credits for individuals giving to parties and candidates. The tax-credit provisions enabled the Conservative party to broaden its financial base, and made it possible to build an extremely successful direct-mail operation, to launch the "500 Club" for $1,000 donors, and to stage more and larger fund-raising dinners. On the day in 1976 that Joe Clark was elected Tory leader, John Laschinger, then the party's national director, reported to Stanfield that the last bills outstanding from the 1974 election had finally been paid and the party would be a few dollars in the black after the leadership convention.

Although the 1974 legislation should have made it possible for any well-managed party to avoid red ink, parties are frequently not well managed and they do get into trouble, lots of it. They get into trouble especially when they find themselves abruptly falling out of power and landing in opposition. Inevitably, the inflow of funds slows from a rush to a trickle. Parties can no longer afford the high-spending habits they developed while in office. They are forced to downsize — to reduce staff, cut back promotional activities and candidate recruitment, and even curtail expensive fund-raising operations — thereby digging themselves more deeply into the hole. Meanwhile, parties in power, unless they make themselves grossly unpopular with the cheque-writing public, have fewer problems raising money; they are able to increase spending on personnel, polling, promotional activities — and fund-raising.

The federal Liberals have never recovered, psychologically or financially, from losing office in 1984, the first Mulroney–Turner election. By the end of the 1988 election campaign, they were $4 million in debt. The Ontario Conservatives, who lost power in 1985 and who went through three changes of leadership in five years, suffered even more. By the time Liberal premier David Peterson called the September 1990 election, the Tories owed $5 million to five banks and five trust companies. The poverty, however, was all at the top. As Laschinger assembled the Conservative election organization, he discovered to his astonishment that, although the party was destitute, its 130 riding associations were sitting on a small gold mine. Collectively, they had $2 million in their bank accounts. The party never could get its hands on much of that money; it was still $4.6 million in debt in the summer of 1992.

Political financing laws, with their tax credits for contributors, make it infinitely easier than it used to be to attract money. At the same time, the new election-expense ceilings restrict the amounts parties and candidates can legally spend. In 1988, for example, the three major federal parties raised donations totalling $55.6 million, compared to their combined spending of $21.8 million (about $2 million less than the ceiling) during the two-month campaign period. They did not, however, have $33.8 million in the bank after the election. Due to a loophole in federal election law, some big-ticket items, notably polling, do not count in the calculation of the campaign spending. In addition, revenues raised in 1988 also had to cover their operating expenses in the ten non-campaign months of the year. Operating expenses are always high in the period leading up to an election call as parties do as much of their spending as possible before the campaign officially begins, bringing the expenditure limits into effect. Often they spend more in the run-up to an election than they do in the campaign proper. When this non-campaign-period spending is added — and when allowance is made for the partial reimbursement of election expenses under the Election Expenses Act — the three big national parties had a combined *deficit* in 1988 of $5.5 million.

Table 1

Party Income/Expenses — 1988

	PC	Lib.	NDP
Election expenses	$ 7,921,738	$ 6,839,875	$ 7,060,563
Other 1988 expenses	21,124,672	10,175,612	14,933,202
Total expenses:	$29,046,410	17,015,487	21,993,765
Contributions	$24,542,036	$13,211,364	$17,863,827
Election reimbursement	1,782,391	1,538,972	1,588,627
Other income	688,271	873,004	444,044

	PC	Lib.	NDP
Total income:	$27,012,698	$15,623,340	$19,896,498
Deficit	$ 2,033,712	$ 1,392,147	$ 2,097,267

SOURCE: Chief Electoral Officer of Canada

As Laschinger discovered at the provincial level during the 1990 Ontario election, the picture changes dramatically when the financial position of federal party *candidates* is examined. Candidates often enjoy handsome bank balances while their parties are drowning in red ink. Under the Election Expenses Act, candidates, like parties, are limited in the amounts they may spend. In the 1988 federal election, the limit averaged $47,000 per candidate. But there is no limit on the amount that candidates may raise, or on the size of contributions they may accept. For example, a total of 1,578 candidates, including independents and representatives of minor parties, contested the 1988 federal election. They reported election expenses of $31,341,494 plus personal expenses of $1,732,538, for a total of $33,074,032. However, thanks largely to the tax-credit regime, the candidates were able to raise $32,532,018 in contributions. In addition, they collected $13,734,568 in partial reimbursement of their election expenditures. (Under the act, any candidate who gets 15 per cent of the vote is reimbursed for 50 per cent of his or her election expenses.) The bottom line: The 1,578 candidates had a total income of $46,266,586 and expenses of $33,074,032 — for a *surplus* of $13,192,554. That is, an average surplus per candidate of $8,360.

Table 2 shows how the candidates of the three major parties fared financially in the 1988 federal election.

Table 2

Candidate Finances, Major Parties, 1988

	PC	Lib.	NDP
No. of candidates	295	294	295
Contributions	$13,391,670	$ 9,630,842	$ 6,806,869
Reimbursement	6,055,597	4,655,526	2,839,253
Total income:	$19,447,267	$14,286,368	$ 9,646,122
Election expenses	$11,864,239	$ 9,676,996	$ 7,306,414
Personal expenses	708,752	494,832	368,383

	PC	Lib.	NDP
Total expenses:	$12,572,991	$10,171,828	$ 7,674,797
Surplus	$ 6,874,276	$ 4,114,540	$ 1,971,325
Average surplus per candidate:	$ 23,303	$ 13,995	$ 6,682

SOURCE: Chief Electoral Officer of Canada.
Note: Figures reflect funds raised and spent during the official election period only.

The average Tory candidate had enough money left over in 1988 to cover about half of the amount he or she would be allowed to spend in the *next* election. In the aggregate, the candidates, with the exception of New Democrats, produced surpluses that were larger than their parties' deficits. Or, to look at it another way, the 294 Liberal candidates came out of the election with a combined surplus of $4.1 million — enough to pay off the national party's accumulated debt, if the party had been able to get its hands on its candidates' surpluses. But it could not.

In politics, money is like water: It flows down much more readily than it flows up. Parties use a portion of the money they raise to subsidize campaigns at the constituency levels. Candidates, however, have a choice when it comes to their surplus funds. They may transfer them to their party's national headquarters, never to be seen by them again. Few do that. Or they may — as the vast majority do — keep the money at home by turning it over to their constituency associations, to be used in their next nomination fight or election campaign.

It is not the way the Election Expenses Act was meant to function. It was never intended that candidates who succeed in taking in more contributions than they require to cover their election costs should also enjoy the windfall of a reimbursement of expenses from public funds. It was never intended that candidates, raising money for a specific campaign, should be able to hoard it, tax free, for use in another campaign in the future. And it was never intended that the taxpayer, through the tax-credit system and the reimbursement subsidy, should be asked to underwrite the creation of constituency slush funds.

The public is not told how large these funds are. Candidates are obliged to report the amounts they raise and spend during the period of the election writ (usually just over fifty days). But successful candidates do not stop raising and spending money on election night. Many hold annual fund-raising dinners, cocktail parties, barbecues, and other activities to build up their war chests. Some prominent MPs, according to informed estimates, are sitting on funds in the $400,000-to-$500,000 range. Such huge funds give a sitting member the financial muscle to beat off challengers for his or her party's nomination in the next election, and they give him or her a big head start over other parties' candidates once the election is called. On the other hand, war chests attract pirates, as has happened in several Toronto-area ridings. Interlopers try to take over a party's constituency association to get control of its bank account, then use the money to wrest the nomination away from the incumbent.

Jean-Marc Hamel, the retired chief electoral officer, remembers the debate when a Commons committee was conducting its clause-by-clause study of the Election Expenses Act in the early 1970s. "Jimmy Walker [a Liberal backbencher from Toronto] mentioned the tax credits. They were a Canadian invention and nobody else had ever attempted to use them this way before. Nobody had any clue as to how much money they would generate. You know, would they really bring money in? Jimmy Walker said, 'Well, what will happen if a candidate after an election has a surplus? What is going to happen?' Everybody laughed. Everybody said, 'Come on, Jimmy. That's impossible.' Well, as it turned out, he was the only one who was right."

The old stereotype of an impoverished candidate expending his or her life savings in the pursuit of public office is no longer applicable. Today, relatively few major-party candidates have to reach into their own pockets to finance their campaigns. The tax credit has made money easy to raise, and the reimbursement subsidy to candidates collecting 15 per cent or more of the vote has taken most of the financial risk out of running. There is something wrong with a candidate's organization if he or she does not finish with money in the bank. Table 3, compiled from candidates' financial returns, shows how a selection of MPs or former MPs fared in the money game in the 1984 and 1988 federal elections.

Table 3

Campaign Surpluses, Selected Candidates

Candidate (party)	1984 Election	1988 Election	Total 1984/1988
Lloyd Axworthy (Lib.)	$ 37,360	$ 37,140	$ 74,500
Ed Broadbent (NDP)	20,479	27,119	47,598

Candidate (party)	1984 Election	1988 Election	Total 1984/1988
Joe Clark (PC)	39,442	42,282	81,724
John Crosbie (PC)	39,100	53,543	92,643
Robert de Cotret (PC)	19,003	58,847	77,850
Paul Dick (PC)	54,282	81,803	136,085
Carole Jacques (PC)	3,776	61,571	65,347
Ray Hnatyshyn (PC)	49,936	29,095	79,031
Barbara McDougall (PC)	64,118	106,219	170,337
Audrey McLaughlin (NDP)	—	5,599	—
Sergio Marchi (Lib.)	12,117	61,686	73,803
Paul Martin (Lib.)	—	93,469	—
Don Mazankowski (PC)	36,156	41,400	77,556
Gerry Merrithew (PC)	52,640	86,507	139,147
Brian Mulroney (PC)	66,562	40,662	107,224
André Ouellet (Lib.)	37,997	29,017	67,014
James Peterson (Lib.)	34,923	90,392	125,315
Svend Robinson (NDP)	33,547	47,388	80,935
Gerry St. Germaine (PC)	41,425	100,759	142,184
Tom Siddon (PC)	33,570	69,397	102,967
John Turner (Lib.)	23,937	46,450	70,387
Michael Wilson (PC)	121,637	83,237	204,874

Note: The figures reflect amounts received and expended during the period of the election writ only. They do not include amounts raised or spent before the elections were called or after voting day — amounts that candidates and constituency associations are not required to report. The surplus is calculated by adding contributions collected to the expense reimbursement received, and subtracting from this total the candidate's campaign and personal expenses, as reported by his official agent. Audrey McLaughlin and Paul Martin were not candidates in 1984.

Canada's leading expert on election law, Jean-Marc Hamel, is one of many who worries that money is distorting the political system. While political parties struggle to pay their bills, candidates — current and past — are sitting on small fortunes. Their fortunes are largely built of public funds, through the tax credits and the reimbursement of expenses. Yet there is no control at all over how the money is used. He says:

> We [at the chief electoral office] get a report and we see that
> the candidate has a $90,000-odd surplus, but because he or she

obtained more than 15 per cent of the vote, they are entitled
to reimbursement of half of their election expenses. So we send
them a cheque for $25,000, which is a bit ridiculous. Then
the money is transferred to the constituency association, which
is not defined anywhere in law. We completely lose track of
that money. We have no idea what use is made of it. . . . People
were concerned that the Election Expenses Act would give the
parties too much power, that the parties would have lots of
money and the candidates would still starve. It's just the opposite. The parties are starving. . . . Some constituency associations have pretty fat bank accounts. [Their surplus] could
be used for all kinds of purposes because it's pretty well the
decision of whoever controls it — the constituency association,
the previous candidate, the sitting MP, or one of his friends,
or his wife, or whoever.

The most élite group in federal politics is the unofficial $100,000
Club — candidates who have raised $100,000 in contributions in
a single election campaign (roughly eight weeks in duration). In
the 1984 election, the club had only two members — Tories Bud
Sherman, who raised $103,783 in a losing campaign in Winnipeg,
and Michael Wilson, soon to be finance minister, who took in
$144,225 for his re-election bid in the Toronto suburb of Etobicoke.
With fund-raising techniques becoming increasingly proficient, the
club expanded to ten members in the 1988 election.

Table 4

Candidate Fund-raising: The Top 10, 1988 Election

Barbara McDougall (PC, Ont.)	$ 130,626
Larry Schneider (PC, Sask.)	124,788
Gerry St. Germaine (PC, B.C.)	123,427
Kim Campbell (PC, B.C.)	116,488
Paul Martin (Lib., Que.)	114,070
James Peterson (Lib., Ont.)	112,118
Gerry Merrithew (PC, N.B.)	108,015
Paul Dick (PC, Ont.)	105,989
Michael Wilson (PC, Ont.)	105,568
John Fraser (PC, B.C.)	101,770

SOURCE: Chief Electoral Officer of Canada. Contributions are amounts
raised during the election period only. Dinners and other annual fund-

raising events are not included, unless they took place during the writ period.

Money loves power. Five of the ten members of the $100,000 Club in 1988 were ministers in the Mulroney government (McDougall, St. Germaine, Merrithew, Dick, and Wilson). A sixth (Campbell) would join the cabinet after the election, and a seventh (Fraser) was a former minister who had become speaker of the Commons. Paul Martin would shortly run for the Liberal leadership (and lose to Jean Chrétien). Peterson was no stranger to power; he is the older brother of then Ontario premier David Peterson. Only Schneider could be considered to be a backbencher. And, of the ten, only one — St. Germaine — failed to win his seat in that 1988 election.

If three backroom managers were asked whether money wins elections, they would come up with three different answers: Yes, No, and It Depends. It Depends comes closest to the mark. A party or a candidate must have a minimum amount of money — enough to be taken seriously and to pay for the essential elements of the campaign. The minimum is, in effect, an entry fee to the contest — be it a national or provincial election, constituency-level election, or a leadership convention. At the other end of the spectrum, however, more is not automatically better. Beyond a certain point, additional spending may become counterproductive. A party can waste so much money and effort on non-essentials that it loses its focus. Candidates may actually spend themselves out of contention — as Brian Mulroney did in his flashy first campaign for the Conservative leadership in 1976. Canadians are not comfortable with politicians who pursue a prize too ardently, especially politicians who spend more in the pursuit than the prize seems to be worth. Somewhere between Not Enough and Too Much is the Right Amount to spend. The Right Amount will depend on the type of race being run (national, provincial, constituency, or leadership), on the state of the competition, on the mood and expectation of the electorate, on any national or provincial trends that may be occurring, and on the profile of the spender.

Conspicuous spending would be out of keeping, for example, with the frugal, ordinary-folks profile that the NDP cultivates, and it would jeopardize the chances of any NDP candidate so ill-advised as to be seen spending too lavishly. Wendy Walker, a union activist and campaign organizer who is now an Ontario civil servant, remembers working for Rosemary Brown in the 1975 NDP leadership campaign (won by Ed Broadbent, with Brown second). Somehow, the candidates managed to campaign within a spending limit of $15,000. At most stops, organizers booked a hotel room for the candidate only; his or her workers bunked with friends or paid for their own hotel rooms. Walker and three others drove in a Volkswagen from Toronto to Winnipeg, site of the convention. They were there for eight days. "We were all broke," Walker says. "We only had a couple of hotel rooms. We took turns trying to sleep in shifts on floors and beds and chairs and stuff. Nobody slept. . . . What I've never been able to figure out is how you spend $2 million or $3 million on a leadership campaign. If I had that kind of money, I wouldn't know what to do with it. . . . Hospitality is a fine line to walk in the NDP. Plush hospitality suites with lots of free stuff are not well considered."

Leadership conventions defy any traditional cost-benefit analysis. As a general proposition, the candidate who spends the most money generally wins the leadership race. But leadership races are also generally won by the candidate who was the favorite when the race began. It is an open question whether the candidate wins because he or she has the most money to spend, or whether the candidate is able to raise the most money because he or she is favored to win. Backroom organizers know that financial receipts are often a harbinger of a candidate's progress. The flow of donations increases when contributors sense that a campaign is gaining momentum. In 1985, for example, with his Conservatives still in power in Ontario, Bill Davis decided to retire. His industry minister, Frank Miller, was the odds-on favorite in a four-way race to succeed him. Miller's front-runner status was reflected in his fund-raising; he collected nearly $2 million in contributions while spending "only" $1,235,815 in his leadership campaign (he won on the third ballot).

By the same token, donations slow to a trickle when supporters sense that a candidate is faltering. But one thing is clear: A leadership candidate who has little apparent chance of winning when a race begins will not improve the odds by trying to spend his or her way to victory.

Table 5 examines the utility or futility of money spent by candidates in selected leadership campaigns. The cost per vote is determined by dividing a candidate's total reported spending by the largest number of votes he or she received on any one ballot. (An asterisk denotes a winner.)

Table 5

Cost Per Vote, Selected Leadership Campaigns

	Spending	Vote (Best Ballot)	Cost Per Vote
Canada			
1967 PC			
Robert Stanfield*	$ 150,000 (est)	1,150	$ 130
1968 Lib.			
Pierre Trudeau*	300,000 (est)	1,203	249
1976 PC			
Joe Clark*	168,353	1,187	142
Claude Wagner	266,538	1,112	240
Brian Mulroney	500,000 (est)	419	1,193
Flora MacDonald	152,704	239	639
Paul Hellyer	287,786	231	1,246
Sinclair Stevens	294,106	182	1,616
James Gillies	192,847	87	2,217
1983 PC			
Joe Clark	1,900,000	1,325	1,434
John Crosbie	1,800,000	858	2,098
Peter Pocklington	965,000	102	9,461
1984 Lib.			
John Turner*	1,600,000	1,862	859
Jean Chrétien	1,500,000	1,368	1,096
John Munro	625,000	93	6,720
1990 Lib.			
Jean Chrétien*	2,440,000†	2,652	920
Paul Martin	2,370,000†	1,176	2,015
Sheila Copps	806,000	499	1,615
Ontario			
1982 NDP			
Bob Rae*	22,000	1,356	16
1982 Lib.			
David Peterson*	100,000 (est)	1,136	88
1985 (Jan.) PC			
Frank Miller*	1,235,815	869	1,422
1985 (Nov.) PC			
Larry Grossman*	841,000	848	992

1990 PC			
Michael Harris*	569,000	7,175‡	79
Newfoundland			
1979 PC			
Brian Peckford*	60,000	331	181
1989 PC			
Tom Rideout*	344,000	403	854
New Brunswick			
1989 PC			
B. Baird-Filliter*	90,000	1,021	88
British Columbia			
1986 Social Credit			
Bud Smith	450,000	219	2,055
1991 Social Credit			
Norman Jacobsen	144,000	169	852
Mel Couvelier	180,000	331	544

Notes: Spending figures are from candidates' reports, where available; otherwise, from published estimates.

† The 1990 Liberal leadership contest had a per-candidate spending limit of $1.7 million. Both Chrétien and Martin reported spending that came within the limit. However, certain classes of expenditure were not subject to the limit. The figures are the spending totals reported by Chrétien and Martin. They include the amounts — $284,000 in Chrétien's case, $277,000 in Martin's — that were "taxed" by the Liberal party from contributions to the candidates. But they do not include a variety of expenses that candidates were not required to report.

‡ In 1990, the Ontario Conservatives, borrowing a page from the Parti Québécois, elected their leader by a province-wide vote of party supporters.

Increasingly, parties are addressing the problem — financial and perceptual — of excessive spending by imposing expenditure limits on leadership campaigns, as the federal Liberals did, half-heartedly, in their 1990 race. When the NDP chose Audrey McLaughlin to succeed Ed Broadbent in 1989, each candidate was limited to $150,000 — or $50,000 less than Nova Scotia Tories set for their provincial leadership campaign two years later. When the Ontario Liberals chose Lyn McLeod as their new leader in 1992, the spending limit was $250,000.

Spending limits help level the playing field, but they are an imperfect remedy. In most instances, the limits apply only to certain types of expenditure while exempting other types. A candidate's "personal" expenses, including all travel costs, are frequently exempted from the limit. When the Ontario Tories elected Michael Harris in 1990, the limit was ostensibly $500,000. It did not apply, however, to salaries paid to campaign organizers and workers, nor to money spent on polling.

Spending limits established by parties are utterly unenforceable. No party, after the last leadership poster has been taken down and the last balloon burst, is going to turn its candidates' financial reports over to forensic accountants to make sure that no one understated his or her expenses. No party is going to strip its new leader of his or her position because the candidate unknowingly (or knowingly) overspent. Brian Mulroney refused to file the required financial report following his first attempt to win the Conservative leadership in 1976, the only candidate who failed to file. It never occurred to the party to try to prevent him from running again in 1983.

David MacNaughton, who managed Don Johnston's campaign for the national Liberal leadership in 1984, the year that John Turner won, does not believe in spending limits. "Leadership campaigns are expensive things to run," he says. "Anybody who thinks you can put on a limit of $250,000 is crazy. . . . Everybody lies. [However,] I think limits are academic at the present moment. The problem is the money. You can't raise it. Paul Martin blew his brains out on spending [in the 1990 Liberal leadership]. He should have been a guy who raised lots of money. I don't know how much money he lost on that, but it was lots. It came out of his pocket."

While MacNaughton was running Johnston's losing campaign in 1984, Eddie Goldenberg was campaigning for Jean Chrétien, also unsuccessfully. "The money was very hard to raise," Goldenberg remembers. "There was almost a self-imposed control. I think the way to control spending is to have shorter campaigns." Much of Chrétien's money in 1984 and again in 1990 went for telephone bills that ran into six figures. "A great deal of the expense in our campaigns also went into provincial headquarters," says Goldenberg. "We were expected to have a headquarters in each province. If you don't, you don't love us, was the way they looked at it."

When John Laschinger flew to Vancouver in May 1986 to take over Bud Smith's campaign for the B.C. Social Credit leadership, after Bill Bennett stepped down, his first challenge was to set a budget that the candidate and his fund raisers alike could live with.

After many meetings, three budgets were drafted — low ($375,000), medium ($500,000), and high ($750,000). Smith felt the high budget was realistic and he was confident that his fund raisers could collect $750,000 without difficulty. Laschinger and others believed Smith would be courting financial disaster — and inviting a crippling post-convention debt — if he started at the high end. A "modular" approach was finally agreed on. The budget was set at $375,000 with provision to approve additional spending as it became obvious that funds would be available. In fact, Smith was never perceived by Socreds or by the general public as having much chance of defeating either Bill Vander Zalm (the eventual winner) or Grace McCarthy. The money never did pour in, although spending broke through the budget constraints, reaching $450,000 by time the race was over. Smith ended in fourth place — and more than $200,000 in debt. If the high-end budget had been adopted, he might well have bankrupted himself.

The Royal Commission on Electoral Reform and Party Financing, reporting in 1992, recommended bringing national party leadership campaigns under the same general regime that applies to general elections. Reports would have to be filed — including a preliminary report from each candidate the day before the convention votes. The tax-credit system would be used. Candidates would be required to disclose the size and source of all contributions of $250 or more. And individual leadership contestants would not be allowed to spend more than 15 per cent of the amount that their party had been permitted to spend in the most recent election. In the 1988 federal election, the limit for a party fielding a full slate of candidates was just under $8 million. This would produce a leadership ceiling of $1.2 million, although the royal commission recommended that parties be able to set ceilings below the statutory maximum if they wished. A $1.2 million limit — roughly 50 per cent less than was spent by the principal contenders at the 1983 Conservative and 1990 Liberal conventions — would force the two old parties to rein themselves in.

The problem of enforcement, however, would remain. There is no way that parties can compel candidates to submit reports that account for every cent of their spending, even if they go over the limit. And when a convention is over, a party is preoccupied with healing the wounds opened during the leadership campaign. The last thing it wants to do is to open new wounds by imposing sanctions on candidates who have exceeded the limit.

In fairness, it is impossible for candidates and their managers to maintain iron control over spending in the frenzy of a leadership race, particularly in convention week. John Rae gives a small illustration from the 1984 Chrétien campaign. "A poll came out which showed that Mr. Chrétien was more popular in the country than Mr. Turner. It was a significant poll, and we had a choice to make. The vote was on Saturday and the poll came out on the Friday, the day before. What do you do? You go to the printer and get it printed [for distribution to all delegates]. And that was $1,000 or so, I forget the figure. Those are things that you do. Money in politics is very important to keep the machine going, but you're not spending for very exotic purposes. . . . Nothing very elaborate."

Late in the 1983 Conservative leadership race, *Maclean's* magazine ran a cover story on John Crosbie as "The Tory to Watch." Crosbie organizers loved the story and agreed eagerly when a company that distributed *Maclean's* offered them 8,000 unsold copies for "just" $1 per copy to give delegates. Another (unbudgeted) $8,000 was added to Crosbie's campaign debt.

Legislated controls on political financing address perceptions as much as they address real problems. But perceptions are important. It is important to practitioners that the public view the political process as being open, fair, and honest. A legal requirement to disclose the source and size of contributions helps to dispel the perception that large corporations or wealthy individuals are able to influence politicians and governments through their financial donations. A statutory limit on campaign spending reassures the public that all contestants have an equitable opportunity to win.

In practice, if vested interests want to influence the political process, there are more effective ways to do it than through campaign contributions. A big businessman who wants special consideration for his company will gain more influence by, say, lending a vacation home to a party leader or creating a job for a cabinet minister's spouse or dropout son than he will by making a $50,000 campaign donation. And limits on campaign spending will not seriously deter parties or candidates who feel they must spend more than the law contemplates. They simply spend as heavily as they choose before the election writ is issued, then scale down during the campaign period.

Maybe it does not matter. In Canada, at least, there is no obvious correlation between money spent and electoral success. "You can't buy an election because you're limited to the kinds of times you can buy on radio and television," says veteran Tory strategist Paul

Curley. "If you want to buy an election, it's pretty hard to do. . . . You can spend what you want in terms of written materials, but do they have any impact? A lot less than electronic communications." Eddie Goldenberg, the Chrétien adviser, agrees: "You don't necessarily have to spend more money than the other party to win. [But] there's a certain base that has to be spent."

There are two big differences between Canada and the United States. U.S. incumbents have a much larger advantage than Canadian incumbents — 95 per cent of sitting members of the U.S. House of Representatives win re-election, versus 75 per cent of Canadian MPs.[2] And the electoral process in the United States involves sums of money undreamed of in Canada. A challenger trying to win a House seat in Washington can expect to spend $600,000 or more — at least twelve times as much as a major-party candidate will spend in a typical Canadian constituency. A candidate for the U.S. Senate may end up spending $20 million to $24 million — as much as the three main parties in Canada, combined, spent in the 1988 federal election. "If you talk to U.S. congressmen," says John Rae, "they will tell you that part of every day — 80 per cent of their time — is spent raising money." Jean-Marc Hamel remembers how startled he and members of the Royal Commission on Electoral Reform and Party Financing were when they were told by a U.S. senator during a symposium at Harvard University that he spends 95 per cent of his time fund-raising.

In a study for the royal commission, researcher Keith Heintzman argues that money is more important to challengers than to incumbents. A reduction in spending limits would benefit incumbents because they enter a campaign with a marginal vote advantage of 7 per cent, he says, by virtue of the recognition factor. But raising the ceilings would assist challengers by enabling them to spend more to become better known. Heintzman calculates that an increase of 30 to 40 per cent in expenditure limits would put challengers on an equal footing with incumbents. His research suggests that a 1 per cent increase in spending produces an additional 0.21 per cent in votes.[3]

Examination of spending and voting patterns in thirty federal swing ridings in Ontario suggests, however, that as long as the principal candidates have enough funds to be competitive, a few thousand extra dollars will make little or no difference. The thirty ridings are ones in which the spread between the winner and the second-place finisher in the 1984 election was 10 per cent or less of the vote cast. Money was no advantage — only eleven of the thirty contests were won by the candidate who spent the most. It was the same story in the same seats in the 1988 election — only ten of the thirty went to the biggest spender. Thirteen of these thirty swing ridings changed hands in 1988, but only one went to the biggest spender. The other twelve were won by the second- or third-rank spender.[4]

Money is important in politics in Canada. It buys the polling and the television time. It is the grease that keeps the machine running smoothly. But it is not the only thing that makes the political world go round. That is as it should be in a democracy.

9. BAGMEN AND OTHER HEROES

"Absence of money means absence of chances of winning.
Money is where it is."
— Paul Curley, Tory strategist and lobbyist

The 1979 federal general election — the one Pierre Trudeau was to lose to Joe Clark — was not going at all well, and everyone in the Liberal backroom knew it. Trudeau knew it, too. With three weeks to go in the campaign, he invited two reporters, Mary Janigan of the *Toronto Star* and Mark Phillips of the CBC, to join him for dinner in the front cabin of his campaign aircraft. As the meal progressed, Phillips asked Trudeau about a theoretical argument that he had advanced in the past: that a prime minister has the constitutional right in a minority situation to attempt to form a government, even if his party is outnumbered by an opposition party. Would Trudeau, Phillips asked, consider carrying on if the Liberals won fewer seats than the Tories on election day? Trudeau, who normally refused to respond to hypothetical questions, made the mistake of answering Phillips. He would have "no hesitancy," he replied, in saying that he would be inclined to put the Liberal program before Parliament to test the support of the smaller parties. Then he answered in the affirmative when Phillips suggested he might try to carry on if the Liberals were about five seats behind the Conservatives, but not if they were ten seats behind.

When the story broke, as it did on the television news that night, it caused a sensation. It also dealt a body blow to the staggering Liberal campaign. The Conservatives were overjoyed. They excoriated Trudeau for arrogance. And they rushed to their mailing lists, sending letters to thousands of Tory supporters, warning them that Trudeau was proposing to use a constitutional subterfuge to cling to power — and urging them to send money at once to stop him from winning enough seats to make the attempt. The response was overwhelming. "It was the most successful fund-raising thing we'd ever done," recalls Paul Curley, who was party treasurer at the time. "We raised about $2 million!"[1]

The story reveals three things. First, political fund-raising is most successful when conducted with an air of urgency and with a specific objective. Second, giving can be stimulated more by negative motives than by positive ones; in this case, Tories gave money to help get rid of Trudeau. Third, computerized direct mail has become an absolutely vital tool for today's bagmen.

It was not always so easy to raise money. The Liberals discovered that very early on, in the 1920s, when, under the leadership of Mackenzie King, they tried to put the party's finances on a regular, secure footing. They asked each of the 240-odd Liberal constituency associations across the country to contribute $250 annually towards the upkeep of the national office in Ottawa. The effort was a dismal failure.

So was a 1943 attempt by the Progressive Conservatives to democratize their financial base by mounting a national Popular Finance Campaign, as they called it. This is how their leader, John Bracken, described it in *Public Opinion*, the party's monthly newsletter: "The money must come from those who are interested — the people themselves. I am, therefore, asking for your financial support for our organization. We desire small contributions from large numbers of people. The contributions will be used to build an organization with no other purpose than to bring about better conditions in Canada." Party canvassers were instructed not to ask for more than $25. A target of $1 million was set, seemingly a modest-enough goal for such a high-minded appeal. But the campaign was a disaster, failing even to cover its overhead. "No old-line party had ever publicly asked for money before, and suspicion, apathy, and tightfistedness killed the project," historian Jack Granatstein concluded.[2]

Political fund-raising entered the modern era, at the federal level at least, with the enactment of the Election Expenses Act in 1974. Until then, most fund-raising activities in the Liberal and Conservative parties were conducted in the shadows. Their bagmen, as anonymous as they were influential, quietly put the touch on big corporations and wealthy individuals to raise the major portion of funds to meet the parties' financial requirements. Because there was no public disclosure, no one beyond a party's inner circle knew who was contributing, how much they were giving, and what favors or promises they might be extracting in return.

The 1974 Election Expenses Act required parties and candidates to disclose the sources and amounts of all contributions over $100. It also broadened the base of political giving by establishing tax credits for donations, with the credits weighted to encourage small contributors; a $100 donation, for example, earned a tax credit of $75. The disclosure requirement changed the pattern of corporate contributions. Companies that were used to giving very large amounts to the party in power and smaller amounts (or nothing at all) to the opposition parties realized that, with public disclosure, they would have to defend their contributions to, among others, their shareholders. Retired senator John Godfrey, who was the country's most proficient bagman in his years as the chief fund raiser for the federal Liberals, says that, prior to 1974, some large federally regulated enterprises, such as chartered banks, would give as much as $125,000 to the government party in election years. Most large companies gave nothing, or close to nothing, in non-election years. Once the new act with its disclosure provisions came into force, two things happened. The big corporate donors started to give approximately equal amounts to the government and op-position. And they spread their contributions over the normal four-year parliamentary cycle, replacing large election-year donations with more modest annual contributions. Instead of giving $100,000 in election year, for example, a company might give $25,000 or $30,000 a year for four years. The parties were grateful for the cash flow between elections.

Jack Godfrey is a rarity — an old-time bagman (a label he wears proudly) who was happy to come out of the closet. When the 1974 legislation was first introduced, he worried about publicly identi-fying corporate contributors. "I thought it would do more harm for cabinet ministers to know how much these guys gave. Before they had no idea really, and absolutely no interest. However, I have changed my mind." One reason he changed his mind was the fact that disclosure discourages tollgating — the practice of squeezing political donations from firms that obtain government contracts. Between 1957 and 1963, when the Tories under John Diefenbaker were in office, tollgating was rampant, according to Godfrey. He laughs at the recollection:

Alex McBain was the chief tollgater in Ontario for the Conservative party and he was chairman of the United Funds, the mutual funds of which I was president. He was a retired old Scottish banker. Honest as hell. He didn't seem to see anything wrong with [tollgating]. He got a list of government contracts. He'd phone up [for a donation] and say, "Well, I see they were very good to you." Alex used to tell me this and, of course, he said he told them they should give to the Liberals as well, which I knew was bullshit. And one day a young architect got a government job and he was really thrilled about it. Then he got a call from Alex McBain wanting "suitable recognition" for the Conservative party, and he didn't know what to do, whether it was proper or not. . . . I said I thought he should give, but he should give equally to both parties — it was quite a big contract, so maybe $1,000, something like that — and he should call Alex McBain and say he's going to give and wants, of course, to give to each party and who should he contact in the Liberals to make a donation to them. So he phones Alex and Alex's comment was: "Piss on the Liberals, to hell with the Liberals, let them raise their own damn money."

The Liberals did raise their own money — and some of them, like backroom boss Keith Davey, maintained a policy of selective ignorance about the origins of the money that they spent on election campaigns. "I've never known, in campaigns I've run, where the money has come from," Davey says. "I rather deliberately don't try to find out."

Godfrey, meanwhile, had to wrestle with contributors who wanted to attach strings to their donations. Before the 1972 federal election, the Liberals approached Canadian Pacific for a contribution, but CP chairman Ian Sinclair, later a senator, was not in a giving mood. As Godfrey tells it,

CP Air was trying to get the franchise to fly to Madrid and somewhere else. There were several things they wanted and . . . [Liberal fund raiser] Maurice Riel was told by Sinclair that he wouldn't make any contribution until he found out whether or not he was going to get these things. And whether or not he got them, of course, would influence whether he contributed or not. . . . So when I heard this, I phoned Maurice Riel and I said, "You go and phone Mr. Sinclair and give him my

compliments and tell him there's no way he can get Madrid
or any of the other things unless he gives [right now] — and
I want to get a cheque in forty-eight hours. . . . You tell him
to make his decision and tell us right now. If he doesn't, he's
holding out, then there's just no way we can give it [Madrid]
to him. People'd say we're giving it to him so we can get a
contribution. The party isn't for sale and the government isn't
for sale. Tell him that." . . . He made the contribution. . . . I
told Trudeau what I'd done afterward. I told him not to be
influenced one way or the other.[3]

The links between political contributions and political favors are
too pervasive, too insidious, to be eradicated by any financing law
— as periodic scandals in Ottawa and in Ontario and other provinces
demonstrate. But legislation at least brings practices like tollgating
within public scrutiny. Any firm that gives disproportionate sums
to the party in power, while courting government business, sticks
out like a sore thumb in the disclosure reports, which are avidly
read by journalists and opposition politicians. "I saw that one of
the big chartered accountancy firms gave the Conservatives $82,000
[in 1990]," Godfrey says. "That's way too much. There's no way
that isn't tollgating. When I was running it for the Liberals, the
biggest ones, Peat Marwick and so on, would give $5,000 a year
to each party, and Clarkson Gordon would give around the same.
But to give $82,000, that just stinks, as far as I'm concerned."

Bill Knight, director of the New Democratic Party campaign in
the 1988 election, says the two fundamental changes in Canadian
politics in the past two decades have been the use of television and
the opening up of political financing with the 1974 legislation. A
membership-based party, the NDP used the act's tax-credit system
to magnificent advantage — raising tens of millions of dollars in
small donations to overcome, virtually overnight, the huge financial
edge that the two older parties had traditionally enjoyed, thanks to
their ability to attract large corporate contributions. The tax credits
also enabled the NDP to reduce its financial dependence on the labor
movement; union contributions, says Knight, still account for about
30 per cent of the NDP's funds, but it is thousands of small, individual supporters who now give the NDP its financial muscle. The
New Democrats can compete on an equal footing with the Liberals
and Conservatives in terms of polling, television, assistance to candidates, campaign aircraft, staff, and technology. "In 1984, we

brought in technology, a special sound system for Ed Broadbent (then national leader), to smooth out his voice in terms of the high pitch part of it."

Every campaign manager and fund raiser in the country was astonished by the difference that the Election Expenses Act made. By opening political financing to public view, the act made it respectable for people who had never given money to politicians to start contributing to parties and candidates. The tax *credits* — which were much more generous than the tax *deductions* allowed for religious and charitable donations — meant that a $100 political contribution (which carried a $75 tax credit) cost the donor only $25. It was like opening a fire hydrant. The money gushed out, flooding the parties with undreamed-of cash. They were soon raising more money than the act allowed them to spend during election campaigns. The New Democrats, quick to tap their large membership base, benefited immensely, as did the Tories who went into direct-mail fund-raising in a major way. Oddly, although it was a Liberal government — the 1972–74 minority Trudeau administration — that had introduced the expenses legislation, the Liberals were slow to take advantage of the law. Their early efforts at direct-mail solicitation were a disaster; they simply did not know how to do it. Even with the tax credits, they failed to pull in enough money to cover their mailing costs. By 1978, the ruling Liberals' revenues had fallen behind the opposition Tories', although they were still ahead of the New Democrats'.

Passed in 1974, the election-expenses law did not come into force in time for the federal election that year. The 1979 election — the one the Liberals lost — was the first to be fought under the new spending limits and disclosure requirements. Table 1 shows the rise in the number of contributors and in amounts raised by the three major parties between 1979 and 1990.

Table 1

Party Fund-raising, 1979–1990

	Liberal		Conservative		NDP	
	No.	Amt.	No.	Amt.	No.	Amt.
1979*	17,226	$ 5,220,520	42,948	$ 8,375,716	65,031	$ 4,741,281
1980*	22,606	6,217,795	37,884	7,564,120	63,699	4,920,447
1981	31,826	5,095,158	55,597	6,949,797	57,580	3,855,812
1982	34,688	6,104,367	62,278	8,193,660	67,900	6,984,881

	Liberal		Conservative		NDP	
	No.	Amt.	No.	Amt.	No.	Amt.
1983	42,338	$ 7,285,115	117,716	$ 14,108,012	67,058	$ 8,590,942
1984*	35,631	10,553,316	114,485	21,145,920	81,261	10,371,018
1985	32,355	5,570,822	90,906	14,565,652	98,680	6,284,316
1986	41,664	10,619,007	65,467	15,117,750	92,014	7,795,658
1987	35,118	8,832,377	48,510	12,761,155	89,278	6,697,083
1988*	37,911	13,211,364	67,926	24,542,036	120,703	18,754,770
1989	23,859	6,324,012	49,635	13,801,368	90,771	13,864,694
1990	42,035	12,036,486	34,887	11,046,654	116,339	15,438,908

SOURCE: Chief Electoral Officer of Canada
* General election year.

Election campaigns give fund-raising a clear objective and a sense of urgency. As the table indicates, parties redouble their efforts to raise money in election years, increasing both the number of their contributors and the amount of their receipts. In the 1988 election, for example, all three parties raised far more than the $8 million each was permitted by law to spend for national campaign purposes. There were also four leadership conventions in the twelve-year period (Liberals in 1984 and 1990, Tories in 1983, and NDP in 1989) which created special interest in those parties in those years. These distortions aside, the figures show how the New Democrats and the Conservatives used the Election Expenses Act to broaden their base of financial support. In 1979, the NDP were in third place in money raised, but they soon caught up to the Liberals, and by 1989 overtook the Tories, too. The Tory decline in contributors and receipts following their election victory in 1988 reflected the persistent unpopularity of the Mulroney government. Opinion polls are a reliable barometer for fund raisers. A gain of five percentage points makes the money pour in; a loss of five points reduces the flood to a trickle.

Table 1 deals only with the national parties reporting under the federal statute. Most provinces have their own political finance legislation. Some are patterned on the federal legislation. Some go beyond it. Ontario, for example, limits the size of contributions. Quebec bars contributions from corporations.

Table 2

Election Finance Legislation in Canada

	Limits Size of Contributions	Limits Expenditures	Tax Credit	Disclosure of Larger Donors
Federal	no	yes	yes	yes
Nfld.	no	no	no	no
P.E.I.	no	yes	yes	yes
N.S.	no	yes	yes*	yes*
N.B.	no	yes	yes	yes
Que.	yes	yes	yes	yes
Ont.	yes	yes	yes	yes
Man.	no	yes	yes	yes
Sask.	no	yes	no	yes
Alta.	no	no	yes	yes
B.C.	no	no*	yes	no

* Nova Scotia allows tax credits and requires disclosure for contributions to provincial parties, but not for contributions to parties' constituency associations. British Columbia does not limit election expenditures but does require them to be publicly reported after the election. Only Ontario has moved, gingerly, into the area of leadership contests — by limiting campaign periods and requiring disclosure of all expenditures by category and of the names of all major suppliers and all donors of more than $100.

The three main legislative elements — spending limits, disclosure, and tax credits — are enthusiastically endorsed by fund raisers in all parties. "[The federal legislation] was an absolutely superb thing," says Terry Yates, who was the Tories' chief fund raiser at the time. "It got us out of the nineteenth century and into the twentieth century. . . . It gives you more credibility and believability and gets you away from the 'slime' factor."

Some of the applause for political financing laws is self-serving, of course, and some of it is self-congratulatory. Not only have these laws brought fund-raising out of the closet, they have proved to be cash cows. And the cows' richest cream comes from direct mail.

Robert Odell helped introduce direct-mail methods to political fund-raising for the Republican National Committee in Washington in the 1960s. In those days, direct mail consisted of hand-typed "personalized" form letters to prospective contributors; they were stuffed in envelopes, stamped, and hauled to the post office. A laborious and not particularly productive process, it did little to broaden the Republicans' base of donors. Then, in the fall of 1964, actor Ronald Reagan, later to be governor of California and president of the United States, went on television to appeal for support for the Republican presidential nominee, Senator Barry Goldwater, who was running against Democratic president Lyndon Johnson. "It was one of those historic moments in political history, when Reagan went on television and made a public televised appeal for support, political support, to vote for Barry Goldwater," says Odell. "He closed with a message asking for financial contributions. Reagan's appeal just worked like magic. Literally tons of mail came in as a result of that. One-dollar cheques, one-dollar bills, five-dollar bills, cheques for this and that. It brought in a couple of million dollars."

Even more important than the money were the names and addresses. Until then, the Republican National Committee had to go through state committees to raise most of its money. Now it had its own mailing list, a large-enough list to raise serious amounts of money, a list of people who cared enough to send money in response to Reagan's appeal and who in all likelihood would give again when asked.

Good lists are central to the success of all direct-mail campaigns, as the Republicans were soon to discover. In 1972, the RNC raised $8 million for Richard Nixon's re-election by direct-mail appeals to small contributors. When the Watergate scandal broke a year later, the party's big donors bolted. Only 5 per cent of the Republicans who customarily had given $1,000 or more annually continued to contribute after Watergate. The Republicans looked frantically to their small supporters for help. Odell and his colleagues organized a special mailing to contributors, telling them their party was in trouble and urging them to look beyond the Watergate headlines to the health of the Republican National Committee and the very survival of the U.S. two-party system. The letter ran to eight pages. Odell says:

> People will read long letters if they're informative and if they're about things they're interested in. It wasn't just another direct-mail message. We knew we were in trouble and we needed to convey this message to people who were our friends. These are the people we count on to fund the party, day in and day out. I can recall very clearly the look of that letter. It was printed on one side of a piece of paper, so the eight sheets of paper were there. We used rough-edged paper to give it a

different kind of look. Then we followed that letter up to those who did not respond with another letter. We called the first one, the eight-paged letter, "The Blockbuster" and the second one "Son of Blockbuster." Those two letters would have to be in the top five or six of the most successful direct-mail packages I've been associated with.

Between 40 and 50 per cent of the Republicans who received the "Blockbusters" responded with cheques or cash, an unheard-of response rate.

At about the same time, Canada's Conservatives were gearing up for a federal election — fought in 1974 without the benefit of the new election-expenses law (which had been passed too late for the election) — and for the new era of fund-raising that would begin when the law came into effect. Malcolm Wickson, the Tories' campaign chairman in 1974 and a former national director of the party, was determined to acquire modern political tools, especially for fund-raising. (Later, the party retained Odell as a consultant, and the American expert is still working behind the scenes to design the Tories' direct-mail campaigns.)

Wickson regularly sent staff members to meet Republican back-roomers in Washington, Detroit, and Columbus, Ohio, and to find out more about fund-raising techniques that could be adapted to Canadian needs. On a trip to Columbus in 1973, John Laschinger, then the Tories' national director, learned about the Ruby Red Grapefruit Co. Ruby Red Grapefruit was simply a Florida-based outfit that sold citrus fruit by mail, but its mailing list was highly prized by political fund raisers in the United States. Ralph Goettler, a Republican fund-raising consultant, explained the elements of soliciting funds by mail: "You have to write to people who have money and who trust the mails. The best list in the U.S.A. for both percentage response and size of donation is the Ruby Red Grapefruit list. This is a list of people who put $40 in the mail and trust the postal system to deliver them a case of quality grapefruit."

It sounds simple. Find Canadians who have money and who trust the mail, send them a letter, and wait for the cheques to pour in. But it is not that simple. The first challenge is to find these elusive people who have money and faith in the postal service. The process of finding them is known in the direct-mail trade as "prospecting." In the summer of 1974, the Conservatives were flat broke, having been crushed by the renascent Trudeau Liberals in the so-called wage-and-price-control election that spring. But Laschinger persuaded the Tory treasury committee to advance him $50,000 to go prospecting. It was enough to enable him to buy lists and to send initial letters to prospects. The response was encouraging; enough money came in to pay for the mailings.

The economics of direct mail are not complicated. The initial mailing to prospects should yield enough revenue to cover the cost of the mailing. Those who do respond with contributions — a 1 per cent response rate is considered good — are put on an active list, known as the "donor file," to be solicited again and again and again. Another mailing goes to a fresh list of prospects. The contributions pay the prospecting costs, the contributors go on the donor file, and the process keeps replicating itself.

In 1984, the year the Mulroney government came to power, the Conservatives — having started from scratch ten years earlier — had 80,000 names on their donor file. They raised $7 million by direct mail that year. Table 3 shows Odell's projections, prepared in late 1983, for the Tories' 1984 direct-mail campaign.

Table 3

Prospecting for New Names

Letters to be sent	2,525,000
Cost of mailings	$1,083,000
Response rate	1%
Average donation	$50
Anticipated gross revenue	$1,262,500
Net Income	$179,500
Names to be added to donor file	25,250

Renewals & General Appeals (donor file)

Letters to be sent (8 mailings)	669,000
Cost of mailings	$545,850
Response rate (range)	18% to 9%*
Average donation (range)	$70 to $58*
Gross revenue	$4,925,230
Net income	$4,379,380

* The rate of response projected for the first mailing to the donor file was 18 per cent, dropping to 9 per cent by the eighth mailing; the average donation was projected to decline from $70 on the first mailing to $58 on the eighth.

In fact, the Tories exceeded Odell's projections, with a net income of $7 million from the direct-mail campaign — or about one-

third of all the money they took in during the 1984 election year.
Direct mail alone produced more than enough money to cover all
the Conservatives' reportable expenses during the official eight-
week election period. (The three major parties were limited to
spending $6,391,497 apiece during the 1984 campaign; the Tories
reported spending $6,388,941.)

The key to successful political fund-raising by direct mail is to
get that crucial first donation. Once an individual has contributed
to a political party, there is a good chance that he or she will
continue to give, year after year — and perhaps several times a year.
Odell finds Canadians give more than Americans. "I think it's more
than just the tax credit. It's also true in non-political activity that
Canadians on an individual basis are more generous than they are
in the United States. They may not make as many contributions
per year — that's the suspicion — but each contribution they make
is on average higher than you would find in the United States."

But Canadians are also more likely than Americans to be influenced in their political giving by trends in the opinion polls. When
a party slips in the polls, its donations decline. Or as Odell puts it,
"The donor base, like the electorate, is much more fluid in Canada.
In other words, the sense of loyalty to party and leader amongst a
broad scale of people out there is much more fluid in Canada than
in the United States."

The array of devices employed by the fund raiser is much the
same in the two countries, however. One is to make individuals
feel that, by making a donation, they are not only supporting the
democratic process, but are also making their voice resonate in the
corridors of power. Another is to reinforce, not challenge, the re-
cipient's preconceptions. A successful direct-mail campaign does not
seek to persuade voters to change their minds on issues or personalities. It preaches to the converted. As Odell says:

> We're going to people who basically agree with us. We benefit
> if we have an enemy. People give against as much as they give
> for. The enemy for us in the Republican party in the 1960s
> was certainly the Kennedys. Now, they might have been at
> 60 per cent in the opinion polls, but with conservative Re-
> publicans all across the country if they weren't at zero, they
> were very close to it. That was our marketplace. It was a straw
> man, but it had to be credible because the donor is very sensitive
> to faults. . . . [Donors] are after the perception that a person is
> bad, and if they can justify that perception by what they see

on television, what they see in the daily newspaper, and if you're buttressing their basic opinion about someone, some policy, some attitude, you'll see the reaction [in donations]. We were able to pillory Jimmy Carter on the Panama Canal issue. Many Republicans who contributed were against giving up the Panama Canal, and they contributed over and over again as long as that issue was alive.

Cynical? Yes. Effective? Undoubtedly.

Equally effective are the tactics fund raisers employ to make contributors believe they are more than just another name at the bottom of a cheque. The tactics are essentially the same whether the solicitation takes the form of a personal call on big-business people by a party bagman in search of a $50,000 donation or a computer-generated "personalized" letter mailed to thousands of strangers in pursuit of $50 contributions.

The "membership ploy" is a particularly effective device. People like to belong to groups, and they are flattered to be asked to join a cause. Credit card companies, such as Diners Club and American Express ("membership has its privileges"), have long exploited the "belonging" instinct. Small contributors to political parties are often given wallet-sized cards attesting to their membership in some otherwise illusory club or organization. The card idea worked in political fund-raising in the United States, so the Tories appropriated it and introduced a PC Canada Fund card. There was a brisk debate among top Conservatives at the time as to whether Canadians would actually donate money on the promise of a meaningless and valueless piece of pasteboard. Terry Yates, who, as chairman of the PC Canada Fund, was the party's chief fund raiser, was one of the doubters — until election night 1979. "We were out in Spruce Grove, Alberta, the night Joe Clark won, and here's this guy walking around the arena, and on his chest he'd pinned his PC Canada card," Yates recalls. "It worked. I nearly died."

For larger contributors, the Tories stole another Republican innovation. The GOP in Ohio had created something called the Early Bird Club, with "membership" reserved for supporters who made donations of $1,000 or more in the first quarter of each year — when all parties experience cash-flow problems. Every year, the Early Birds received a limited-edition print of a specially commissioned painting by a prominent American artist. Many hung the prints proudly in their offices or homes. In Canada, the Conservatives created their equivalent "club" — the 500 Club, so named because the original objective was a membership of five hundred people. Yates commissioned and personally paid for the first two paintings. The idea worked. In fact, it worked so well that, rather than use the device exclusively to raise money early in the year, as the Ohio Republicans did, the Tories turned the 500 Club into a general fund-raising campaign, with "membership" open to any individual who donated $1,000 at any time during the year.

The Tories have added a few bells and whistles that reek of selling privileged access — access to the top people in the party and (since 1984) in the government. Members of the 500 Club are routinely invited to receptions whenever the prime minister and other prominent Tories come to their community. Twice a year, on average, members are invited to Ottawa (at their own expense) for a day-long briefing by key cabinet ministers on the government's plans for dealing with the issues of the day. They also get to hear and to question the prime minister. It is an opportunity for individual contributors to let off steam, to tell the PM and his colleagues what they think the government should be doing. And when they get home, they can tell friends and associates that they have been to the capital, heard the real lowdown, met the prime minister, and given him a piece of their mind.

It is heady stuff. It makes Tories feel very important. For a mere $1,000, they can be insiders. Membership in the 500 Club quickly exceeded the target of five hundred; soon three thousand Conservatives were paying $1,000 — or $3 million a year — for the pleasures and privileges of membership. In the 1988 election year, the 500 Club brought $6 million into Tory coffers. The party did it by peddling privileged access and insider status, and by creating the illusion, at least, that political influence is as close as a supporter's chequebook. Purists may squirm. Conservatives are content.

Most fund-raising gimmicks, large or small, succeed by implying access and influence. At the upper end of the fund-raising game, no corporate chief executive whose firm donates $50,000 to the party in power really believes that his or her generosity empowers him or her to pick up the phone and tell the prime minister to fire the minister of finance. As often as not, however, large contributors do believe that their money buys the right to have their views considered respectfully by those in authority. And they believe that if, for some reason, they need access to the politicians at the top, their financial support will secure that access, if not to the prime minister, certainly to members of his cabinet. (In fact, CEOs of important corporations seldom have trouble gaining access to the ministers of their choice, regardless of whether their firms make political contributions. Bagmen, however, do not go out of their way to point this out when they are soliciting donations.)

"A lot of people give money because they think it will give them some influence," says Hugh Mackenzie, who was chief of staff to Frank Miller, the last Tory premier of Ontario.

> I think that peaked during [David] Peterson's term when the Liberals became quite formal about the process . . . and they started talking about "$1,000 and get to meet a cabinet minister." A lot of people give money, traditionally have given money, because of a perceived influence they have on people in power. . . . Everybody in politics has ears, and the only question is who do they listen to? So one positions himself so that he gets listened to. That doesn't mean you get special privileges because you give money. But the fact is [a donation] puts you in a position where you're known, and gives you an opportunity to express your opinion. But I think anyone would be naive to believe that people who give regularly, and with some generosity, to political parties don't do it so that they'll be in a position to influence the process. And I am one who doesn't believe that in itself is a bad thing. It's a question of how [influence] is used.

At the lower end of the fund-raising game, among prospective small contributors, the illusion of being able to influence the powers that be comes in the form of a questionnaire that accompanies a direct-mail appeal for money — a questionnaire that asks the recipients to give their views on selected subjects for the benefit of the party leadership and policy makers. Such questionnaires are complete frauds. But they can be highly effective. Shortly after he became chairman of the PC Canada Fund, Finlay MacDonald, now a senator, had an argument with Bob Odell about the appropriate letter to send to prospects. Odell proposed a test. They rented a list of 800,000 names, and MacDonald and Odell each wrote a letter to part of the list. MacDonald laughs at the memory:

> Bob said, "You write your letter and I'll write mine." I wrote a letter which was succinct, which was Churchillian, which was magnificent. It didn't bring in enough to cover the cost of stamps. His long letter brought in a piss-pot. I said, "This

is fraudulent." He said, "What's fraudulent?" I said, "This quiz, this questionnaire." He sent the questionnaire to the list — "It is important that you answer these questions because they will be shown in confidence to the leader. One: Do you believe in motherhood? — yes or no. Two: Do you think underprivileged people should have an equal opportunity in life? — yes or no. Three —" and the backroom of the PC Canada Fund was up to its ass in these responses. They were burned. They were never seen by anybody. And they raised $600,000. As a matter of fact, we got a complaint from the direct-mail association because our campaign wasn't up to [their] code. . . .

The next item in the fund raiser's bag of tricks also surprised MacDonald. He was told that he, as chairman of the PC Canada Fund, was expected to send a certificate of appreciation to everyone who contributed money in the direct-mail campaign. And he was to get the leader, Joe Clark, and the party president, then Montreal lawyer Peter Blaikie, to sign the certificate, too. "We were sending a graduation certificate to everybody who'd given to the Conservative party," MacDonald says. "We were thanking them for their magnificent contribution to democracy. 'To John Smith, with sincere thanks for saving democracy and doing such and such and so and so, etc.' I started to vomit. I had to sign this thing — only to find the next time I went to some guy's house, that he'd taken down the magnificent painting over his fireplace. And in its place was one of those appalling little certificates."

Small contributors are not the only ones whose egos can be massaged to advantage. Toronto media entrepreneur (Baton Broadcasting) and sometime Tory fund raiser Douglas Bassett raised money for Larry Grossman in 1985 in the first of two Grossman campaigns for the Ontario Conservative leadership. Bassett approached a leading member of the Toronto Jewish business community whom he figured would be good for a very substantial cheque for Grossman, who is also Jewish. To Bassett's dismay, the businessman, who had probably heard that Grossman was a long shot to beat Frank Miller, offered Bassett $5,000. Thinking quickly, Bassett refused. He said he did not want to embarrass him by accepting such a small donation when one of the man's closest business associates was contributing $50,000. Bassett left empty-handed. The next day, however, a cheque for $35,000 was delivered to his office.

Although the 1974 Election Expenses Act turned a historically secretive activity into at least a semi-transparent one, no political finance legislation, federal or provincial, can eliminate the whispered promises or unspoken undertakings that may be exchanged between bagmen and donors in the course of fund raising. No law short of the Criminal Code — if that — can stamp out bribery and other corrupt practices. But the 1974 legislation, by imposing limits on election spending, made the playing field more level than before. By requiring disclosure of contributions, it made the process open. By providing tax credits to donors, it made political giving both respectable and financially attractive.

The act also opened the doors to an unprecedented flood of money. But politics is an increasingly costly business. Today, the financial demands of national parties are outstripping the ability of their bagmen to find and tap new sources of revenue. What's more, the 1974 law perpetuates the distortion in the political finance system that is created by the concentration of excess funds at the bottom — at the candidate-constituency level — and by the accumulation of deficits at the top, at party headquarters. Surplus money does not move up through the system to enable parties to meet present needs. Witness the fact that Tories, Liberals, and New Democrats all ran deficits at the national party level in 1988, a federal election year. Their combined red ink came to $5,523,126 for the year. Yet their 884 candidates in 1988 reported a combined election surplus of $12,960,141.

Until the legislation is changed to require candidates and their constituency associations to share the wealth and to assist their central parties, the parties will grow weaker, more ineffectual, and less able to function as national institutions in the life of the country.

The Election Expenses Act has also failed to democratize the process of political financing to any important and lasting degree. Fewer than 2 per cent of Canadians contribute to federal parties and candidates in election years. And in non-election years, the proportion of political givers is closer to 1 per cent. Three out of four Canadians care enough about their democracy to exercise their franchise in national elections, but only one in fifty cares enough to support the political process financially.

The signs are not encouraging. The Conservatives, who led the way in broadening their base by importing direct-mail techniques, have reverted to their comfortable old habit of relying on the corporate sector. In 1983, the year before they came to federal office, the Conservatives attracted contributions from a record 99,264 individuals (as opposed to businesses and commercial organizations)

— a record that stood until it was broken by the NDP in the 1988 election year. But since the Tories formed the government in 1984, the number of individual contributors has declined, year after year, while corporate contributions have increased. In 1983, the Tories got 65 per cent of their revenue from individuals and 34 per cent from business. By 1990, the figures were also reversed — 57 per cent from business, 42 per cent from individuals.[4]

Parties in power have to work harder to raise money from small individual contributors; unlike the opposition parties, they cannot invite prospective donors to take a stand against the government or government policies by making a contribution. What is more, big money loves political power; corporate contributions fall into the laps of government parties, assuming, of course, they are free-enterprise parties. The dependence of government parties on the corporate sector — and on such devices as the 500 Club — for their financial well-being raises anew the issue of undue influence. It is an issue that will not go away.

PART THREE

THE FRONTROOM

ALL THE ACTIVITY AND EFFORT IN BACKROOM politics are directed to one end: the advancement of the politicians in the frontroom — to help them secure a nomination, to get elected, to win a leadership convention. Normally, frontroom politicians are grateful for the help. Once in a while, however, they wonder. . . .

Joe Clark's decision to put his job on the line at a Conservative leadership convention in 1983 created a frenzy in Tory backrooms. Across the country, prospective candidates, strategists, organizers, and fund raisers huddled in dozens of secret meetings. One particularly conspiratorial group convened in Toronto in early February 1983, determined to persuade William Davis, then premier of Ontario, to contest the federal leadership. Security was tight for the meeting, which took place in the office of the Ontario Tories' top bagman, Bill Kelly. To avoid leaks, the meeting did not begin until after the secretarial staff had left for the day. Then the whisky was poured, the cigars were lighted, and the plotting began. But unknown to the conspirators, the air-conditioning in the office tower was turned off at the end of the working day. The cigars set off the smoke alarms, and the secret deliberations came to a rude halt when twenty firemen in full equipment suddenly burst into Kelly's office.

Davis thought better of being a candidate.

10. CAN YOU HELP ME GET ELECTED?

"Ambition is what makes the whole process go, ambition and timing. You don't have ten times to [run] in your lifetime."
— Liberal John Rae, leadership campaign manager to Jean Chrétien

It was 1972 and the hall in Burin, Newfoundland, was packed to the rafters for the election-campaign appearance of Newfoundland's favorite son, patronage boss, and orator extraordinaire, Don Jamieson, then transport minister in the Trudeau Liberal government in Ottawa.

Jamieson was in full oratorical flight when a heckler at the back of the hall, a huge fisherman — tall, heavy, muscular — opened up.

"Liar!" he shouted.

Jamieson kept talking.

"I said you're a liar!"

Jamieson ignored him.

"You're all liars," the man bellowed.

At this point, a backroom assistant to Jamieson, David MacNaughton, decided it was time to go to his candidate's assistance. He went over to the heckler and, in his most diplomatic manner, said: "Excuse me, sir, but I work for the minister and maybe you'd care to speak with him after the meeting. I can arrange it."

MacNaughton, now a public-affairs consultant and lobbyist, laughs at the memory. "He was a big son of a bitch and he looked down at me and said: 'Fuck you.' Then he grabbed me by the back of the neck and he picked me up — literally, he picked me up right off the ground. I was up in the air. And he takes me out back and tries to beat the shit out of me. I had to get three guys to pull him off." Meanwhile Jamieson continued his speech without missing a beat. Later, he gave his helpful young aide a lecture. "Look, I didn't mind the god-damned heckling," Jamieson said. "But what was really distressing for everyone was to see you up in the air with your legs going like crazy and this guy hauling you out back."

People like MacNaughton who labor in the backrooms of politics do not often encounter physical abuse or public humiliation in the line of duty. In fact, they usually steer clear of public political events, or else they linger well back on the fringes of the crowd where they can observe without being observed. They value their anonymity. They are not in politics for the recognition or the glory — there is no Place Keith Davey in Ottawa nor even a tiny Norman Atkins Parkette in Toronto. Backroom workers are not in it for the money — most are volunteers who take time away from paying jobs to work in a campaign; only a relative handful ever get patronage appointments. They are in it for a bouillabaisse of motives — loyalty to a cause, faith in a party, belief in a leader or some other frontroom politician, a desire to serve, or a yen to experience the thrill of the combat. In many cases, they are in it for the simple reason that someone came to them and uttered the six most seductive words in the political lexicon: Can you help me get elected?

Helping people get elected is what backroom politics is all about. Three campaigns are described in this chapter. One was a municipal election, one federal, and one provincial. John Laschinger was campaign director or strategist in each. The three campaigns all presented the same challenges: to assess the candidate's strengths and weaknesses; to identify the obstacles to his or her election; to determine the opponents' weaknesses and figure out how to exploit them; to draft the strategy; to assemble the organization; to run the campaign; and to win the contest. Two of the campaigns followed their strategic plans, and were successful. The third, in Newfoundland, failed when key strategic advice was not implemented. But the essential elements were the same. Municipal, federal, or provincial — it is all part of the same game of politics.

June Rowlands for Mayor

June Rowlands wanted to be mayor of Toronto in 1991. At least, she assumed she wanted to be mayor. She was one of those politicians who seek public office without any clear sense of what they want to do with power once they have it. If Rowlands had a vision for Toronto, she did not share it. If she harbored hopes and dreams, they were never evident to the members of her campaign organization. When asked why she wanted to be mayor, she would reply by listing the problems — from high property taxes to crime in the streets — that she saw facing the city of Toronto. She wanted to solve those problems, she would say. How did she propose to solve them? If she knew, she did not say.

Rowlands was no dream candidate for a campaign manager. A sixty-seven-year-old grandmother, she was too old, too dated in her thinking, and unable to comprehend the demographic changes that had transformed Toronto since the Second World War from the WASP bastion of Canada into a multicultural mosaic in which Anglo-Saxons found themselves no longer the commanding ethnic group. She seemed oblivious to the needs and feelings of minority groups. Even her supporters wondered whether she had ever met a police officer whose word she would not take on the spot in preference to the word of a black crime suspect.

Her assets were her name, her experience, her proven ability to win white middle-class votes, and the monied coalition of downtown business leaders and lawyers, some of them involved in the real estate development industry, who put their financial and organizational muscle behind her. Their motives were not selfless. They feared that Toronto would be a less congenial place for business, especially for developers, if the other principal candidate, Jack Layton, running on the New Democratic Party ticket, became mayor.

To these big backers, Rowlands was a safe candidate. A rightwing Liberal, she could count many Conservatives among her supporters. She had been a member of Toronto City Council from 1976 to 1988; for half that time she was the council's budget chief, distinguishing herself by holding civic spending down during the recession of 1981–82. In early 1988, having retired from elected politics, Rowlands was appointed by the then Liberal government of Ontario to a three-year term as chairman of the Metro Police Services Board, the commission that oversees the six-thousand-member police force of Metropolitan Toronto.

As head of the police board, she developed a genuine concern about crime and violence, along with the conviction that black youths were responsible for a disproportionate amount of Toronto's crime, especially drug-related offences. And when Rowlands thought something, she had a habit of saying it, without considering the consequences of her words. Her candor was her strength, but it was also her weakness. As she was to put it to a public meeting sponsored by the Jamaican-Canadian Association during the mayoral election: "If you take a look at the major-crime sheets every morning, you will get a very clear impression that the number of black youths that are creating problems is out of proportion to the size of the population of the black community in this city. Now that happens to be the truth."

Her views did not sit well with the NDP, which defeated David Peterson's Liberals in 1990. The new premier, Bob Rae, decided not to renew Rowlands's appointment when her term expired in early 1991. Her replacement was a young Chinese-Canadian lawyer, Susan Eng. Within weeks, an upset Rowlands announced she was going to run for mayor, to succeed Arthur Eggleton, who was retiring after eleven unremarkable years in the city's top job.

At another time, or under other circumstances, Rowlands's candidacy might have been stillborn. When she made her announcement in May 1991, six months before the election, she had no money, no organization, and no strategy. The next month, she retained John Laschinger as her campaign manager, although he had never run a campaign at the municipal level before. Her supporters on Bay Street started raising money, and Laschinger hired a Liberal polling firm, Goldfarb Consultants, to do her polling.

The Rowlands strategists knew her performance as city budget chief would work to her advantage against Layton, who carried the image of being a free-spending radical at a time when Toronto and the country were caught in a deep recession. They also knew that the views of their candidate — "Mummy Cop," as the cynics called her — were not nearly as unpopular among the sort of Torontonians who take the trouble to vote in municipal elections as the news media thought they were. Her reputation, from her police-board days, as a hardliner on law and order would win her more votes than it would lose her.

Rowlands, however, would be weak on issues where Layton would be strong, including housing and the environment, which are always good NDP causes. But if Layton wanted to win, he was going to have demonstrate that, as mayor, he would be able to work with business leaders, that he would help recession-crippled small business, and that he could get along with the police. These were the strategy assumptions of the Rowlands backroom from the beginning.

With the election due in November, Martin Goldfarb produced his first poll in the fourth week of July:

Table 1

Popular Support (%) for Toronto Mayoral Candidates, July 1991

June Rowlands	40
Jack Layton	34
Susan Fish	21
Betty Disero[1]	5

SOURCE: Goldfarb Consultants

Although the six-point lead was a narrow one, it gave Laschinger room to manoeuvre. The Rowlands strategy was the classic front-runner strategy: always consolidate; always emphasize the issues that are most important to existing supporters; do not dilute the effort by trying to appeal to supporters of other candidates.

Because he was trailing, Layton should have followed the opposite strategy: do not worry about consolidating existing support; concentrate on expanding the base by emphasizing issues that will attract additional support. Layton failed to do it. He tried, inexplicably, to campaign as though he were the front-runner. He directed his campaign effort to the people who were already supporting him (and who had nowhere else to go); he failed to broaden his base; he made no attempt to show that he could work with business-community leaders, small businessmen, and the police. His strategy was a fatal miscalculation.

In his July poll, Goldfarb asked respondents what they thought was the most pressing problem that would face the new mayor. He then asked them what they thought was the second-most pressing problem. Consolidated under broad headings, the responses looked like this:

Table 2

Most Pressing Issue (%)
(first and second responses combined)

Economy and taxes	35
Housing	34
Environment	27
Safety and security	25

SOURCE: Goldfarb Consultants

Goldfarb broke the responses down into considerable detail. Rowlands had a slight lead in the electorate's assessment of who could best create jobs and keep taxes down, and a wide lead in controlling drugs and crime, and in working with the police. Layton had a large lead in dealing with the environment, representing the poor and the disadvantaged, and increasing the supply of affordable housing.

A closer look at Goldfarb's numbers shows how the voters perceived the two main candidates in July and again in October, a month before the election.

Table 3

Which candidate is best at . . .

	Late July		Mid-October	
	Rowlands	Layton	Rowlands	Layton
Creating jobs	13%	11%	41%	21%
Keeping taxes down	14	10	41	17
Controlling crime	27	9	50	21
Controlling drugs	22	11	Not asked	
Working with police	33	8	Not asked	
Dealing with environment	12	22	25	38
Increasing affordable housing	10	33	25	45
Representing poor and disadvantaged	12	31	27	46
Working with racial minorities	14	21	29	37

SOURCE: Goldfarb Consultants

When they reviewed the July numbers, Rowlands's strategists were worried by the narrowness of her support. She was strong on law and order, had a shaky lead on economic and tax issues, and was weak on all other fronts. Goldfarb proposed opening an ad-

ditional front — education. Others suggested she widen her range
of issues to include health, poverty, and other social concerns. Laschinger refused. Rowlands had no public identification with education and, given her tendency to speak without thinking, was
likely to shoot herself in the foot if she tried to campaign on social
issues with which she was unfamiliar.

The numbers drove her strategy. The numbers said Rowlands
was leading. The strategy was to keep her there by protecting and
consolidating her base; unlike Layton, she did not need to attract
new support to win. The challenge was to keep the campaign tightly
focused on law and order and economy/taxes to the exclusion of
all other issues. There would be no new front.

Between July and October, Rowlands consolidated her advantage
over Layton on law-and-order issues and widened her narrow July
lead on issues of the economy and taxation. Layton failed to expand
his base because he did not establish any credentials of his own for
being able to stimulate economic growth, curb property-tax increases, or combat crime. Rather than try to demonstrate that he
would be a responsible, prudent mayor, he unveiled policies on
thirty issues — policies he acknowledged might cost Toronto taxpayers $1 billion to implement.

As the news media saw the contest, the only burning issue in an
otherwise boring campaign was Rowlands's views on matters of
race and crime. Following Rowlands's suggestion to the Jamaican-
Canadian Association that young blacks were responsible for a disproportionate amount of major crime, a third candidate, Susan Fish,
denounced her as a racist. Layton declared Rowlands unfit to hold
office.

The public, however, did not see it that way. As shown in the
bottom line of Table 3, in July, Layton had a 21–14 lead over
Rowlands on the question of the candidates' ability to work with
racial minorities. The spread in October, following her comments
to the Jamaican-Canadian Association, was about the same (37–29).

Goldfarb's numbers talked more loudly than the ugly words that
were traded on the hustings. As her strategists saw it, the voters
who were going to make June Rowlands mayor did not care whether
she sounded like a racist. The more her opponents, and the press,
raised the spectre of racism, the more it solidified her strength on
the law-and-order side of the ledger. The spectre of racism did not
make Mummy Cop mayor of Toronto, but it did not impede her
pursuit of the office.

She polled fifty thousand more votes than Layton. She had started with a small lead and built it into an election-day margin of nearly two to one. She did it by following a carefully thought-out strategy that resisted the temptation to try to soften her views or make her candidacy more attractive to a larger number of voters. It was a consolidation strategy that turned her perceived liabilities — especially her controversial opinions on matters involving race and law and order — into assets by using them to reinforce her core support. Rowlands was the first municipal candidate in Toronto history to run such a tightly controlled, focused, strategic campaign.[2]

David MacDonald for MP

In August 1988, Laschinger got the kind of telephone call that backroom politicians learn to expect. "Lasch, I'm in trouble," said David MacDonald, would-be Conservative candidate in Toronto's Rosedale riding. "We've only got two weeks left until the nominating convention, and we found out last night when we handed in all the memberships we've sold that Doug McCutcheon's outsold us by a couple of hundred. Can you give me a hand?"

MacDonald was not an ordinary candidate for a nomination in an ordinary riding. Then fifty-two years old, he was a United Church clergyman who had represented a Prince Edward Island riding in Parliament for fifteen years. A Red Tory, he was known for several things: his courage in opposing the Trudeau government's use of the War Measures Act during the 1970 FLQ crisis in Quebec; his commitment to the causes of world peace and Third World development; and his loyalty to Robert Stanfield and Joe Clark when they were leaders of the Conservative party. MacDonald was secretary of state and minister of communications in Clark's cabinet in 1979. After losing his P.E.I. seat in the 1980 election, MacDonald was made co-ordinator of Canadian famine relief and, later, Canadian ambassador to Ethiopia. When he decided in 1988 to seek the Tory nomination, he knew he had some hurdles to surmount. He had been out of the country for most of the previous four years. He had lived and worked in P.E.I. and in Ottawa, but never in Toronto. As a Clark loyalist, he could not expect any help from Prime Minister Mulroney or from Tory party headquarters. Although Rosedale had no objections to Red Tories (one of the species, David Crombie, the former mayor of Toronto, having held the seat for ten years), it liked to know that whoever it sent to Ottawa would be welcomed into the cabinet — as were Crombie and his predecessors in Rosedale, Liberal Donald S. Macdonald and Conservative David Walker. To the voters of Rosedale, partisan affiliation was less important than political clout. And given MacDonald's status as an outsider in the Mulroney party, there was no guarantee that he would be welcomed into a Mulroney cabinet.[3]

Giving MacDonald a "hand" in August 1988 meant finding a way for him to win the Rosedale nomination even though he had been out-campaigned in the vital first phase — recruiting supporters by selling party memberships. It also meant, Laschinger knew, taking on the assignment as a favor for a old friend, without a fee. He agreed to meet MacDonald and his main organizers the following evening.

Name recognition was important in Rosedale. There were three candidates, and all were well-known. Douglas McCutcheon, son of the late Conservative senator Wallace McCutcheon, a Bay Street financier who became a Diefenbaker cabinet minister, was the right-wing candidate. He drew his support from the wealthy north end of the riding. Nancy Jackman, sister of Hal Jackman, one of Canada's wealthiest men, who became lieutenant-governor of Ontario in 1991, had her roots in the north but most of her support came from the high-rise and working-class areas south of Bloor Street. A feminist, she was firmly identified with the poor and the disaffected. For the most part, her supporters were not traditional Tories; many had joined the party only to support her. David MacDonald's support was spread — thinly — across the riding. But because all three candidates enjoyed high recognition, the impression that they made, favorable or unfavorable, at the nominating convention might well prove decisive.

MacDonald needed a combination of good organization and sound strategic planning. It was the organization's job to overcome McCutcheon's advantage in memberships sold by making sure that a higher proportion of MacDonald supporters than McCutcheon supporters turned out for the nomination. The organization did its job; although McCutcheon had sold 200 more memberships, his lead on the first ballot was a mere five votes — thanks to two leaders of Toronto's Filipino community, Tony Cruz and Dr. Francisco Portugal, who delivered a bloc of 150 new Tory party members to vote for MacDonald.

Laschinger directed his strategic planning to the speech that MacDonald would make prior to the voting. He was helped by Susan Fish, later to be a mayoral candidate in Toronto, and Keith Norton who, like Fish, had been a cabinet minister in the Bill Davis

Ontario government. There was a crucial difference between MacDonald's nomination campaign and the June Rowlands mayoralty campaign. Rowlands was the front-runner from the outset; her campaign strategy concentrated on consolidating her support and reinforcing her lead. A similar strategy would have been fatal for David MacDonald. In the close Rosedale nomination race, the worst mistake he could have made would have been to adopt a Rowlands-style front-runner strategy by addressing his nomination speech to his own supporters to the exclusion of other delegates whose votes he would need as the balloting proceeded. Paul Hellyer's speech at the national Tory leadership convention in 1976, the one that chose Clark, was a notorious example of that kind of mistake. Hellyer railed against Red Tories and other progressives in the party. His right-wing supporters were delighted, but the speech destroyed his leadership chances by alienating more moderate delegates.

McCutcheon made the Hellyer mistake. He delivered a stridently right-wing, free-enterprise speech that left his own supporters cheering wildly and the MacDonald and Jackman delegates sitting resolutely on their hands.

MacDonald, in contrast, spoke as much to Nancy Jackman's supporters as to his own. He talked about several issues of concern to the Jackman group, including AIDS, poverty, the homeless, and the environment, earning some applause from Jackman supporters in response. The 150 Filipino-Canadians cheered wildly, although no one was sure how much, if any, of MacDonald's remarks they understood. Jackman finished third on the first ballot and was eliminated, leaving McCutcheon and MacDonald (who was just five votes behind) to fight it out on the second ballot. About half of Jackman's supporters, having no further interest in the proceedings, left after the first-ballot results were announced. Those who remained went heavily to MacDonald, as he defeated McCutcheon by fifty-one votes on the second ballot. The outcome could have been the reverse, if McCutcheon's organization had succeeded in getting out his vote, and if he had thought to pitch his appeal to the delegates whose votes he would need on the second ballot.

Laschinger also managed MacDonald's campaign in the general election that fall. It was a desperately close affair in Rosedale — the closest in the country — and it turned on the issue of free trade. As a Tory candidate, MacDonald supported the Canada–U.S. Free Trade Agreement that Mulroney and U.S. president Ronald Reagan had signed in January 1988. But he knew that, as a parachute candidate facing an established Liberal opponent (Bill Graham, a university professor who had been working the riding since being defeated in the 1984 election), he faced plenty of obstacles, without also having to contend with free trade. And, like Canadians elsewhere, most Rosedaleans did not like the trade deal. In fact, they were downright surly about it. Laschinger's pollster, John Mykytyshyn, asked Rosedale voters to identify the most important problem facing Canada and to rate the Mulroney government's handling of that problem. This, it will be recalled, was in a riding that had been solidly and unrepentantly Tory for a decade:

Table 4

Issues — Rosedale, September 1988

Free trade	34%
Environment	22
Economy	8
Housing	8
Other issues	28

Government Handling of Most Important Issue

Excellent job	2%
Good job	7
Fair job	39
Poor job	50

SOURCE: John Mykytyshyn

Although Mykytyshyn found that only 37 per cent of respondents in Rosedale supported the free-trade agreement compared to 52 per cent who opposed it, Laschinger strongly advised MacDonald that the worst thing he could do as a high-profile Conservative would be to waffle on the campaign's most important issue. Voters will vote for politicians with whom they disagree, but they will not vote for politicians who appear to be unsure or vacillating on issues that the voters believe to be important. Laschinger told MacDonald that he should be aggressive in his support of the trade agreement and hope that voters would give him credit for his conviction, if not for his position. This strategy also played to two groups within the poll sample — probable and soft Tory voters — who were, Mykytyshyn found, neutral or mildly positive on the trade agreement. These were the voters whose support MacDonald needed most urgently. He concentrated on them, stood by free trade, and, for all practical purposes, wrote off voters who were opposed to the agreement.

The strategy worked — barely. After three recounts, MacDonald was declared elected by just 80 votes — 22,704 to 22,624. He needed all the help he got in that campaign.

Tom Rideout for Premier

Brian Peckford always trusted his nose. He was premier of Newfoundland from 1979 until he retired undefeated ten years later. Every three years, he would go around the province, sniffing the political breezes, then call John Laschinger in Toronto to tell him he thought it was time to have an election. Laschinger, playing it safe, would commission a poll, but Peckford's nose was always right.

Tom Rideout, who succeeded Peckford as Newfoundland Conservative leader in 1989, did not have the Peckford nose. He wanted to secure his own mandate from the people but was not sure whether it would be safe to call an election. He asked Laschinger, who had run his campaign for the leadership, to arrange to have a poll taken.

It looked as though Rideout would not be needing much help from Laschinger or anyone else. The poll seemed too good to be true — and it was, as events were to prove. Allan Gregg's Decima Research conducted the poll in the last week of March 1989. It found that Rideout's Tories had a huge lead over the Liberals under Clyde Wells — 52 per cent to 31. Thanks to a computerized permanent voters' list (eliminating the need for door-to-door enumeration), Newfoundland's elections are the shortest in Canada, just three weeks. There was no way, surely, that the Liberals could overcome a twenty-one-point deficit in twenty-one days.

Most prominent Newfoundland Tories urged Rideout to call an election without delay. There was some bad economic news that could not long be withheld from the people. The state of the provincial economy was worsening daily; Ottawa was poised to make changes in the unemployment insurance system that would enrage Newfoundlanders by reducing protection for seasonal workers, such as fishermen; a long postponement in the development of the Hibernia offshore petroleum reserves was becoming inevitable. And there was that irresistible twenty-one-point lead in the Decima poll.

Laschinger and Rideout hesitated, however. They phoned Gregg in Toronto. Gregg remembers the warning he gave them:

I said I have seen the exact same data with John Turner [in the 1984 federal election] and Bill Vander Zalm [in B.C., in 1986], and it can go either way. With Turner, what he failed to understand was that he had to be seen as an agent of change and to run against the past — and against Trudeau, very particularly. And exactly the same condition was there with Vander Zalm. Exactly. [British Columbians] were completely and utterly turned off on the incumbent [William Bennett], but they were prepared to extend the benefit of the doubt to a new guy. But as soon as there was evidence that the benefit of the doubt was misplaced, they would turn on you. I remember saying [to Rideout] they'll shed the Tory party the way a snake sheds its skin if you don't [run against the past]. But Rideout was congenitally unable to run against the party — as was Turner — whereas Bill Vander Zalm had no qualms whatsoever. The campaign slogan we developed for Vander Zalm was, "For a fresh start to B.C., vote Socred." That was as outrageous as the one we did in Nova Scotia — "Vote John Buchanan and the New PCs." There was not a new thing there. There was not a new person, not a new idea. But it worked. Newfoundland could have been saved. It really could have. The guy there [Rideout] just couldn't do it.

Rideout ignored Gregg's warning and called the election. By the mid-point of the three-week campaign, it looked like smartest thing he had ever done. Decima took another poll and reported that the Tory lead had *increased* to twenty-six percentage points. The party leaders debated on television, and the pundits solemnly agreed: advantage Rideout. Yet, on April 20, 1989, the people of Newfoundland and Labrador went to the polls and elected Clyde Wells and a majority Liberal government.

Table 5

Newfoundland, 1989

| | Decima Polls | | Election (April 20) | |
	March 27–28	April 8–9	Pop. Vote	Seats
PC	52%	58%	48%	21
Lib.	31	32	47	31
NDP	11	5	5	0
No Opinion	6	6	—	—

Note: April poll numbers do not add to 100 because of rounding.

How could certain victory become crushing defeat? How could a lead of twenty-six points disappear in eleven or twelve days?

The clues are in the first Decima poll, the one on which Rideout made his decision to call the election. Gregg asked Newfoundlanders whether, on the one hand, they thought the Conservative government would stay much the same with Rideout replacing Peckford, or whether, on the other hand, they thought the selection of Rideout would mean a new approach to government in Newfoundland. Only 40 per cent thought there would be a new approach; 56 per cent thought the government would stay the same (4 per cent had no opinion). Yet 76 per cent of the respondents had negative views of the performance of the Peckford government, rating it either fair (44 per cent) or poor (32 per cent). Probing deeper, Gregg found that 59 per cent agreed with the suggestion that the Peckford government had started off well enough ten years earlier, but that its performance had worsened in its final couple of years.

It was clear to Gregg that Newfoundlanders were unhappy with the government Peckford had given them towards the end, that they wanted a different kind of government, and that because Rideout was seen as being much the same as Peckford, they could not achieve change by voting Conservative. Rideout should not have called an election unless he was prepared to present himself as an agent of change by campaigning against the Peckford government (of which Rideout himself had been a part). If Rideout was unwilling to do that, no amount of help from pollsters and strategists would save him.

While Decima was polling the province, Laschinger had John Mykytyshyn tracking eight swing ridings. The Tories' chances, he found, fell apart on April 16, just four days before the voting. On that day, the Conservative lead began to slip away in the eight ridings. Also on that day, Mykytyshyn detected a steep climb in the proportion of voters who regarded Rideout as being a political clone of Peckford. If, earlier, they had been prepared to give the new premier the benefit of the doubt, they no longer were. The "sameness" factor that Gregg had reported in his province-wide poll before the election call was suddenly being translated into voting intention — and the intention was to vote Liberal to achieve change. As Gregg had warned, Newfoundlanders shed the Tory party the way a snake sheds its skin.

Rideout's miscalculation changed the course of Canadian history. Along with the prime minister and the other nine premiers, Peckford had signed the Meech Lake constitutional accord in 1987 and the Newfoundland House of Assembly had approved it. The Wells government reopened consideration of the accord, something a Rideout government would never have done. In June 1990, fourteen months after his stunning victory, Clyde Wells killed the Meech Lake accord by not letting it come to a vote in the Assembly. Wells, the man who might never have been premier — if Rideout had been able to cast himself as an agent for change — precipitated a national constitutional crisis.

11. SO YOU WANT TO BE LEADER

Party leadership is the prize at the end of the political rainbow. Few people enter public life planning to spend their careers as backbenchers. Not many are so well adjusted or so realistic about their own capabilities that they go into politics thinking that they will be doing very well to spend a few years in a cabinet portfolio before coming home to the family shoe store or to their old teaching job at the high school.

Most people do not burn with an ambition to be leader when they enter politics, but the idea is there, lurking in the back of their minds. As they see their peers climb the political ladder, they start to dream. Who knows, maybe some day, with a few breaks, they, too, could be the leader of their party. And maybe, with a few more breaks, they could be even prime minister or premier. And why should they not dream? Look at the calibre of some of the individuals who have made it to the top, they tell themselves. If those people can do it, why not . . . ?

Ambition is an insidious thing. Some of the dreamers reach for the prize. A majority fail to grasp it, but their failure does not discourage others from trying. Newspaper morgues are full of the names of politicians whose ambition exceeded their grasp, who reached for leadership they could never attain. At the federal level alone, it is a roll call of futility: Donald Fleming. Alvin Hamilton.

Michael Starr. Wallace McCutcheon. Paul Hellyer. Allan Mac-Eachen. Joe Greene. Frank Howard. Jack Horner. Pat Nowlan. Sinclair Stevens. Jim Gillies. Heward Grafftey. David Crombie. Michael Wilson. Peter Pocklington. John Munro. Gene Whelan. John Roberts. Mark MacGuigan. Simon de Jong. Ian Waddell. John Nunziata. These were not fringe or nuisance candidates. All were serious politicians. All wanted to be leader. None, realistically, had a chance of ever making it. And none would be content until he had made the attempt, regardless of the cost to health, emotions, and his family's financial security and well-being. For too many of them, the costs were greater than the prize. (See Appendix B for a full list of leadership-convention results, federal and provincial, from 1967 to 1992.)

It was six weeks after the dramatic Progressive Conservative leadership convention of 1983. Brian Mulroney had defeated Joe Clark on the fourth ballot. John Crosbie was eliminated when he finished third on the third ballot. Still smarting from the defeat, Crosbie's campaign manager, John Laschinger, was invited to a dinner party where the host seated him next to a Mrs. Dawson, who had been a voting delegate at the convention. Laschinger asked her how she had voted.

MRS. DAWSON: I voted for Mike Wilson because he's from Ontario, as I am. Besides, Mulroney was just too slick — I didn't trust him. Clark's a wimp, and Crosbie couldn't speak French.
LASCHINGER: I see. What did you do on the second ballot?
MRS. DAWSON: I voted for Crosbie.
LASCHINGER: Great, but what about his lack of French?
MRS. DAWSON: Well, I didn't trust Mulroney at all, and Clark was a wimp.
LASCHINGER: What about the third ballot?
MRS. DAWSON: Oh, I voted for Joe Clark.
LASCHINGER: Why? Crosbie was still on the third ballot.
MRS. DAWSON: I know, but during the break between the second and third votes, I stood on the floor in front of Clark's seats and I felt so sorry for him and his wife. And besides, Mulroney was so untrustworthy.
LASCHINGER: And you voted for Clark on the fourth ballot?
MRS. DAWSON: Oh, no. I voted for Mulroney!
LASCHINGER: What? I thought you said you couldn't trust him.

MRS. DAWSON: That's right. But Clark was such a wimp!

Four votes cast for four different candidates on four ballots! If it is not megalomania or blinding ambition, what is it that persuades politicians to expose themselves to the vicissitudes of leadership campaigns and the eccentricities of convention delegates? If they knew what they were getting into, most of them would recoil from the idea of running for leadership. Some do not know what to expect. Others, who do know, run anyway. They are the masochists.

There are two hard truths that prospective leadership candidates must learn before they decide to take the plunge. The first is that people will lie to them. It is a national characteristic: Canadians do not like to disappoint people. Anyone with leadership aspirations has to expect that convention delegates (even ones they think of as friends and devoted supporters) will look them in the eye and declare: "I'm with you all the way." They would swear it on a bible. Then they go to the polling booth and vote for someone else. It is known as the "Flora Syndrome" — after Flora MacDonald, who ran a spirited, populist, and, in the end, cruelly disappointing campaign for the Conservative leadership in 1976, the convention that chose Joe Clark. Hundreds of Tories told MacDonald that they admired her, that they thought it was time the Conservatives had a woman leader, and that they would be voting for her. On the day of the voting, more delegates were wearing her buttons than the buttons of any other candidate. Her workers counted 283 delegates with "Flora" buttons enter the polling booths for the first ballot; only 214 votes came out. MacDonald finished sixth, and the experience left her feeling betrayed.

When campaign managers calculate first-ballot support, they have to allow for a "lie factor." Its size will depend on such things as

Table 1

The Lie Factor

Newfoundland — Brian Peckford, 1979	16%
Ontario — Larry Grossman, 1985 (2 campaigns)	10
British Columbia — Bud Smith, 1986	20
Newfoundland — Tom Rideout, 1989	16
Nova Scotia — Tom McInnis, 1991	25

the prominence and strength of the candidate, the type of campaign the candidate has run, the closeness of the race, and so on. By comparing pledges of support with first-ballot results, Laschinger calculated the "lie factor" in six of the provincial leadership campaigns that he has run.

The second hard truth is that candidates can expect financial trouble. Unless they are so wealthy that they can write a personal cheque to pay off their campaign debts — and few politicians have that kind of money — they can expect to be hounded by creditors if they lose. Money behaves just like an uncommitted delegate. It tries to go with the winner. A successful candidate usually manages to raise enough during and after the campaign to cover his or her expenditures. Losing candidates are not so lucky. They almost always find themselves in debt. The 1976 Tory leadership race was the first that gave the public a clear glimpse of the financial burden that goes with defeat.

Table 2

PC Leadership Candidates' Reports, 1976

Candidate	Contributions	Expenditures	Vote on 1st Ballot
Joe Clark	$ 157,897	$ 168,353	277
John Fraser	54,542	116,107	127
James Gillies	133,913	192,847	87
Heward Grafftey	40,442	83,845	33
Paul Hellyer	81,957	287,786	231
Flora MacDonald	126,319	152,704	214
Brian Mulroney*	250,000 (est.)	500,000 (est.)	357
Patrick Nowlan	26,931	58,635	86
Richard Quittenton**	4,541	9,336	0
Sinclair Stevens	114,064	294,106	82
Claude Wagner	163,860	266,538	531
Total:	$1,154,466	$2,130,257	

* Mulroney refused to file a financial statement, as required by the party.
** Quittenton withdrew the day before the voting, too late to get his name off the ballot.

The candidates had accumulated $1 million in debts chasing a job that paid less than one-tenth of that amount. By today's measure, the 1976 figures seem puny. In the 1990 Liberal leadership campaign, for example, the top two candidates, Jean Chrétien and Paul Martin, both spent more than $2.4 million (how much more is not known because, under the Liberals' lax rules, candidates were not required to report all classes of expenditure). In other words, Chrétien and Martin each spent more than all eleven Tory candidates combined had spent fourteen years earlier. Or, to look at it another way, the five Liberal candidates in 1990 spent a total of $5.9 million, just $900,000 less than the Liberal Party of Canada spent on its national campaign in the 1988 general election.

Pledges of contributions are often forgotten after a leadership race has been run and lost (which is why smart bagmen make sure they collect all of their candidates' pledges — and get the cheques to the bank — before the voting begins). New financial angels are all but impossible for a defeated candidate to find. Pursuing an impossible dream of leadership can cause a politician years of financial hardship.

John Crosbie raised $1.3 million in 1983 and spent $1.8 million. It took his Newfoundland cronies Frank Ryan and Basil Dobbin a full year of begging and arm twisting to raise enough to clear the debt. In his ultimately unsuccessful struggle to retain his leadership, Joe Clark spent at least $1.9 million — more than ten times as much as he had spent to win the job in the first place seven years earlier. The 1983 campaign left Clark with a debt that dogged him for the next few years. Donald Johnston spent $1.2 million in futile pursuit of the Liberal leadership in 1984, but, even with his big-business contacts in Montreal, managed to raise only $900,000. Paul Martin came out of the 1990 Liberal leadership convention with a second-place finish and a debt rumored to be in the range of $1 million. Michael Harris had to mortgage his home in North Bay to keep his campaign for the leadership of the Ontario Conservative leadership alive in 1989. When he won, enough money came in to pay off the $40,000 mortgage. For Tom McInnis in Nova Scotia, however, it was a different story. He put up $20,000 of his own money to get his campaign going for the Nova Scotia Tory leadership in 1991. When he lost, McInnis was broke. He had a friend write a $10,000 cheque to pay his campaign strategist after the convention. It bounced.

Most politicians who are contemplating running for their party's leadership know the campaign will not be easy. Few, however, anticipate the exceptional stress to which they and their families will be subjected. Some candidates find it more than they can bear and they crack under the pressure. One leadership aspirant fell completely apart; his wife was devastated to find him in bed with a young boy. Brian Mulroney's bout with depression and alcohol following his leadership defeat by Joe Clark in 1976 — his bitterness made deeper by distress over his $250,000 campaign debt — is detailed by author-journalist John Sawatsky in *Mulroney: The Politics of Ambition*.[1] Claude Wagner was never the same after his failure to win that same convention. In 1978, he accepted a Senate appointment from the Liberal government and died the following year, a broken man. Robert Winters, who ran second to Pierre Trudeau in 1968, refused to join the new leader's cabinet, abandoned public life, and died suddenly not long after. Richard Quittenton, the quixotic candidate who ran for the Tory leadership in 1976 only to pull out on the eve of the voting, was fired as president of St. Clair College in Windsor by the college's NDP-controlled board of directors. Both John Fraser and Flora MacDonald took many months to bounce back after their defeats at that 1976 convention, as did Jean Chrétien after he lost the Liberal leadership to John Turner in 1984.

Preparing a candidate's family for defeat is not normally the job of a campaign manager, but the responsibility sometimes falls to him. Laschinger remembers walking down a concrete corridor in the Pacific Convention Centre during the 1991 B.C. Social Credit leadership convention with his arms around the shoulders of candidate Norman Jacobsen's two youngsters. He talked to them about the possibility that their father would lose, what it meant, and how they should respond to defeat. Eleven-year-old Torre Jacobsen took it all in and declared, resolutely, that regardless of the outcome, he was very proud of his dad. One hour later, however, the results of the first ballot were announced, and sobs racked the boy's body as he saw his father eliminated from the race.

The unwritten rules of the game change when politicians decide to become leadership candidates. They lose their privacy and their freedom to be themselves. Even their clothing and their personal idiosyncrasies come under a microscrope.

When Robert Stanfield won the Conservative leadership in 1967

— at the first big American-style convention in Canada — he had been premier of Nova Scotia for eleven years. He was his province's most popular politician since Joseph Howe. He was nationally known and universally respected. He reeked of integrity. What was good enough for Nova Scotia, however, would not do at all for national politics and national media exposure. To start with, there were his clothes. Stanfield in those days favored suits of dark blue and dark grey, colors that made him appear even more gaunt than he was, emphasized his humped back, and reinforced the public's misperception of him as a dull, dour man. On television he looked about as upbeat as an undertaker on his way to a night course.

Then there was the problem of his slow, hesitant speaking style. Stanfield's speeches were renowned for their long pauses — so long that, as someone put it, his listeners could nip out for a fast beer and make it back without missing a sentence. Although his handlers eventually managed to persuade him to wear suits of softer colors, they were never able to do much with his speaking style. And they got nowhere at all when — after Pierre Trudeau appeared on the scene and started dating singer-actress Barbra Streisand — they suggested to Stanfield that he might invigorate his image by also being seen in public with a glamorous movie star. "Would you believe with Gloria Swanson?" he replied drily. Some make-overs are not meant to be.

Today, the make-over begins before a politician declares his leadership candidacy. One of the first things a campaign strategist does is to go through the candidate's clothes closets to see what, if anything, of the wardrobe is usable for the campaign. "If you really want to be leader," Laschinger told Tom McInnis, a provincial cabinet minister who was trying to decide in 1990 whether to enter the Tory leadership race in Nova Scotia, "you're going to have to stop dressing like a farmer and start looking like someone who wants to be premier." The next thing the strategist does is to take the candidate out to buy a new wardrobe, usually after seeking professional advice on colors, fabrics, and styles that will best project the desired image.

Not only do the clothes reinforce the image, the process of dressing the candidate up, of treating him or her like a TV star, is important psychologically. It enhances the candidate's own sense of worth. Clothes can also serve other useful purposes for would-be leaders and leaders. Media consultant Nancy McLean recalled preparing Brian Peckford, the new, raw leader of the Newfoundland Conservatives, for his first television debate, against Liberal leader Don Jamieson, an old pro and veteran TV performer, in June 1979:

> Brian Peckford was a bit daunting for the public, a bit over-whelming. . . . He was so bombastic, and so passionate, and so driven, and he was going into a debate with Jamieson, a sea-soned older man. I thought it was going to look like this young street fighter, a teddy boy with pointed shoes and sideburns, coming in and trying to kick the stuffing out of this poor old guy. And we talked and talked and talked about it, but you know Newfoundland politics: if the roof doesn't come off, the event didn't happen. So I bought him a suit that was several sizes too small and sent him into the debate and he was con-trolled. . . . He was physically restrained to some extent by the straitjacket of the suit. He couldn't even scratch his nose. Everybody said they'd never seen him perform like that.

The elimination of a candidate's irritating mannerisms or habits is simple common sense. Male candidates also should not wear ties that are too bland or too loud. They should not wear cowboy boots. They should avoid funny hats, because they do not seem funny — only foolish — to television viewers who are not in on the joke. Their clothes should be clean and of above-average quality (no polyester), and fit well. Shoes should be polished and comfortable. Socks should be black (for television). Men's hair should be freshly trimmed, washed, and combed. Shaggy is out.

While a man can get away with a good suit for most occasions, plus a casual outfit (sweater or blazer) for informal events, women candidates require a more extensive wardrobe. They will need three different outfits each day — for morning, afternoon, and evening. They should be what political handlers call "power clothes" — clothes that project an image of authority, competence, and con-fidence. The styles should be fashionable but not out in front of the fashion parade. And they should not appear too masculine. Regardless of the season, a woman candidate's wardrobe should be lightweight so that she can remain cool in overheated meeting rooms and under television lights. She will need to budget at least $50 a week for drycleaning to keep her power clothes fresh during a campaign. Veteran handlers advise that she have her hair styled once a week and washed each evening. Nail polish should be well maintained and subdued in color. Comfortable shoes with low heels are essential.

Unlike a male candidate, a female candidate must keep with her at all times a travel kit containing cosmetics, personal toiletries, clothes brush, toothbrush, toothpaste, and spare pantyhose. She will need to have someone with her to look after the travel kit as she campaigns — plus another person at her home to answer the phone, do the grocery shopping, run to the drycleaner, and keep the house in some semblance of order during the campaign.

Male and female candidates alike have to remember that they are on display every minute of the campaign. They must discipline themselves not to fidget or scratch when the cameras are pointed in their direction. They should never drink liquor or beer in public, although one glass of wine at a head table may be tolerated. And no smoking.

(Ontario's Bill Davis was an exception to the no-smoking rule. In his early days, he favored cigars, which conjured up all the wrong political and public health images. Even the seemingly imperturbable Davis needed something to do with his hands when he was tense or impatient. So he took up a pipe, which he was forever cleaning and filling, though seldom actually smoking. Even now, in political retirement, he finds it calming when he is in an aircraft to pull out a pipe and clench it tightly between his teeth, unlighted, as the plane prepares to land.)

Most leadership candidates fail to understand how utterly the campaign will take over their lives. For the duration of the race, the candidate's closest friend, most intimate confidant, and constant companion will be not his or her spouse but the campaign manager. The campaign manager, in turn, has to know when to be a friend and a faithful supporter, and when to be an uncompromising critic — even a bully.

John Crosbie is one of the great stump speakers in Canadian politics — witty, impassioned, and often caustic. He is also thoroughly undisciplined. When he stands up to speak, no one (including Crosbie himself) is quite sure where his rhetoric will carry him or how long it will take to get there. He regards a speech text as a burden, a lead weight on his eloquence. At the 1983 Tory leadership convention, at which he ran third behind Mulroney and Clark, Crosbie made the best speech of the eight candidates. It did not happen easily or by chance. Work on the speech began weeks in advance, and from the outset Crosbie was determined to speak off the cuff; there was to be no script.

A leadership-convention speech is uncommonly difficult to write and to deliver. It has to be punchy, almost staccato. It has to hit all the right "hot buttons" — the "top of the waves" of the subjects that the delegates expect to hear addressed. It has to give the impression of being thoughtful and having substance, without going into a lot of boring detail. Candidates have to sound as though they are saying something significant; empty platitudes echo hollowly in a large arena and, especially, on television. Speeches have to hold the attention of audiences in two completely different settings — delegates in the cavernous reaches of a convention hall and families in the intimacy of their living room. The candidates must display some familiarity with both official languages. And their presentation must be precisely timed so that they complete their remarks within the allotted time. If they don't, the convention chairman has the authority to order the candidate to sit down or to cut off power to the microphone, making the candidate appear thoroughly unprofessional.

As campaign manager, Laschinger was determined that Crosbie would use a text and would follow it faithfully. The trick was to shame him into it. Early one Sunday morning two weeks before the convention, he put Crosbie in a hotel room in Ottawa with Tom Scott, a Toronto advertising executive, for a practice run in front of a video camera. Crosbie was tired and out of sorts. Without a text, he delivered a "short" version of the opening remarks he would be required to make at the policy sessions scheduled for candidates at the convention. It was dreadful — rambling, disjointed, pointless, and far too long. He blathered on for sixteen minutes — eleven minutes longer than he would be allowed to speak. Crosbie was so humiliated, particularly in the presence of Scott, a stranger, that he refused to watch the replay on the monitor. He turned away and stared at a newspaper, pretending not to listen as Laschinger and Scott discussed the deficiencies of his performance on the screen. But later that morning he grudgingly agreed to use a text, both for the policy sessions and for his major address to the full convention.

Crosbie, a proud man, was subjected to even greater humiliation. His inability to speak French had become a campaign issue, and Laschinger was determined to have him meet the criticism head-on by opening his convention speech in French. It was not a lot of French — just three short paragraphs — but it was more than Crosbie could manage. A tutor, the girlfriend of one of Crosbie's Quebec organizers, was recruited. Every day for the final week of the campaign, she made Crosbie rehearse the three paragraphs, over and over again. When finally he rose to present his carefully crafted speech to the delegates at Ottawa's Civic Centre, he managed to deliver the three little paragraphs competently enough that delegates were able to recognize them for what they were — a peculiar Newfoundland variation of something that sounded vaguely like French. Crosbie did not fool anyone about his ability in French, but he showed that he wanted the leadership badly enough to risk embarrassing himself in front of his party and a national television audience.

The most dangerous natural enemy of the leadership candidate is fatigue — bone-numbing exhaustion. A general election is a stroll in a park compared to marathon leadership races. A federal election campaign lasts fifty-plus days, while a leadership campaign can stretch for five months, and even longer. A major candidate will spend six days a week on the road, making speeches, courting delegates, and sweet-talking financial backers, and one day a week at the home base for planning and strategy sessions. A small amount of time is built into each day's schedule to let the candidate gather physical and mental forces, to phone home, and to wash socks.

Candidates sometimes rise to exceptional levels of endurance. Three weeks before the 1983 Tory convention, Laschinger got the phone call that campaign managers fear. It was very late on a Thursday night near the end of an especially exhausting week for Crosbie — a heavy travel schedule with 5:00 a.m. starts to days that stretched to midnight. It was 11:00 p.m. in Alberta when Ross Reid, a Crosbie aide, called from the candidate's hotel room in Edmonton to Laschinger, still at work at campaign headquarters at 1:00 a.m. in Ottawa, to report that Crosbie was ill. Oh, my God, I've killed him, was Laschinger's first thought. I've worked him too hard and his heart has given out. The pace of the campaign had been relentless, and the previous twenty-four hours would have exhausted anyone, let alone someone like Crosbie, who was overweight and had a family history of heart trouble. There had been a late-night flight from the British Columbia interior to Calgary for campaign engagements, including a speech at noon, followed by a flight to Edmonton for separate meetings with then premier (and Tory power broker) Peter Lougheed and leadership candidate Peter Pocklington (whose delegates Crosbie coveted), followed by a fund-raising dinner attended by twenty heavy hitters who were each contributing $5,000 to the Crosbie campaign. They were puzzled by the candidate's insistence on eating his dinner standing up.

Laschinger burst out laughing when Reid explained that it wasn't Crosbie's heart that was causing the problem, but his hemorrhoids. He had been in excruciating pain all day. The hotel doctor had seen him and would operate in the morning. Next morning, Crosbie was in the hospital waiting room in Edmonton, hiding behind yet another newspaper and hoping he would not be recognized, lest his delicate condition become public knowledge.

No one was fooled. Nurses walking past pointed at the familiar, portly figure screening his face with the newspaper; they sniggered and wandered off, discussing his symptoms in loud voices. The doctor performed the operation, removed the hemorrhoids, and sent Crosbie on his way with a sanitary napkin stuffed between his cheeks to control the bleeding. The candidate went off to meet two Edmonton businessmen who wanted to get a look at him before deciding whether to contribute to his campaign, then he flew to Ottawa. Crosbie did not miss a single campaign engagement. He had the constitution of an ox, and needed it.

A candidate also needs to be able to resist the temptation to try to be his own campaign boss. Frontroom politicians, as a rule, are not managers; they tend to be great doers and poor delegators. Having been involved in the hands-on running of their local constituency campaigns, candidates may think they can successfully manage their own leadership operation. A wise candidate will resist that temptation, and will accept that a certain amount of chaos is inevitable in a ramshackle organization, spread thinly from coast to coast, which by the end will encompass 500 to 1,500 individuals, the vast majority of them untrained volunteers who may be bursting with enthusiasm but who have everyday jobs and everyday lives to distract them.

"In a campaign, one of the hardest things is that you have to involve a lot of people, and that involvement can't be hollow," says John Rae, manager of Jean Chrétien's Liberal leadership campaigns. "But at the same time you have to maintain a consistency of purpose and consistency of performance. If you get deterred from doing that because of the pulling and shoving and tugging that goes on, you're going to be in trouble."

The pulling, shoving, and tugging can be kept to a minimum if the candidate identifies and appoints four central members of the campaign team and leaves them to build and direct the rest of the organization. The four key appointments are:

— Campaign manager (to oversee the whole operation)
— Finance chairman (in charge of fund-raising)
— Comptroller (to police spending)
— Key adviser/close friend (someone whom the candidate knows well and trusts to represent his or her interests in the campaign planning)

A well-run leadership campaign needs two clear weekly schedules — one for the organizers and one for the candidate.

Weekly Schedule: Campaign Team

Day		Event	Candidate attends
Sun.	— afternoon	Strategy group mtg (3–4 hrs)	yes
	— later	Review of next 10 days of tour	yes
Mon.	— noon	Budget committee meets	no
	— evening	Campaign operations mtg	no
Tues.	— evening	Policy/issues mtg	no
	— later	Communications mtg	no
Wed.	— noon	Tour planning mtg	no
	— evening	Convention Week planning mtg	no
Thurs.	— noon	Fund raisers' mtg	no
Fri.	— evening		
	OR		
Sat.	— morning	Organization mtg	no

Weekly Schedule: Candidate
John Crosbie, Week of May 15, 1983

Sun.	— morning	off
	— afternoon	Strategy, tour mtgs
	— evening	Fly to Vancouver
Mon.	— 6:45 a.m.	Wake up call

	— 7:35	Surrey, delegate breakfast, 200 people, remarks
	— 10:45	Fly to Victoria
	— 12 noon	Chamber of Commerce lunch, speech, 20 mins.
	— 1:30 p.m.	Private meeting with delegates
	— 3:00	Fly to Vancouver
	— 5:45	Fund-raising reception, 200 people, remarks
	— 7:50	Reception for delegates, 130 people, remarks
	— 9:40	To bed
Tues.	— 5:00 a.m.	Wake up call
	— 7:30	Fly to Prince Rupert
	— 10:15	Tour port facilities
	— 11:35	Private meeting with delegates
	— 12 noon	Lunch with delegates, speech
	— 2:00 p.m.	Fly to Smithers
	— 3:05	Reception for delegates, remarks
	— 4:15	Fly to Prince George
	— 6:15	Reception for delegates, remarks
	— 7:30	Community dinner, 450 people, remarks
	— 9:30	To bed
Wed.	— 5:00 a.m.	Wake up call
	— 6:00	Fly to Kamloops
	— 7:30	Chamber of Commerce breakfast, 350 people, remarks
	— 8:45	Private meeting with delegates
	— 10:00	Fly to Kelowna
	— 12 noon	Chamber of Commerce luncheon, remarks
	— 1:30 p.m.	Private meeting with delegates
	— 2:30	Fly to Penticton
	— 3:30	Reception for delegates, remarks
	— 5:20	Fly to Cranbrook, dinner on board
	— 7:30	Reception for delegates, etc., 300 people, remarks
	— 9:40	Fly to Calgary
	— 11:10	To bed
Thurs	— 8:30 a.m.	Wake up call

	— 9:40	Telephone calls
	— 11:15	Meet PC Youth, remarks
	— 12 noon	Lunch and speech, 20–25 mins. plus Q & A
	— 1:20 p.m.	Press conference
	— 2:05	Fly to Edmonton
	— 3:45	Meet Premier Lougheed and PC caucus, remarks
	— 5:10	Private meeting, Peter Pocklington
	— 6:30	Edmonton Club reception
	— 7:30	Dinner, speech, 10–15 mins. plus Q & A
	— 10:00	Return to hotel, bed
Fri.	— morning	Emergency surgery (unscheduled)
	— later	Meet potential supporters; Fly to Ottawa

No matter how brilliant his strategy, how efficient his organization, and how insurmountable his lead may seem to be, the candidate will inevitably be surprised by the closeness of the convention. Few leadership races are dominated by a single candidate who so overpowers all opponents that the outcome is never in doubt. Most contested conventions go two or more ballots. In 94 per cent of cases, the candidate who leads on the first ballot goes on to win, although the victory may be a close thing. Robert Stanfield in 1967, Pierre Trudeau in 1968, and William Davis in Ontario in 1971 all led from the start of the balloting but had to hang on to win. Occasionally, a candidate moves out of the pack and overtakes the front-runner. John Robarts did it at the Ontario Conservative convention in 1961. Joe Clark did it in 1976, moving from third to first. And so did Brian Mulroney in 1983. He ran in second place for three ballots, whittling away at Clark's lead — reducing it from 217 votes on the first ballot to 64 on the second, to 22 on the third. Mulroney finally moved ahead and won on the fourth ballot, by 1,584 votes to 1,325. His margin — 259 votes, or 8.9 per cent of the 2,909 votes cast on the fourth ballot — made his victory seem easier than it really was. It had been a very narrow triumph. In 1992, Lyn McLeod, after running second on the early ballots, pulled ahead of Murray Elston to win the Ontario Liberal leadership on the fifth ballot.

In the final analysis, what the delegates to leadership conventions want more than anything else is to be with a winner. Like it or not — and most leadership aspirants do not like it at all — the determining factor in a delegate's decision often has less to do with friendship, loyalty, policy, character, or even leadership ability than it has with winnability. Can the candidate win the convention? Could he or she, as leader, win an election?

Consider the responses to the following polls shown in Table 3 taken prior to four provincial Tory leadership conventions.

Table 3

Question: How important is it that you support and vote for the candidate who is going to win the leadership? Would you say that it is very important, somewhat important, not very important or not important at all?

	Very	Somewhat	Not Very	Not At All
Ontario — Oct. 1985	41	31	15	12
Nfld. — Feb. 1989	54	25	9	9
Ontario — Dec. 1989	29	26	26	13
Nova Scotia — Oct. 1990	38	33	17	9

SOURCES: Ontario polls by Decima Research; Newfoundland and Nova Scotia by John Mykytyshyn.

In the four races, roughly one-third to one-half of the voting delegates thought it was *very important* to be with the winner; one-half to three-quarters thought it was either very or somewhat important to support the winner. It is for this reason that it is crucial for a candidate to be perceived (rightly or otherwise) to have early momentum. A convention is a bandwagon waiting to happen.

Win or lose, a candidate's life will never be the same. In one sense, it is less disrupting to lose than it is to win. A loser, if he or she is well-adjusted, can put defeat in the past, but a winner assumes new responsibilities that change his or her life dramatically, probably for many years. The average stay for leaders who came and went in the three major national parties between 1960 and 1990 was nine and a half years.

Defeat, however, can be devastating. It may be the first serious setback that a leadership candidate has experienced in an entire political career. John Rae thinks the toughest adjustment may be coming to terms with friends, or former friends, who refused to support the candidate or who actively campaigned for one of the opponents. The sense of betrayal, of being let down, can be enor-

mous. Even candidates who enter a leadership campaign understanding the odds manage to convince themselves that they have
a real chance of winning. They discover that everyone is surpris-
ingly nice to them as the campaign goes on. What they do not
realize in time is that the less chance they have, the nicer people
will be to them.

Veteran Liberal backroom manager Senator Keith Davey remembers offering friendly advice to Eugene Whelan, Pierre Trudeau's
agriculture minister, when he decided to clap a green stetson on
his head and join the race for the Liberal leadership in 1984. "Gene
was one of the few guys that I told I thought it was okay if they
ran," says Davey. "I said, 'Sure, go for it, Gene. I know you well
enough to know you'll have a lot of fun and you'll enjoy it — on
two conditions: as long as you know that you can't win, and as
long as you've got the money.' Well, of course, that lasted for
about forty-eight hours, and then he began to think he could win. . . .
I could give you a long list of people [like that]. . . . I say it's
megalomania. They say it's ego."

Few people handle defeat as well as Joe Clark did. He saw his
leadership determinedly undermined by Mulroney and others following the Conservative election defeat in 1980. He lost his job
to Mulroney in a bitter leadership fight in 1983. And he ended up
serving Mulroney, loyally and discreetly, as a senior member of the
cabinet after the Tories returned to power in the 1984 election. It
was a class act.

For the politician who is determined to seek the prize at the end
of the rainbow, there are a few rules that will improve his or her
leadership odds.

RULE ONE. A candidate should always operate on the assumption
that the convention will go to more than one ballot. Of fifty-eight
leadership races in Canada between 1967 and 1992 that had more
than two candidates, forty went to two or more ballots.[2] In contrast,
every presidential convention held by the Republicans and the
Democrats in the United States since 1948 and 1952, respectively,
has ended with just one ballot. When a convention goes beyond
one ballot, survival (and ultimately success) is determined by a candidate's ability to attract the votes of delegates who came to the
convention supporting another candidate. Contestants who alienate
their opponents, or their opponents' supporters, do so at their peril.

RULE TWO. A candidate should ensure that he or she has adequate support from the parliamentary or legislative caucus. Caucus support is important — especially for candidates who are not elected members — because it sends a signal to rank-and-file delegates that the candidates, although they may be outsiders, are acceptable to those whom they seek to lead. When Brian Mulroney ran for the Tory leadership in 1976, he had only one supporter in caucus. He lost. In 1983, he had more than twenty caucus supporters and won the leadership.

RULE THREE. A candidate who waits until a leadership convention is called before he or she starts to campaign is too late. Delegates are generally people who have been active in the party over the years and they make up their minds over a period of time. Often they make their first-ballot choices for reasons that are outside the context of the leadership campaign. They may decide to go with a particular candidate because months or even years earlier he or she came to a fund-raising event in their riding, or sent workers to help in a byelection, or wrote a note of condolence when someone's mother died.

RULE FOUR. Before declaring, a leadership candidate should commission a poll of party members and delegates to establish issues and strategy. Polling is important in a leadership race for the same reasons that it is important in a general election.

RULE FIVE. A shrewd candidate will understate and overachieve. A candidate who makes exaggerated claims of delegate support will lose any momentum he or she might have when the first-ballot results are announced and fewer votes than had been predicted are won. Conversely, if the candidate is stronger on the first ballot than the pundits and the delegates expect him or her to be, a bandwagon effect may be created. Campaign managers generally instruct their candidates not to talk about numbers at all before the balloting takes place.

RULE SIX. A leadership campaign must have a hard-nosed S.O.B. to serve as the organization's comptroller. Inadequate financial controls will kill the candidate after the convention, if not before. The John Crosbie leadership campaign of 1983 was a financial nightmare. With more than 1,500 Crosbie volunteers, delegates, friends, constituents, observers, and hangers-on in Ottawa for convention week, expenditures soared out of control — from an initial campaign budget of $700,000 to $950,000, to $1.2 million, to a final tally of $1.8 million. Some of the bills were unpaid for a year. Senator Finlay MacDonald was working for Joe Clark in that 1983 race and he saw the same thing happen. "You are incapable of controlling costs at a certain point," says MacDonald. "Suddenly the bills come in and you say, 'What the hell's this? Who authorized it?' Well, nobody authorized it. 'Well, who said we'd pay for the twenty thousand ham sandwiches and soft drinks that are being delivered?' Nobody knows. Somebody says, 'I think it was so-and-so.' Of course, there comes a point of desperation when you realize the jig may be up and you'll spend freely and you'll figure that somehow there's a fairy godmother who will get you out of it. The main thing is to get back, to perpetuate ourselves in power — spend, spend, spend. . . . It got away from us."

Clark's campaign ended up costing $1.9 million, perhaps more, as he lost to Mulroney. When his friends were unable to raise enough additional money to pay off the debts, they negotiated with creditors to accept fifty cents on the dollar.

RULE SEVEN. A campaign must be professional, but never lavish. Mulroney's first leadership campaign in 1976 illustrated the peril of conspicuous overspending. It was not just that he spent twice as much as any other candidate, it was the visible way he spent it — including renting the Coliseum next to the convention hall in Ottawa for a free concert by Quebec singer Ginette Reno (her fee: $10,000) with free beer and free pizza for all. Thousands turned out. But the voting delegates worried: Why was Mulroney spending so much? Whom was he trying to impress? Where was the money coming from? How was he going to pay it back?

RULE EIGHT. Candidates should identify a solid base of early financial support to begin a campaign. Too many candidates pour their own money, in many cases money they can ill afford to invest, into their campaigns. Fund raisers should be appointed before candidates declare, and they should make sure their bagmen have money in hand before they commit themselves irrevocably to running. If they cannot raise money before they start, they will have more trouble trying to raise it later. Prudent candidates who cannot find early money will reconsider their decision to run.

RULE NINE. A candidate must know, and be able to articulate, his or her reasons for wanting to be leader. Brian Peckford in Newfoundland was one of the few who had a coherent response when Laschinger put the question to him on their first meeting prior to the 1979 provincial Tory leadership campaign. Peckford told him:

> I have been attracted to public life and have a natural instinct to be involved in the eye of the storm. I have travelled the province since I was ten. I have seen things that I haven't liked and fundamental things I want to change — the development of rural Newfoundland; our political system, both the legislature and the cost of elections; the direction of the province's energy development, both hydro and the offshore; and other areas of development, like the fisheries, where we have to get the best deal for Newfoundlanders. I see a changing Newfoundland. As I look at the 'eighties, we are on the threshold and we need effective resource management to manage this expansion and to get the economic rent we require. Our resource-management policy will weave into our overall social policy, which takes care of the old, the poor, and the sick, and it weaves into our cultural approach.

It was an impressive, impromptu performance by a raw, untutored young politician who in those days was known mainly for his fiery temper and burning ambition. Peckford won the leadership and the election that followed. He served as Newfoundland's premier for the next ten years.

A leadership campaign is only as good as its candidate. The good candidate has a sense of self and of purpose. He or she does not try to be all things to all delegates by contorting his or her personality, ideas, and style to match the characteristics he or she thinks they are looking for in a leader. Candidates who do adapt too readily will be seen for what they are — superficial, insincere, and cynical. Megalomania will carry a politician only so far.

PART FOUR

LOOKING AHEAD

THE CANADIAN POLITICAL SYSTEM, AS WE KNOW IT, is in its last days. The people are fed up with the opportunism and cynicism of politicians in the frontroom and backroom alike. Their disenchantment is seen in their low regard for politicians – lower than for any other occupational group – in the decline in partisanship that is eroding the base of every traditional party, and in Canadians' flirtation with the Reform Party and other protest movements. If today's mainstream parties do not satisfy the public's demand for a political system that is less manipulative, more open, fairer, and more responsive to the needs and wishes of the electorate, they will not survive.

And the future is pressing in. Political polling — so crucial to campaign management — is threatened by new technology. Politicians who are still stranded in the age of print — who cannot pack their hopes, dreams, and policies into TV clips of ten seconds or less — are teetering on the brink of redundancy.

12. THE BLACK ARTS

"There's a backlash building — a serious irritation — with the black arts of politics. The political élites fail to acknowledge how the irritation affects not simply marginal voters or participants in the system, but upper-middle-class, professional, formerly politically active voters."
— New Democrat Robin Sears

Every year, pollster Martin Goldfarb surveys Canadians to determine the degree of esteem in which they hold various professions, occupations, and institutions in Canadian life. Ranking the responses on a scale of one to a hundred, he calculates a "level-of-respect index." The annual index seldom contains good news for Canada's politicians, but the 1992 edition was the most depressing ever. Politicians ranked dead last in public esteem, lower than even journalists and rock musicians.

To make this depressing news even more discouraging, the level of respect for politics and politicians has been declining from year to year. For example, since the 1988 federal election, which re-elected a majority Mulroney Conservative government, respect for Parliament has dropped thirteen percentage points (from 44 to 31), while respect for cabinet ministers has slipped by twelve points (39 to 27) and for politicians in general by eleven (35 to 24).

This loss of respect reflects the growing alienation of the Canadian public from the politicians whom they elect to represent them, but who too often seem to be pursuing their own agendas, which have little in common with the wishes of the people. There is a crisis of confidence in the ability of the political process to serve the electorate. And the crisis affects all mainstream politicians and traditional parties.

Table 1

Level of Respect 1992   **Rank out of 100**

Farmers	73
Doctors	69
Skilled tradesmen	68
Small businessmen	67
Police	65
Organized religion/churches	57
Journalists/newsmen	54
Economists	54
Union leaders	49
Rock musicians	43
Car dealerships	38
Parliament	31
Cabinet ministers	27
Politicians (in general)	24

SOURCE: Goldfarb Consultants

The crisis is documented in the monthly drum roll of opinion polls that report fluctuations in party support. The Tories won the November 1988 federal election with 43 per cent of the popular vote. After a two-month honeymoon with the populace, they went into a nosedive, falling behind the Liberals and New Democrats. Conservative support dropped below 20 per cent in early 1990, and continued to fall to record depths of support for a party in government. Before long, the Tories were flirting with single digits. One day in late 1991, pollster Michael Adams of Environics Research Group fed the poll numbers into his computer and came up with a startling projection: If an election were held then, the Conservatives would win just one seat in all of Canada.[1]

As the government's popularity collapsed, so did Prime Minister Mulroney's approval rating. Goldfarb asked Canadians in early 1992 who they would prefer as their next prime minister. Only 8 per cent chose Mulroney. As the government grappled with the national-unity crisis in mid-1992, the Tories' popularity improved somewhat. But the challenge of devising a winning strategy for the Conservatives for an election expected in 1993 was testing all the intellectual resources of Allan Gregg, the Tory pollster-guru. He described the challenge that confronts the Conservatives:

The majority of the people will not give us any benefit of the doubt until the evidence is overwhelming. We have to prove that Brian Mulroney is prepared to admit his mistakes, that he has become more honest and more trustworthy. . . . In the public's eye, he's gone from being Willy Loman [the protagonist in *Death of a Salesman*] — the guy who was prepared to kiss any ass to win favor, to get the population with him — to being Idi Amin — a guy who's got his own view, who doesn't listen and, in the end, just doesn't care about the consequences of that. [Tories] have to address that weakness even when they have no credibility — because until they address the weakness, they just can't get out of the mire.

Superficially, Mulroney was to blame for the mire that the Tories were struggling to escape. At a more fundamental level, however, the problem was the inevitable product of the public's loss of faith in the political process. Only new, untested (and largely unscrutinized) protest parties or single-issue parties were escaping the public's mounting dissatisfaction with the political system. The traditional parties, growing weaker by the year, were losing their status as important national institutions. Membership in a political party had become virtually meaningless. The parties were increasingly incapable of mobilizing any sense of national purpose or will — on the Constitution, the economy, the environment, or any other issue. And the parties themselves were largely to blame. Their leading spokesmen seemed only too willing to say anything and to promise anything to win election, with no honest intention of keeping their commitments after the votes were counted. Their backroom managers, also more preoccupied with electoral success than with good government, ran campaigns that were often as cynical as they were effective. Politicians in both the frontroom and the backroom were not responding to the public's growing irritation with what Robin Sears calls the "black arts of politics." They failed to address Canadians' demand for greater openness and fairness in the political system.

Canadians tend to assess their political system by comparing it to that of the United States. By that yardstick, we seem to be doing relatively well. We have a much higher voter turnout than the Americans do: Traditionally, 75 per cent of eligible voters cast ballots in Canadian federal elections, compared to 50 per cent or fewer in presidential elections — largely because the U.S. voter-registration system acts as an obstacle more than an inducement to voting. We have avoided the worst financial excesses of U.S. politics by enacting legislation at the federal level and in many provinces to limit the amount of money that parties and candidates may spend during campaigns, restrict the amount of television advertising they may do, and require the public disclosure of the sources of political donations. These measures may not necessarily make the Canadian system more democratic than the U.S. version, but they have made the playing field more level here than there.

In Washington, congressmen typically devote 80 per cent, or even more, of their time to raising money for their next campaign. In the presidential election of 1988, *each* candidate for his party's nomination — for the *nomination* alone, not for the post-convention election campaign — was allowed to spend a staggering $26.6 million. To put that amount in perspective, the budget for just one candidate for a nomination would have paid for the combined national campaigns of the Progressive Conservative, Liberal, and New Democratic parties in the general election that same year, with about $5 million left over. Or, to look at it another way, that $26.6 million, converted into Canadian dollars, would have covered the reported election expenses of all 884 Tory, Liberal, and NDP candidates in 1988.

Four years later, in 1992, the U.S. business tycoon Ross Perot became an overnight sensation and an instantly credible independent candidate for the presidency for two reasons. First, he was not a politician in the usual sense. Second, he was prepared to put $100 million of his own money into his quest for the White House.

Although some Canadian politicians take smug satisfaction from the fact that Canada has not had a Watergate scandal — not yet, at least — the Canadian public is as disenchanted with their politics as Americans are with theirs. Only one-third of Canadians have a favorable impression of their politicians, and only 40 per cent, according to a 1990 Gregg poll, think they are trustworthy (down from 63 per cent ten years earlier). And only 32 per cent think their politicians are competent.

The disrepute in which politicians and the political system find themselves will make it even more difficult in the future than it is at present to encourage capable men and women to seek public office. As fewer good people are prepared to risk their reputations and personal careers by standing for election, mediocrity takes stronger hold and the public's cynicism grows deeper.

Michael Adams argues that the public cynicism has created a

generation gap in Canadian political leadership. The baby-boom generation, which was keenly interested in politics in the late 1960s and early 1970s, is shunning the political process in the 1990s, he says. Male "boomers" in particular — now thirty-five to forty-five years old — who would otherwise be moving into positions of leadership in politics, are devoting themselves to non-political careers instead. "When you talk to these people, they tell you that they think anybody who would go into public life is crazy to give up their personal freedom that way," Adams says. "These are modern people who have families and kids and want to live balanced lives and basically are very cynical about politics now. You're not getting a lot of people from that generation interested in public life. Consequently, we're left with an older generation of people who are in their late forties and in their fifties."[2]

Public disenchantment is caused by more than the seeming inability of politicians to resolve problems, large and small. It is also partly due to a feeling of exclusion. The people feel they are powerless, that they are not consulted or involved in the decision making at the centre. The political backrooms must shoulder some of the blame. Party strategists and managers devise and run campaigns in which discipline and control take precedence over spontaneity, and in which direct human contact between the politicians and the voters is deliberately kept to a manageable minimum.

If a politician wants to know what the people are thinking, his or her campaign managers probably will not call a town hall meeting for the candidate to meet and listen to constituents. Chances are they will hire a pollster to provide a "scientific" reading of the public mood by conducting a poll or convening a few focus groups. If the politician wants to convey a message, he or she may still do it in the old-fashioned way: by going out and making speeches in hope that the groups of voters whom the campaign is targeting will turn out to hear the word. But it is more "efficient" these days to let computers do the talking. One "personalized" letter, written and signed by a computer and sent to a list of target voters identified by another computer, will raise more money and win more votes than a candidate who makes a dozen speeches or knocks on a thousand doors. And if this "research-driven voter contact," as computer-generated letters are known, is not sufficient, the practitioners of the black arts in the backroom have other devices. These include "spin doctors" to massage and manipulate the press and "media strategists" to harness the most potent weapon in politics today: television. As every such artist knows, one television commercial

— especially one that abuses the opposition — is worth more at election time than a candidate's exemplary record of devoted attention to the concerns of his or her constituents.

The alienation of the electorate is reflected in declining support for the major parties and in the rise of sectarian parties that are based on no principle more profound than regional grievance or ethnic ambition. The Reform Party of Canada gained enough of a following among alienated Western Canadians, supplemented by some support in Ontario, to pull even with, or marginally ahead of, the governing Tories in some of the national polls. And, as the national-unity debate tormented the nation in 1992, pollsters found that four out of every ten Quebeckers said they were prepared to vote for the separatist Bloc Québécois in a federal election.

Among the two dozen lesser parties vying for attention and support, the reactionary, know-nothing Confederation of Regions party made inroads in eastern Canada, establishing itself as the official opposition in the New Brunswick Legislature. Voters in the 1990 Ontario election were so disillusioned with the available choices that a record number — nearly 7 per cent — wasted their vote on independents or fringe-party candidates.

The fragmentation of political support increases the influence of protest parties out of all proportion to their numerical strength, and raises the spectre that it may become impossible in Ottawa (as in Italy) for any one political leader to control enough parliamentary seats to govern for more than a few months before losing the confidence of the House. Major parties may well be forced to form alliances with regional parties. But if the Conservatives or Liberals were forced to look, for example, to the Reform Party for support in Parliament, the price of that support could be painfully high — the elimination of official bilingualism, perhaps, or the dismantling of expensive national programs, such as universal medicare.

A generation-long decline in partisanship bedevils the major parties as they try to rebuild their bases of support. Not only do most Canadians no longer vote the way their parents did, they do not vote the same way from one election to the next. Voters are so volatile that some change their minds two or three times in the course of a seven-week election campaign. To the astonishment of pollsters, the 1988 federal election produced a "double reverse," the first known one in Canadian history. The Tories went into the campaign with a comfortable lead, lost their momentum, and fell behind the Liberals after the leaders' debate on television, then rebounded by concentrating their attack on the credibility of the leader of the Liberal party, John Turner. The Conservatives won easily.

In 1991 and again in 1992, Goldfarb Consultants asked a national sample of 1,600 Canadians about their political affiliation. Their responses contained sobering news for political leaders and backroom politicians.

Table 2

In terms of federal politics, do you consider yourself to be ...

	1991	1992
Conservative	19%	14%
Liberal	30	26
NDP	22	16
Bloc Québécois	9	9
Reform Party	6	7
Other	6	2
None of the above	7	24

SOURCE: Goldfarb Consultants
Note: Numbers do not add to 100 because of rounding.

Goldfarb's findings do not surprise Allan Gregg. "You've got a population that's really questioning all of its political beliefs," the Tory pollster says. Gregg continues:

> They've been told that if you work hard, really put your mind to it, you can get anything you want. Now, people are saying maybe that's not the case. They're told progress is normal, but maybe tomorrow will be worse than today. We're told that government solves all your problems. Yet the same government can't organize a two-hole outhouse.
>
> And that, I think, has really taken partisanship and thrown it out the window. It's the same way you see very little brand loyalty in shopping any more. The person who's been told for forty years that Tide is new and improved comes to the conclusion: B.S. It isn't improved. All of a sudden, his commitment to Tide is out the window. . . . And that's what I think is happening in the political process: people aren't anchored the way they were. . . .
>
> I've got 30 per cent of the electorate saying they are casting

their votes today for a party they have never voted for. Never! Thirty per cent! Half of them say they're only voting that way because they're pissed off at their old vote. There's nothing that attracts them to the new one at all. That's 15 per cent of the electorate. That's huge, huge, huge numbers — millions of people voting for entirely negative reasons in a brand-new way they've never voted before.

Canadians are moving to new parties more out of anger against the old than out of affection for the new. And they are singularly unenthusiastic about the current crop of leaders. In February 1992, for example, 15 per cent of people polled told the Gallup organization that they would vote for the Reform Party. But in the same month only half that many — 8 per cent — told Goldfarb Consultants that they wanted Reform leader Preston Manning as Canada's next prime minister. Other leaders fared little better. The Liberals' Jean Chrétien was the choice of 19 per cent for the next prime minister, followed by the NDP's Audrey McLaughlin at 16 per cent, Lucien Bouchard of the Bloc Québécois at 9 per cent, and Mulroney tied with Manning at 8 per cent. The real "winner" was Anybody Else at 30 per cent. (Ten per cent refused to say.)

Every leader (except Bouchard) is less popular than his or her party. The decline of partisanship in the old parties, the absence of genuine enthusiasm for the newer parties, and the yearning for Anyone Else other than the available alternatives show how profoundly Canadians are disillusioned with their political system and politicians.

Too much of what goes on in politics appears to be pure opportunism. Too many frontroom politicians do not seem to stand for anything that matters to the people. Too many backroom politicians seem to be cut from the same cloth as Charles Colson, the Republican fixer who said he would walk over his grandmother if it would help Richard Nixon. Too many rumors and too much loose talk drifting out of the backrooms suggest the employment of practices that, if not illegal, would not bear close ethical scrutiny.

Public confidence in the political system will not be restored until the whole system — frontroom and backroom — is made more open and more accessible. The public is entitled to see for itself that the system is fair, honest, and truly democratic. Nothing less will relieve the electorate's pervasive disenchantment with, and distrust of, politics and politicians.

13. THE ROAD TO REFORM

"The very nature of politics is that people don't *heed fact and logic. It does no good to say that people* should; *they wilfully don't. . . . Frustration, imprecision, and impermanence are of the essence of political life."*
— American historian Theodore Roszak, 1972

It is one of the strengths — as well as one of the frustrations — of the Canadian political system that it resists change and fights attempts to reform it. This is true both of the way political parties run their organizations and of the way the political process works to elect representatives and to hold them accountable to the people. If the system was not so stubborn in its resistance to change, it would be vulnerable to every impractical idea or harebrained scheme — of which there have been many — that has been advanced by well-intentioned reformers over the years.

As the country heads towards another election, the pressure for reform is greater than it ever has been. Some of the pressure comes from the most potent new political force of recent decades, the Reform Party of Canada, which is demanding far-reaching changes. It groups its reforms under the inoffensive-sounding heading of "direct democracy," although the changes would do as much to undermine the role of elected representatives as they would to improve the health and vigor of the Canadian democracy. Pressure for reform also comes from the Lortie Royal Commission on Electoral Reform and Party Financing, whose four-volume report was published in early 1992. The royal commission went so far as to hand the government pre-drafted legislation incorporating its specific recommendations so that, Parliament willing, the reforms could be implemented in time for the next election.

Pressure — less specific but no less insistent — also comes from the general public, from people of all political persuasions, who feel that somehow the Canadian political system has slipped from their control and assumed a life and a direction of its own. Elected politicians feel this pressure from the public and they know that the demand for reform is based on a legitimate concern, a sense of ill-being that crosses partisan boundaries. And backroom politicians feel the pressure, too. They know that their job — electing candidates, leaders, and governments — becomes increasingly difficult as the public loses faith in the ability of the system to serve their interests. As the public gives up on the system, it becomes impossible for campaign managers to recruit candidates, raise money, conduct polling, and engage the voters' attention long enough to present the merits of one's own side and the demerits of one's opponents.

The reforms that are most frequently proposed fall into three broad categories: reforms in the way representatives are selected; reforms to provide greater citizen influence in decision making (including the so-called direct democracy); and reforms that would rehabilitate the existing system without destroying it, so as to provide greater fairness in the competition among parties and candidates, to open all operations to more public scrutiny, and to guarantee equal access to women and minority groups.

In the first category, the target of reformers is — and has been for decades — the first-past-the-post system of electing members to Parliament and provincial legislatures. In Canada, as in the United States and Britain, the candidate who gains a plurality of the votes in his or her constituency is declared the winner. It is not necessary to win a majority of the votes cast. The first-past-the-post system favors the party that wins the most popular vote — and enhances the odds that the election will produce a majority government. It also punishes smaller parties that win a slice of the popular vote in many constituencies, but not enough votes anywhere to elect members — and makes it that much tougher for a minor party ever to become a major party.

Various remedies have been suggested. A preferential ballot would benefit smaller parties by giving weight to a voter's second or third choices. Run-off elections, such as they have in France, would mean that wherever one candidate failed to win a majority of the votes cast on election day, the top two candidates would meet in a second, run-off, election.

But the favorite remedy of those who would reform the first-past-the-post system is proportional representation. "PR," as it is known, is a bad idea that will not go away. It persists because variations of it are employed, with varying degrees of success, in such countries as Italy, Israel, Sweden, Germany, and Ireland. If "PR" were introduced here, seats in Parliament and the legislatures would be distributed among political parties on the basis of their share of the popular vote, regardless of how the parties' candidates fared in individual constituencies. Candidates would be elected from party lists on the basis of each party's popular vote. In its simplest construction, proportional representation would mean that a party that got 10 per cent of the popular vote nationally or province-wide would be entitled to 10 per cent of the parliamentary or legislative seats, even if it did not finish first in a single constituency. With proportional representation, Ontario would not have elected a majority New Democratic Party government in 1990. Instead of winding up with 74 of the Legislature's 130 seats (57 per cent of the seats), Bob Rae's New Democrats would have been entitled under "PR" to only the same percentage of seats as they collected in popular vote — 37.6 per cent or 49 seats (compared to 81 seats for the combined Liberal and Conservative opposition).

Brian Mulroney would not have won a majority government in 1988. With 43 per cent of the vote, the Conservatives would have claimed just 127 of the 295 seats in the Commons (instead of 169). Even in 1984, the year of the great Mulroney landslide (211 of 282 seats, as there were then), the Tories would not have had a working majority. They actually won 50.03 per cent of the national vote. Strictly applied, proportional representation would have given them 141 seats; by the time they appointed a speaker, they would have been outnumbered 141–140 by the opposition. (A variation of "PR" would allocate parliamentary seats on the basis of votes received by province or region. The Liberals, for example, took 13.7 per cent of the vote in Alberta and 18.2 per cent in Saskatchewan in 1988, yet failed to elect a single member from either province. With "PR," provincially applied, they would have been awarded three seats in Alberta and two in Saskatchewan.)

Over the past thirty years, proportional representation has enjoyed spells of high popularity among academics (who like to tinker), some practising politicians (who should know better), and a good many grumpy voters (who feel that their region or pet cause — abortion and capital punishment come to mind — is not being given the weight it deserves in the far-off capital). The Macdonald Royal Commission on the Economic Union and Development Prospects for Canada considered alternatives to the first-past-the-post system, including proportional representation, in its report in 1985. The Lortie Royal Commission took a short, sour look at "PR" before recommending against it.

Nevertheless, "PR" persists as a highly salable idea in the political marketplace. Its big appeal is the hope (spurious or otherwise) that it will produce a Parliament or a legislature whose membership more closely reflects the ideological bent of the electorate. Its backers also see it as a way to redress the chronic underrepresentation of women and ethnic minorities. In most countries that have adopted proportional representation, political parties establish the order of lists of candidates — a candidate's rank on the party list determining the likelihood that he or she will be elected. By putting more women or ethnic candidates high on its list, a party can increase their representation in its caucus.

So far, common sense has prevailed to keep "PR" out of the Canadian political system. It is a prescription for political instability (witness Italy and Israel), a guarantee of chronic minority government, especially at the federal level in a nation where political priorities and party preferences vary widely from region to region. Proportional representation would increase the authority of backroom politicians (by empowering them to determine the pecking order of the party's candidates) at the expense of ordinary constituency voters. It would frustrate communities that voted to be represented by, say, a white male Tory farmer, only to find that, thanks to "PR" and the party lists, their MP would instead be a female Liberal lawyer or black New Democrat teacher.

The popular notion of a Triple-E Senate — a new Senate whose members would be elected (perhaps by "PR") rather than appointed, which would have effective powers, and in which each province would have an equal number of seats — straddles the first two categories of reform. It would change the way members of Parliament's Upper House are selected. And it is intended, with its third E — equal — to increase the influence of citizens of small provinces and outlying regions in the decision making at the centre. It addresses the chronic complaint of Canadians from outside Ontario and Quebec that their interests are not reflected adequately in the House of Commons, where representation is based on population. An equal Senate in which all provinces would have the same number of seats would increase the influence of worthy Canadians in small places like Stettler, Alberta, and Summerside, P.E.I., at the expense of presumably less worthy Canadians in big places like Toronto, Montreal, and Vancouver.

Although a Triple-E Senate would do nothing to improve legislative capacity of Parliament, it gained a prominent place on the national agenda because it had prominent backers, including Preston Manning, the leader of the Reform Party, and Donald Getty, the Tory premier of Alberta, who saw it as a way, among other things, of countering what they regarded as Quebec's insatiable demands for greater political and constitutional power.

In its proposals for "direct democracy," the Reform Party is putting a new gloss on old ideas that have been kicking around for a century. As the Royal Commission on Electoral Reform noted, there are three instruments of direct democracy.[1] The first is the recall, which can be used by constituents to vote on the performance of elected officials (and to terminate their term before its normal conclusion). The second is the citizen initiative or direct initiative (by which legislation is proposed by citizen petition and, if enough signatures are obtained, is submitted directly to the voters for approval — independent of the legislature). The third is the referendum, either advisory or binding. Legislatures occasionally use advisory referendums, or plebiscites, to help them gauge public sentiment before proceeding with some extraordinary measure. Binding referendums are used in some places to ratify constitutional amendments. They can also be used to put legislation before the public for a final decision — for binding approval or binding rejection.

The instruments of direct democracy came out of the populist movement in the United States in the 1890s and early 1900s. American populists argued that the legislative process was controlled by big business and wealthy vested interests. Bribery, graft, and other forms of corruption were widespread and the recall, in particular, was a device to enable voters to get rid of crooked politicians — not, as the Reform Party would have it today, to remove from office representatives who do not follow the wishes of their constituents. As Manning admits, "The main value of having a recall provision is its existence as a threat, since its employment is quite cumbersome."[2] He is right, but the fact that the leader of a national party would deem it necessary to arm the people with a club to wave over the heads of their representatives speaks to the growing alienation he finds in the land.

By 1920, populist candidates had won seats in state legislatures across the U.S. Midwest. Many states adopted the devices of direct democracy — recall, citizen initiatives, and referendums. Although the populist movement spread to Canada (and lingers today in the Reform and Social Credit parties), direct democracy did not win the acceptance that it did south of the border.

In the period from 1913 to 1919, the legislatures of all four western provinces passed legislation that provided for referendums and citizen-initiated referendums. But the British Columbia legislation was never proclaimed by the provincial cabinet. Saskatchewan submitted its legislation to the voters as a referendum question in 1913, and the voters turned it down. Manitoba's direct-legislation law went all the way to the Judicial Committee of the Imperial Privy Council in London, which ruled it unconstitutional (on the ground that it unilaterally reduced the powers of the lieutenant-governor by permitting the adoption of laws without his consent). Alberta never used its direct-legislation law. It was finally repealed in 1958 by the Social Credit government led, ironically, by Preston Manning's father, Ernest Manning.

As the populist movement faded and was absorbed into the mainstream parties, the populist belief that an elected member owes his or her paramount responsibility to his or her constituents and constituency association was replaced by the concept of responsibility to the member's party and cabinet. The Reform Party's call for direct democracy can be seen either as a throwback to an earlier populist era or as a renewal of a suppressed but never extinguished desire to bring government closer to the people. Direct democracy would wreak havoc on the traditional party system. It would be virtually impossible for any government to operate with the twin clubs of recall and citizen-initiated legislation hanging over its head.

Manning tries to play down the potential for dislocation. "The number of names required to launch a citizens' initiative should be high enough to prevent frivolous use of this exercise," he writes. He suggests a minimum of 3 per cent of the population — or about 780,000 signatures — to force a referendum on a piece of citizen-inspired legislation. He is vague about the recall of elected members, except to say that the threshold of signatures to compel a vote to remove a member and force a byelection would have to be quite high. "We are not saying that a nation that has averaged one national referendum per century should suddenly start to have one every second Tuesday," Manning continues. "But we are saying that there must be some reasonable middle ground where, at least from time to time, on important issues, the public can have a direct say in certain key national decisions. . . . We advocate these measures as a necessary complement to parliamentary democracy, to make the government more representative and responsible than at present."[3]

The popular appeal of the Reform Party means that the old-line parties can no longer disregard the clamor for change and renewal. They will ignore at their peril the alienation that exists among millions of Canadians who feel they are not represented by today's politicians playing today's political games by today's rules. They will also ignore at their peril the growing desire of Canadians to have more control over their lives, their governments, and their politicians.

If the politicians — in the backrooms as much as in the frontrooms — do not embrace reform, they will risk becoming irrelevant. Worse, they will invite radical innovations like recall petitions, citizen-initiated referendums, and even proportional representation as the public seeks ways to increase the accountability of their politicians. Politicians must come to grips with reforms that fall into the third category — reforms that would change the system to achieve greater fairness in the competition among parties and candidates, greater openness in all spheres of political activity, and equal access for women and members of minority groups, both as candidates and as managers in the party backrooms.

The political parties should be the starting-point for reform. The emphasis should be on strengthening them, not undermining them. Today's parties are reasonably efficient election machines. They can assemble an organization, raise and spend election funds, commission polls, make commercials, flood the postal system with junk-mail appeals for votes, and get their leader on the television news virtually every night with just the right "sound bite."

Between elections, however, Canadian political parties are irrelevant. They do not play any significant role in the life of the country. No one — not even their own members — looks to political parties for ideas, for inspiration, for leadership on the concerns of the day. No one is interested in the parties' policies between elections. No one even knows the identities of the national presidents of the three major parties. Starved for funds, the parties busy themselves trying to scrape up enough money to pay the interest charges, at least, on their debt at the bank. The parties are tired, they are lethargic, they seem incapable of stirring themselves to useful activity. If they all went out of business tomorrow, most Canadians would not notice — until the next election.

Yet Canada needs more national institutions, not fewer, to advance understanding and reconciliation. We are rough on those we do have, making their health and survival secondary to the short-term considerations of spending control and partisan advantage. The Canadian Broadcasting Corporation is compelled by the government to close television stations at the precise time when, in the interest of national unity, it should be expanding its reach and its national service. Via Rail is emasculated, making it more difficult for Canadians to visit other Canadians in this huge land. The Economic Council of Canada and the Science Council of Canada are abolished, not because the country has no need for intelligent economic and scientific direction, but simply because the Mulroney government did not like the two councils.

Political parties are national institutions in their own way. With encouragement, they could play a part in bringing Canadians together. They could help to involve their members and other Canadians in the great national and global causes of the day. They could help a grumpy people to feel better about themselves and their country by making them part of the decisions that affect their destinies. Properly led, inspired and nurtured, political parties can be a force for reconciliation, not for alienation.

The road to reform starts at the top, with the leaders. Parties will be stronger and more relevant when leaders learn to accept dissent among their followers as natural, healthy, and inevitable. Nothing squeezes the life out of a political party like a leader who will not brook public dissent or disagreement from his or her caucus. One of the chief complaints about today's politics — that elected members are so enslaved by party and cabinet discipline that they do not dare speak out for their constituents — could be addressed by reforming parliamentary procedures.

All parties pay lip-service to parliamentary reform, but parties in power become very nervous when it is suggested that it is not necessary that they always get their own way in Parliament or legislatures. Governments find it hard to accept that the sky will not fall if they lose the occasional — or more than occasional — vote in the chamber. In every parliamentary year, however, there are only two or three times when votes must be taken that are clearly tests of confidence in the administration. The main vote on the Speech from the Throne is one such occasion. The budget is another (as Joe Clark's Conservative government discovered to its chagrin in December 1979). And from time to time there are items of legislation that are so fundamental to the government's program that its fate must rest on their passage; the Mulroney government's goods and services tax and the free-trade agreement with the United States would clearly fall into this category.

On most major measures, and all routine ones, however, members should be free to vote as their conscience or the wishes of their constituents lead them. It would be a salutary thing if the government knew it could not simply lay on the whips to get its legislation through Parliament, if it knew it had to broker its proposals with the backbenches, as the White House does with Congress. Ministers would have to negotiate with their own supporters and, if they could not line up enough of them, they would have to approach opposition members. The government would have to be prepared to accept amendments in return for support. The result would be better laws and improved morale among backbenchers — and a signal to the people that their representatives do not forget them and their wishes once they arrive in the capital.

Another message that needs to be sent to the public is the word that parties and their leaders are open to new people and new ideas — specifically, that they welcome women and members of minority groups who have traditionally been shut out of the hierarchy of mainstream parties. For too many years, politicians have cynically exploited ethnic groups at election time — and ethnic groups have not hesitated to use their voting clout to extract favors from politicians.

In the 1960s and early 1970s, a required stop for national leaders in the opening stages of an election campaign was Toronto for a session with the publishers of the city's ethnic newspapers. In those days, the ethnic press was the surest way to reach voters who spoke little English or who did not read English newspapers. The meetings between leaders and publishers, however, had less to do with the great issues of the day than they did with the politicians' desire for editorial endorsement and the publishers' wish for reassurance of continued government advertising for their publications. Usually, a meeting of minds was arranged.

The inception of official multiculturalism simply entrenched the system of government subsidies for minority groups, paid by politicians in the none-too-subtle expectation that this expenditure of public funds would produce dividends in the form of workers and votes at election time. Multiculturalism is a boondoggle that now costs federal taxpayers $119 million a year. No politician really expects that he or she can lock up the Italian vote by giving grants to Italian-Canadian organizations in Toronto. Politicians know, however, that they can expect trouble with the Ukrainian vote in Winnipeg if they give money to Italians in Toronto and not to Ukrainian groups in the Manitoba capital. Once a grant is given to one ethnic organization, it becomes painfully difficult, politically, to say no to any other group.

The Reform Party is the only party that advocates the abolition of federal support to ethnic groups, although some politicians in other parties privately agree that multiculturalism grants, having become just another pork barrel, should be done away with. Even some minority-group leaders agree, on the grounds that it is humiliating for ethnic organizations to live on the charity of government.

In recent years, politicians have become concerned about a new practice: the packing of nomination meetings by hundreds of ethnic voters who have become instant party members, their membership fees paid by the candidate who solicited their support and who sent the buses to fetch them to the meeting. As Joey Smallwood emptied the hospitals of St. John's in 1969 and as Brian Mulroney emptied the Old Brewery Mission in Montreal in 1983 — both determined to elect delegates to support their leadership campaigns — so Liberal candidates emptied Italian, Portuguese, Greek, and other community centres to help them win nominations in the Toronto area in the 1988 election. It became a fairly common scene: As the new Liberals piled off their buses, stacks of membership applications and bundles of cash were deposited on the registration desks. "Many of them had never been to a Liberal party meeting before and probably never will be again," said David Smith, a former MP and cabinet minister who was named Ontario chairman of the Liberal campaign committee for the next federal election.[4]

Following their 1988 experience, which was repeated on a smaller scale in their 1990 federal leadership race, the Liberals adopted new rules. Party membership lists were closed in advance of nomination meetings (ninety days in advance in the case of Ontario). All new members were required to pay for their own memberships by personal cheque or money order. Liberal leader Jean Chrétien was authorized to reject any candidate who had been nominated in a way that he felt was unfit or inappropriate.

Changing the rules to reduce abuse, however, does not address the more fundamental problem: how to bring ethnic Canadians into the mainstream of political parties that historically have been dominated by English and French Canadians. The problem is especially acute among visible minorities; from 1965 through 1988, only ten members of visible minorities were elected to the House of Commons.

There is a similar problem in ending the underrepresentation of women: how to bring more women into positions of influence in political parties that are controlled by English and French Canadian *males.*

In both instances, the parties must reach out to recruit capable individuals, then knock down the internal barriers that block their advancement. For women, the first big barrier is gaining acceptance from the men in the backrooms. Every political organization is happy to have a woman as its secretary; in 1988, 68 per cent of the secretaries of federal constituency associations were women. But women accounted for only 20 per cent of the association presidents and 28 per cent of campaign managers.

Women need the acceptance and support of the men in the backrooms if they are to surmount their next big barrier — securing a party nomination in a winnable riding. Although a record 172 women ran for Parliament in 1988 (40 more than in 1984), a majority were nominated in ridings where they had no chance. In a research study for the Lortie Royal Commission, Lynda Erickson of Simon Fraser University examined the ridings in which female candidates were nominated in 1988. Only 30 per cent of women candidates were nominated in ridings considered winnable for their party, compared to 51 per cent of male candidates. Not only did they find themselves relegated to unpromising ridings, women were more likely than men — 47 per cent to 31 per cent — to face contested nominations.[5]

Given the obstacles, it is remarkable that more women than ever — 39 of them (or 13.2 per cent of all MPs) — managed to win election to the House of Commons in 1988, 11 more than in the 1984 election. Despite steady if unspectacular progress, women, with 51 per cent of the population, remain by far the most underrepresented group in Canadian politics. The situation has not improved dramatically since the Royal Commission on the Status of Women concluded more than twenty years ago that "the voice of government is still a man's voice."

The underrepresentation of women is the most serious issue confronting Canadian political parties today. Pressure for reform is coming both from women within the parties and from women's groups operating outside the formal political structure. The New Democratic Party has set a goal of 50 per cent of its nominations and 50 per cent of its seats going to women. (The NDP has some distance to go; in the 1988 election, women represented 28.5 per cent of its candidates, but only 11.6 per cent of the MPs it elected, a lower percentage than that of either the Liberals or the Tories.) Each of the three principal national parties has a women's commission to ensure female representation on the party's governing bodies. Each party has a special fund to assist women candidates — the Ellen Fairclough Foundation for the Tories, the Judy LaMarsh Fund for the Liberals, and the Agnes Macphail Fund for the NDP. But the funds are to assist women *after* they have been nominated; and the amounts are modest — typically $500 to $1,500 to help with such expenses as child care.

None of the federal parties provides assistance to women when they need it most: during their campaign for nomination.[6] Yet women historically have had far more trouble than men in raising money to contest nominations. The people, mainly male, who give to parties and candidates are more inclined to take a chance with a man than a woman. It is not until a woman has been elected and has established a name for herself, as Barbara McDougall and Kim Campbell have, that the money starts pouring in.

The Royal Commission on Electoral Reform and Party Financing approached the problem of pre-nomination funding for women from two directions. It tried to level the playing field for male and female candidates by proposing a limit on the amount that candidates could spend in campaigning for a nomination. (The limit would be just 10 per cent of the amount that a candidate would be permitted to spend in the election campaign.)

Second, the royal commission proposed a complicated scheme of financial incentives to encourage parties to nominate and to elect women. It recommended that the election-expense reimbursement or subsidy that parties receive be raised for those parties that succeed in getting more women elected. Once a party reached a floor of 20 per cent female MPs (a level no party has ever approached), its subsidy would be increased by a percentage equivalent to the percentage of its women members. In other words, if 25 per cent of the members elected by a party were women, the party headquarters would get a 25-per-cent-larger subsidy. If it elected 30 per cent women, the subsidy would be 30 per cent larger — and so on, until women constituted 40 per cent of the membership of the House of Commons, at which point the incentives would cease.[7]

The commission's incentives would be a handsome windfall to the parties. Based on the level of reimbursement paid in the 1988 election, a party that succeeded in electing 25 per cent women members would collect an incentive payment of about $400,000. But using the enriched level of reimbursement recommended by the commission, the incentive at the 25-per-cent level would be worth much more — about $850,000 to the Tories, based on their 1988 popular vote.

Unwieldy though the incentive scheme is, it moves in the right direction. So do the royal commission's recommendations for annual grants to the parties and for higher reimbursement at election time. The latter — a proposed election-expense subsidy of sixty cents for every vote received in the country — would be worth an extra $1.6 million to the Conservatives (based on their 1988 popular vote) and $1 million to the Liberals, although very little to the NDP. The proposed annual grant to parties, to assist them in non-election years, would be based on twenty-five cents per vote received in the previous election. At present, this would work out to about $1.4 million annually for the Tories, $1 million for the Liberals, and $670,000 for the NDP.

The greatest problem facing political parties today is their own between-elections poverty. The parties are starving while many of their candidates are wallowing in cash. As a rule, parties have trouble raising enough money to cover their operating expenses in non-election years. They hope they can generate enough from the faithful in election years to cover their campaign expenses and, with luck, pay down their deficit. If they are unlucky, they emerge from the campaign with a huge deficit and no prospect of reducing it. The Ontario Conservatives emerged from the 1990 provincial election $5 million in debt. The federal Liberals were at least $4 million in debt in 1992 as they began preparations for the next election. Yet Liberal candidates came out of the 1988 election with a combined surplus as large or larger than their national party's debt. Federal Tory candidates, successful and unsuccessful, amassed an average surplus of more than $20,000 apiece in that election.

Political parties can survive almost indefinitely without much money — no bank wants to force the bankruptcy of a party that might form the next government. But when they are broke they cannot undertake the kinds of reforms that the Canadian people demand. Without money, parties cannot address the underrepresentation of women and minority groups. They cannot hire full-time campaign managers to help qualified but unknown women get themselves nominated in winnable ridings. Without money, they cannot provide the professional training and assistance on polling, fund-raising, and advertising that a candidate needs to win election in the demanding 1990s.

The royal commission suggested several ways to put more money in the hands of national parties. All of them would be at the expense of the taxpayer in the form of higher election subsidies, annual operating grants to parties, or incentives for electing women. But the same end can be served by a different means, without burdening the taxpayer. It is a matter of redistributing the wealth from the bottom up to the top, from candidates to parties. Instead of permitting candidates or their constituency associations to sock their election surpluses away in the bank, the money (as much as $10 million to $13 million following a typical election) should be turned over to the parties, to be held in trust for the next election. Until then, each party could use the interest. If a candidate decided not to run again, his or her surplus would become the property of the party.

Toronto Conservative Ronald Atkey, who was minister of employment and immigration in the 1979 Clark government, thinks national parties are weaker than they used to be because so many of the financial resources have accumulated at the bottom, at the candidate and constituency level. The parties, he argues, should be demanding a larger slice of the funds raised by constituencies. When constituency associations hold annual fund-raising events, the payments are customarily processed through the national party so that tax credits can be issued to contributors. The parties customarily take 25 per cent off the top for this service. Atkey would raise it to 33 or 40 per cent.

If more money is to be pumped into party coffers, the quid pro quo for the public has to be greater openness and greater accountability. It is time — past time — that parties were required to report all their election spending, including the amounts they spend on polling. Polling has become a huge expense. Each of the national parties will spend between $1 million and $2 million on highly sophisticated polling programs in the next election. Yet because polling was deemed to be research it was not classified as an election expense, did not have to be reported, and did not count against a party's spending limit.

Gerald Caplan recalls losing the battle to have polling counted as an election expense. As federal secretary of the NDP in the early 1980s, he advocated that polling be included. The Conservatives were opposed, and the Liberals, after humming and hawing at great length, came down on the Tory side. Today, just about everyone, including the Lortie Royal Commission, accepts that political polling should be treated as an integral part of the cost of political campaigning.

Openness and accountability also dictate that two types of campaign that escaped the 1974 Election Expenses Act should be brought under its scrutiny and control. These are leadership campaigns and campaigns for riding nominations. In Ontario in 1990, David Peterson's provincial government, with all-party support, introduced partial controls on the financing of leadership campaigns. Candidates were required to disclose the sources of their campaign funds and to report their spending in detail, down to payments made to individual suppliers. The legislation did not, however, impose a ceiling on the amount leadership candidates could spend.

Aside from this Ontario attempt at regulation, the only controls on the amounts that leadership candidates may spend — and the only requirements as to what, if anything, they must disclose about the sources of their funds — are contained in the rules that the political parties adopt for their conventions. In 1976, Brian Mulroney thought so little of the Tory party's disclosure rules that he refused to report his leadership spending. And since there was no limit on spending in the 1983 Conservative leadership race, Joe Clark was able to spend more than ten times as much on his unsuccessful defence of his leadership as he had spent to win it seven years earlier. The NDP set an extremely low spending ceiling of $150,000 per candidate for its national leadership contest in 1989. The Liberals in 1990 set a limit of just under $1.7 million. Yet Jean Chrétien and Paul Martin reported spending $2.44 million and $2.37 million, respectively — without breaching the spending limit. This miracle of modern accounting was possible because certain classes of expenditure (including the travel and accommodation of the candidate, fund-raising expenses, and amounts spent before the campaign officially began) did not count against the $1.7 million limit. To confuse matters further, Chrétien and Martin actually spent more than the $2.44 million and $2.37 million they reported, but it was quite all right (as far as the party was concerned) because some expenses did not have to be reported at all.

The amounts spent by candidates for party nominations in constituencies are small potatoes compared to the spending of a leadership candidate. But the potential for abuse is just as great. Prospective candidates are not required to disclose the sources of their funds, or to report the amounts they spend, as long as the money is raised and spent before the election writ is issued. A candidate who expects a serious challenge spends lavishly to make himself or herself known in the months and weeks before the election is called, then scales back spending when the formal campaign period begins.

To counter public cynicism — and to ensure a more open process and fairer competition — there should be enforceable limits on the sums that candidates are allowed to spend on leadership and nomination campaigns. There should also be full public disclosure of where the money is raised and how it is spent. It defies logic to require this disclosure of sources and expenditures in election campaigns — as has been required since 1974 at the federal level — and not to require it at the equally vital stages of choosing party leaders and nominating candidates for public office.

A direct relationship exists between the public's faith in the integrity of the political system and the transparency of the system. The most opaque corner of the system is the corner in which parties make their secret financial arrangements for their leaders or would-be leaders. Mulroney and other Tories raised a trust fund, reportedly $300,000, for Claude Wagner when the former provincial Liberal cabinet minister resigned from the Quebec bench to enter federal politics as a Conservative in 1972. It was not the existence of the fund, but the surreptitious way it was raised, plus Wagner's denial of its existence, that doomed his hopes of winning the Tory leadership in 1976. When Brian Peckford resigned in 1989 after ten years as Tory leader and premier of Newfoundland, he had no money, no job, and no home. Prominent Conservatives organized a fund-raising dinner — with Mulroney as guest speaker — and collected $100,000 so that Peckford could at least buy a place to live. But the fund-raising effort was criticized as a back-door way of financing the retirement of a political leader.

Politics is a cruel and demanding business. It takes its players away from their careers at the peak of their earning power, and by the time it is finished with them, there may be nothing left for them. It is particularly cruel to the most prominent players. Few are as well adjusted as Walter Harris, Louis St. Laurent's finance minister in the 1950s, who, when his days in politics were done, returned home to tiny Markdale, Ontario, calmly picking up where he had left off, preparing mortgages for clients in a small-town law office with a linoleum floor. More, unfortunately, are like John Munro, the Trudeau-era minister from Hamilton, Ontario, who could not get politics out of his blood and kept trying desperately for a political comeback that was beyond his reach.

Some leading politicians are wealthy enough not to be left financially crippled by their years in public life and sure enough of their own instincts to know when to leave, without regrets. Pierre Trudeau was like that. So was Robert Stanfield. But many others, who live on what they can earn, need help while they are in office. Clyde Wells was earning about $200,000 in law practice in Newfoundland when he became leader of the provincial Liberals and found himself taking home a fraction of that amount; he needed an income supplement from the party. John Buchanan was unable to manage his personal finances during his years as premier of Nova Scotia; the Conservative party bailed him out. When John Turner was leader of the opposition, the taxpayers provided him with an official residence, Stornoway. But his wife felt she needed an apartment in Toronto, and the Liberal party paid the $3,000 monthly rent. Brian Mulroney and his wife wanted improvements made to their official residences at 24 Sussex Drive and Harrington Lake that were too ambitious even for the deep pockets of the federal Department of Public Works. The PC Canada Fund, the fundraising arm of the Tory party, quietly picked up at least $324,000 of these bills in Mulroney's first eighteen months in office.[8]

There is nothing wrong with politicians having party trust funds. There is nothing wrong with parties supplementing leaders' salaries, or bailing them out of debt, or renovating their residence. It is wrong only when it is done furtively, behind the public's back. The public is entitled to know where its politicians get their money and to whom they may be beholden. Parties have a responsibility to play it straight with their supporters. People who contribute to political parties might think twice about giving if they were told that their contributions were being used to rent an apartment for one leader's wife or to satisfy the redecorating lust of another leader and his wife. This, of course, is the reason they are not told.

There should be provisions for political parties to create trust funds or to provide other financial assistance to their leaders and other members. But the parties should be required by law to disclose the existence of all such funds or assistance, plus the identity of all recipients, the circumstances under which the assistance is being provided, and the repayment terms (if any). For their part, politicians should be obliged to disclose any assistance received from their party, and they should be forbidden to accept financial aid from private benefactors. And contributors to political parties should be informed that a portion of the funds collected may be used to support the lifestyle of the leader rather than the work of the party.

A few other reforms will help to achieve greater fairness in the competition among parties and candidates. Election-spending limits on parties and candidates have proved their value. They are absolutely essential to protect the public against the eventuality that the party or candidate with the most money will be able "buy" the election. Limits, however, are meaningless when so-called third parties — outside groups with vested interests — are allowed to spend freely to support or oppose one side or another during an election campaign. It does not matter whether the issue is free trade (as it was in 1988) or free love (as it never has been, alas). It does not matter whether the third party is the Business Council on National Issues or the Canadian Labour Congress, the gun lobby or one of the many groups upset about abortion. It does not matter whether the beneficiaries are the Tories, Liberals, New Democrats, or anyone else.

What does matter is that the contest be reserved for the players, free from the propaganda of lavish advertising campaigns mounted by lobbyists. The lobbyists are free to propagandize until an election begins. But once the election is called, they should retreat to the sidelines until the contest is over.

Third-party advertising should be banned outright, not restricted to $1,000 per individual or group as the Lortie Royal Commission recommended. If the principle of restricting the contest to the players is valid, there is no justification for making an exception for outsiders' expenditures of up to $1,000.

The legal argument against prohibiting third-party advertising is based on the guarantee of freedom of opinion and expression in the Charter of Rights and Freedoms. The charter, however, also provides that its freedoms are subject "to such reasonable limits prescribed by law as can be demonstrably justified in a free and democratic society." The need to assure fairness in elections more than justifies the reasonable limitation on the rights of special-interest groups by preventing them from becoming participants in the election campaign.

The same argument — the need to ensure fair competition — applies to another controversial subject: the publication of public-opinion polls. As V.O. Key, an American expert on public opinion, once observed, "To speak with precision about public opinion is a task not unlike coming to grips with the Holy Ghost."[9] The observation is as valid in Canada today as it was in the United States when it was made in 1965.

Nevertheless, public-opinion polls — there were twenty-six national polls published in the course of the seven-week federal campaign in 1988 and may be even more next time — do two things. They distract the news media from the issues and arguments of an election and turn the reportage into the political equivalent of horse-race coverage. (Who's first? Who's second? Who's gaining? Who cares?) Second, the polls do, in the opinion of most pollsters, influence voting intentions. An inaccurate or "rogue" poll can deflate a party's campaign. If it happens late in a campaign — as it did to Conservative leader Gary Filmon in the 1986 Manitoba election — the harm may be irreversible. The poll was wrong, but it was too late in the campaign to undo the damage. There is no guarantee that the Tories would have won that election if the rogue poll had never been broadcast or published, but they would have had a much fairer shot at winning.

Another menace to a fair election is the "phantom" poll — one that is manufactured by one party to halt the momentum of its opponents or to offset the advantage it feels that another party is receiving from the publication of legitimate polls. The most infamous case — the phantom Liberal poll in the 1989 Newfoundland election — is described by journalist-author Claire Hoy in *Margin of Error: Pollsters and the Manipulation of Canadian Politics.*[10]

Published polls had shown that Tom Rideout's Conservatives enjoyed a lead of from six to eleven points over Clyde Wells's Liberals. Having no polls of their own to counter the published polls, the Liberals concocted one. They did it with Wells's knowledge. Four senior Liberals spent fifteen minutes in a conference call debating what the "poll" should show — the Liberals far ahead or locked in a tight race with the Tories. In the end, they decided to make it a tight race. Four days before the election, the St. John's *Evening Telegram* reported the "results" on its front page — a dramatic reversal of election fortunes with the Liberals moving into a lead of 3.5 percentage points. "The whole thing was bullshit," a Liberal insider told Hoy. "The figures were just pulled out of the air. Clyde knew about it." The Liberals won that election.

Common sense suggests that the publication of polls be prohibited in the final ten days of a campaign to allow the effect of false or fabricated polls to fade, to give parties and candidates an opportunity to make their closing arguments, and to permit the voters to render their verdict in peace. The only ones who would be distressed by this ten-day prohibition would be the pollsters and the journalists. Their distress is a small price to pay for more equitable elections.

The road to reform is not an easy one. It is fraught with all the frustration, imprecision, and impermanence that Theodore Roszak, a U.S. historian and social critic who wrote *Where the Wasteland Ends: Politics and Transcendence in Post-Industrial Society*,[11] detected in American political life two decades ago. But the objectives of reform are clear: stronger, more responsible political parties; a more open political process; fairer competition among all parties and candidates.

14. BACK TO THE FUTURE

"Look at the bridge of the Starship Enterprise. *You don't see any newspapers."*
— Pollster Michael Adams

David Croll was a great reformer, a great Liberal, a great figure in Canadian politics. In a remarkable career that spanned nearly seven decades, he served as mayor of Windsor, Ontario (twice), was the first Jew ever appointed to a Canadian cabinet (Mitchell Hepburn, the Liberal premier of Ontario, had him carrying three portfolios in the 1930s), and resigned on principle when Hepburn refused to support his legislation to give workers at General Motors in Oshawa the right to form a union. He enlisted as a forty-year-old private in the Canadian Army in the Second World War and came out a lieutenant-colonel. He was elected to Parliament three times, and was appointed to the Senate by Prime Minister Louis St. Laurent in 1955, when senators were still named for life. It was in the Senate that Croll really blossomed. A politician with a deep social conscience who chose to sit with the Liberals but to sleep (ideologically) with the New Democrats, he is remembered for his work as chairman of the Senate committee on poverty, which reported in 1971. He was the most radical member of the Upper House, perhaps the only truly progressive senator. "I've been a step ahead, never a step behind," he used to say. And he was right. He understood the game of politics better than just about anyone else on Parliament Hill.

On the last day of his life, June 11, 1991, David Croll, ninety-one years old, arrived at his Senate office at 6:30 a.m. and put in his customary eleven-hour work day. In the morning, he attended a meeting of the Liberal Senate caucus to discuss policy and tactics. The Liberals, in opposition, were still smarting from the way Conservative prime minister Brian Mulroney had expanded the membership of the Senate and packed it with eight extra Tories to ram through the controversial goods and services tax.

Croll told his colleagues to stop whining about the past and to start worrying about the future. "What we should be talking about is winning the next election," he said. "And to do that, there are two basic messages that we, as Liberals, need to concentrate on and take to the public. First, we need to say that we support our current medicare system — 100 per cent. Second, we have to say, over and over again, 'Don't trust Mulroney! Don't trust Mulroney! Don't trust Mulroney!'"

That afternoon, as the Senate assembled for its daily sitting, Croll paused to talk to Senator Keith Davey, the doyen of the Liberal backroom. Davey complimented him on his speech to caucus. Croll replied that there was a third thing he had meant to say. "The third basic message that I forgot to mention this morning was that we should say now that the day we regain the government will be the last day of the GST."

When the Senate rose for the day, Croll went to a local restaurant for an early dinner with an old friend, then returned to the Château Laurier Hotel, where he had a room. That evening, his heart stopped.

The three political messages that Croll advanced that day are as old as political campaigns and as contemporary as the next election. They contain the three fundamentals of any successful electoral strategy. Establish a principle (defence of medicare). Attack an opponent's weakness (distrust of Mulroney). Have a plan (to repeal the GST). A strategy that encompasses those three elements may not automatically be a winner, but a strategy that lacks the three is doomed. As cynical as Canadian voters have become, they still expect their politicians to stand for principle. They want them to have a plan or a road-map — and they will vote for a party that has one, even if they don't agree with it (witness the Mulroney Tories on free trade in the 1988 federal election), in preference to a party that has no plan. And the effective way to mobilize undecided voters, and to attract soft supporters of another party, is to attack the other fellow's weakness — and to attack it hard and often.

Politics is the simplest of games, made arcane by the rites and rituals of the backrooms. Politics has sacrificed color and flavor to technology, in the process making politicians more remote from the electorate. They no longer get in a car or a train and go out to talk to the voters. Instead, they deliver their "core message" through a "research-driven voter contact," such as direct mail or phone bank, or they fly over the voters' heads, landing at intervals for a "photo opportunity" at which their "daily theme" is presented in a "sound bite." They employ "spin doctors" to persuade the press to put the desired slant on their message and "media strategists" to devise the perfect television clip.

Campaigns still must have the three elements identified by David Croll, but they have to be tailored for television. A principle is ineffective if it cannot be illustrated on videotape. A plan is hopeless if it cannot be explained in a clip of ten seconds or less. An attack on an opponent is impotent if it cannot be packed into a "killer line." In the modern political backroom, television is everything. It is where the voters of the 1990s get their information and form their opinions. Television's influence, already enormous, is growing at a breathtaking pace. The newspaper has become virtually irrelevant in political campaigns, of interest to news junkies and of curiosity to others who want to know what a paper's critics thought about a politician's performance on television the night before.

Michael Adams's company, Environics Research Group, conducts a regular study of the information-gleaning habits and preferences of Canadians. He sees the public's reliance on — and faith in — newspapers as a source of information declining even more rapidly than daily newspaper circulations are falling in the early 1990s. As younger Canadians lose (or never develop) the newspaper habit, they become dependent on television for all their information needs.

Newspapers are floundering. If the news is important, their readers will have learned all about it from TV long before their newspaper arrives. Newspaper editors react, wrong-headedly, by abandoning hard news to TV and trying to turn their papers into daily versions of what they imagine newsmagazines to be. They try to summarize information rather than report it, emphasizing context over events and trends over news. Instead of chasing stories that television does not have, cannot get, or will not pursue because they do not lend themselves to pictures on videotape, newspapers deliberately make themselves "softer." They seek to entertain first, and inform second. In so doing, they simply drive more readers to television newscasts for their information requirements.

Specialty television services are a relatively recent phenomenon, but their impact has been significant. The introduction of weather and sports channels led, between 1986 and 1991, to a ten-point increase in the percentage of people who look to television rather than to print for information about weather and sports. More significant to backroom politicians — and more discouraging for everyone who loves newspapers — in the same five years there was a similar ten-point increase in the proportion of Canadians who think television is better than print when it comes to interpreting national and international news.

"Ten points in five years!" says Adams. "You just project that. I'm talking 2010. Our children will not be using newspapers the way we do. . . . It's going to be devastating for newspapers. . . . They're gone [in influence]. Newsmagazines? Gone. The only people reading them will be some baby boomers who just love print and who love what only Shakespeare can do."

Although few seers predict the near-term demise of the newspaper-in-print — it retains a portability and ease of scanning that the electronic newspaper cannot match — futurists do argue that the Information Age is finally catching up to the newspaper. Paul Saffo, a research fellow at the Institute for the Future in Menlo Park, California, says traditional newspapers have become outmoded as computers have become society's preferred way of storing information. "We'll become paperless like we became horseless," he says. "There are still horses. But little girls ride them."[1]

There are no newspapers, as Adams observes, on the bridge of Star Trek's *Starship Enterprise*. Before long, there may be no newspapers on the campaign aircraft of political leaders as they hurtle about the country for the exclusive benefit of the television cameras.

There will be other changes. Gabor Apor, media consultant to Liberal leaders, predicts that political candidates will make ever-greater use of professional coaches. In the United States, he says, the first person a candidate hires is a speech and television coach:

> The first signal an individual sends out about his seriousness and the appropriateness and credibility of his campaign is the kind of talent he is able to attract to "package" the campaign. In Canada, it's exactly the opposite. The last person that gets hired is someone like me, and then they ask us to come in the back door, because the shit has already hit the fan. The assumption in Canada is that if someone like me's involved, it means the candidate's in trouble. But there's nothing wrong with learning how best to communicate what you have in your

head or what you have dedicated the next period of your life
to do.

The backroom politicians of the future will make much greater use
than they have of focus groups to devise strategy, develop campaign
policy, and test television commercials. By the spring of 1992, New
Democratic Party focus groups convinced campaign organizer Julie
Davis of two things: that the party had an opportunity to make
significant gains in Ontario in the next federal election; and, pro-
vocatively, that Reform Party prospects in the province were rapidly
diminishing. The late Nancy McLean of the Conservatives liked
focus groups to assess the reaction of real people to the policy
positions that the party was contemplating for the campaign. "They
also give you a litmus test, a very quick disaster check, on the stuff
you're about to put out in terms of advertising on the air," she said
in an interview shortly before her death.

Future campaigns are destined to be even more antiseptic, with
less human contact between politician and voter, than recent campaigns have been. For one thing, all parties — even the NDP, which
is legendary for its ability to array armies of campaign workers —
are having trouble attracting volunteers to staff their backrooms.
Former NDP federal secretary Bill Knight says the parties find themselves competing increasingly with charities and community groups,
such as Big Brothers and Big Sisters, for a limited pool of volunteers:

> Over a twenty-five-year period, there've been fewer and fewer
> people who would come and volunteer to work full-time in
> our campaigns. Now they say, "Well, I'll come in and work
> on a computer, I'll sit on a phone, I'll give you so many hours"
> — like they do for the United Way. In the old days, people
> used to come in, take their lumps in terms of their loss of
> income, and run campaigns full-time. Now it's much more
> sophisticated. There are pay scales, transportation costs cov-
> ered, and per diems.

Organizers find that concern for personal safety, especially among
women in urban areas, is causing the supply of door-to-door canvassers — the traditional lifeline of constituency politicians — to
dry up. Even with direct voter mail and telephone banks, every
party still relies on armies of volunteers who go door-to-door with

brochures to try to persuade householders to support their candidate or party. In a well-organized campaign, a party's canvassers may hit every door in a riding as many as three times. "Ten years from now, are you going to have canvassers going door-to-door in a lot of urban areas?" asks Liberal organizer Hershell Ezrin. "I doubt it." Ezrin sees a silver lining, however. Fewer canvassers will mean more phone banks, and in his view a telephone call is a surer way to get accurate information than an in-person encounter. "People tell you the truth on the phone that they won't tell you at the door. Candidates are notorious for coming back and saying, 'I don't know what you guys are worried about. I just canvassed that area — they're all in favor of me,' and I say to them, 'Listen, how many people do you know that to your face will say, "I wouldn't vote for you over my dead body"?'"

Pollster Allan Gregg wonders if politicians can keep up with new technology that is fast becoming available. He estimates that campaign managers today make use of only about 25 per cent of the technology in their arsenal. If they are savvy enough — and many are not — they can already use sophisticated polling, demographic data, phone banks, and computer-generated direct mail to identify and deliver a custom-tailored pitch to a single specific voter, without going within miles of his or her door.

In the future, there will be much more of the sort of campaigning that Gregg talks about. The process, he explains, may begin with a phone poll to identify the characteristics of swing voters — voters who are potential supporters of the party in question. Then:

> Once you find out that your swing voter is, for example, single women in apartment buildings, then using census data, postal-code data, and telephone data, you can draw the names, addresses, and telephone numbers of people who live in polling areas, who have profiles that correspond most closely to your target-voter profile. And so now you're not dealing with just an apartment on the corner of Willowbank and Oriole Parkway. You are dealing with Ms Jones, Ms Smith — and you can target them. . . .
>
> Then you can start a dialogue to identify, persuade, and change the views of those key voters in those key polls in those key ridings. You start again with the use of polling. You see that the single women in apartment buildings are disproportionately concerned about inflation, cost of living or whatever the attitudinal profile is. You send them a letter from the

leader, usually very personalized, using laser printers. "Dear Ms Jones: You know the cost of living, blah, blah, blah," and out come the paragraphs. Someone gets on the phone three days later saying, "I've got a note here in front of me from our leader. Is there anything else you'd like to —? Oh, I see, you're really pissed off about the seal hunt." What you've done is, you've pre-programmed 150 different paragraphs on different issues and you just type in 53, which is the seal hunt. The next letter goes out. At the end [of the phone conversation], you're asking how likely is it that we can count on your support. [If] she says, "No way," she's gone, out of the system. If she says, "Absolutely, take it to the bank," she's there for election-day activity. If she's kind of somewhere in between, she's not voting Tory and she's got a second choice that's PC, and she's likely to switch, then she becomes the target of subsequent activity. The next letter comes, addressing very particularly the concern she has articulated over the telephone. If someone was very concerned about the seal hunt — "Let me tell you what we want to do — boom, boom, etc."

Another telephone call comes: "Have you received the letter on the seal hunt? Are you happy with it? How likely is it that we could count on your support?" If it's yes, put her on the election-day list. If you've pissed her off, take her name out of the system. If she's in the persuadable category, in comes the third letter. The third letter's always from the local candidate, because he's on the ballot, the leader isn't. "The leader tells me that he's been writing to you about — blah, blah, blah, etc."

Pollsters like Gregg, however, lie awake nights worrying about a new generation of technology that threatens their business. Especially distressing is new call-management telephone technology that permits people at home to identify and screen incoming calls before answering them. Already, fewer residents are accepting calls from polling companies. Pollsters across North America report steep rises in refusal rates — the proportion of respondents who refuse to participate in telephone surveys. According to a 1990 survey in the United States, 36 per cent of people polled had refused to participate in a poll that year. Ironically, the refusal rate on the survey that reported this finding was even higher — 54 per cent.[2] One leading Canadian polling house reports that the refusal rate in its national surveys reached 35 per cent in 1992. Refusals were highest in Ontario (42 per cent) and lowest in the Atlantic Provinces (19 per cent), where people apparently still like to talk to pollsters. (The polling industry says refusal rates are climbing because busy people do not have the time to answer questions. Critics have a different explanation — too many polls, too much telemarketing.)

Pollsters fear that soaring refusal rates may raise their costs to the point that telephone surveys become uneconomic. Even more serious, in their view, is the prospect that so many people will decline to take their calls that they will be unable to draw representative, statistically valid samples for phone surveys. Already, they are looking for other ways to poll. Gregg has experimented with a variation of the "people meter" technology used to measure television viewership. The cost is prohibitive, he says — about $1,000 per respondent to select a panel scientifically, install the meters, and conduct the poll. The other big obstacle is human idiosyncrasy — people do not want strangers connecting unfamiliar devices to their television receivers. "We've done advertising tests where we had to bring in portable VCR recorder-players with the screen built right in because they won't let you attach anything to their TV set," he says. "And if the set has to be serviced, the liabilities are terrible."

Pay-per-view television and interactive TV programming also worry backroom politicians as they peer into the future. If, increasingly, people pay for the programs they watch, how many, they wonder, will pay to watch political programs? Interactive television is already becoming available. It lets viewers choose what they wish to see and what they do not want to see in a program. Most viewers probably will not to choose to watch commercials — which will create a new challenge for political advertising specialists, as well as for normal advertisers.

Canadian politicians are leery about many technological advances. They have some good reasons for trepidation. In 1971, the Ontario Conservatives wanted to emphasize a new, modern image when they assembled at Maple Leaf Gardens in Toronto to elect a leader to succeed John Robarts,who had been premier for the past ten years. The party rented the latest in American voting machines for their convention. But the machines broke down and the Tories had to revert to paper ballots. The humiliating snafu caused the balloting to stretch through the afternoon and evening and into the wee hours of the next morning before Bill Davis was finally declared elected.

Twenty-one years later, in June 1992, the Nova Scotia Liberal party adopted a computerized phone-in system to elect its new leader. For $25, any Liberal in Nova Scotia could obtain a personal identification number that allowed him or her to vote. Party members phoned special 1–900 numbers — there was a separate number for each leadership candidate — and punched their PINs on their touch-tone phone to register their vote. The idea seemed simple but the complications were enormous. The calls — all of them within Nova Scotia — were actually processed by computers in Ottawa, Toronto, and Wichita, Kansas. The volume of calls was so great that the computers could not record the votes. Some Liberals reported making as many as 84 attempts to get through to record their votes. The more often they tried, the more they overloaded the system. Many Liberals suspected that Nova Scotia Tories with touch-tone phones had deliberately sabotaged the balloting. The chaos was so great that the Liberals called off the vote.

Repeating the exercise two weeks later, they succeeded in electing a new leader — John Savage, the mayor of Dartmouth, who defeated poultry farmer Don Downe on the second ballot as 6,999 votes were called in — but it may be some time before other parties experiment with phone-in voting. Apart from the risk of sabotage by outsiders, there is potential for abuse by a party's own members. According to Halifax consultants James O'Hagan and Peter Dwyer, one Nova Scotia Liberal reportedly registered and paid for 250 PINs for his own use. There is also an issue of confidentiality. Because every Liberal who called one of the 1–900 numbers to vote was billed 50 cents per call, the telephone company has a record of who voted for each candidate — or, at least, whose phone was used to cast which votes — in violation of the principle of the secret ballot.

Ross Perot, the billionaire who campaigned briefly for president of the United States in 1992, was an ardent advocate of what some Americans dubbed "teledemocracy." Perot talked about how he would use an "electronic town hall" — perhaps a weekly interactive television program — to help him govern from the White House. As he explained it, the president, congressional leaders and assorted experts would go on national TV to present their views on proposed pieces of legislation. When they were finished, voters would register their verdict by calling in with their touch-tone phones, by pushing special buttons on their television sets, or by some other means. It was all a bit vague, a bit scary, and a bit simplistic. Some people, like Frank Borman, a former U.S. astronaut, did not like the notion of "teledemocracy" at all. Borman, who was once hired by Perot to test the electronic town hall idea, told the *New York*

Times he had concluded that it was a bad idea, one with "enormous potential for manipulating the emotions of people" and for intimidating elected representatives. "You realize as you get older that a lot of issues are very profound and difficult to understand," Borman said. "I don't think you can govern 250 million people with a TV set."

American political scientist Jeffrey Abramson, of Brandeis University, says it is not yet clear whether the faster, more direct routes of communication opened by the new technologies will be used to sustain and enrich conversation among citizens, or whether they will simply put people on the receiving end of more TV ads and more polls. "Democracy demands a concern for, and a familiarity with, the views of others," Abramson continues."When electronic democracy is envisaged as a way of permitting individuals, isolated in their own homes, to respond to direct-mail stimuli while avoiding the meetings and conversations that alone permit an individual to find his interests in a public context, then the communications revolution threatens democracy with the historic ills of faction and balkanization — different interests competing for power with no sense of community or a common good, the winners bearing no responsibilities for the life of the losers in their midst."[3]

Canadian politicians are responding to the proposition advanced in 1982 by the U.S. social forecaster John Naisbitt: "The more high technology around us, the more the need for human touch."[4] Crude home-made placards — or crude placards that look as though they were made at home (even if they were actually mass-produced by a print shop) — are making a comeback at leadership conventions. Politicians are reverting to handwritten notes of appreciation. "It used to be really chic to put thank-you notes on computer and have them turned out professionally," says Tory backroom veteran Senator Finlay MacDonald. "But now everybody knows they come out of the computer, so the politicians write handwritten notes. It's the same thing as writing a note of condolence to the widow of a friend. You don't type it out. It's a handwritten note."

And Gabor Apor sees a shift back to basics in political image making. "In the world we're living in today, not being slick and not being terribly professional is the best characteristic that perhaps you can put forward," he says. "It adds to your sense of sincerity, your sense of integrity, and your sense of reality."

Home-made signs, handwritten notes, less slickness in politicians' images. These do not amount to a dramatic change in the operations of Canadian backroom politics. But anything at all that brings a human touch to our electronic democracy is welcome. Human contact is as vital to the health of the political system today as it was in the days before the pollster, computer, phone bank, sound bite, and TV clip. Back in the days when a politician like David Croll spoke for the conscience of the nation.

APPENDIX A
National Election
Campaign Organization Chart

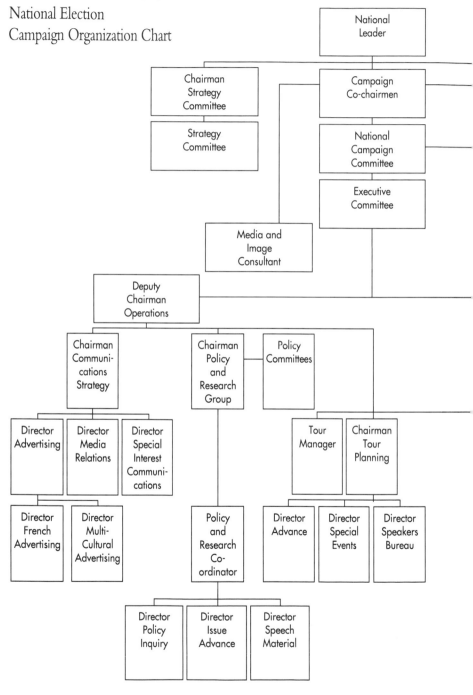

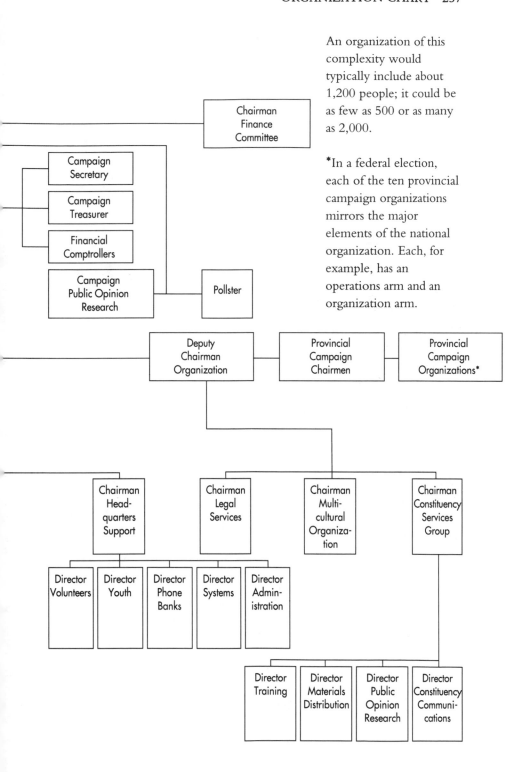

An organization of this complexity would typically include about 1,200 people; it could be as few as 500 or as many as 2,000.

*In a federal election, each of the ten provincial campaign organizations mirrors the major elements of the national organization. Each, for example, has an operations arm and an organization arm.

APPENDIX B
Leadership Conventions in Canada 1967-1992

PROVINCIAL LEADERSHIP CONVENTIONS

NEWFOUNDLAND
Liberal Party of Newfoundland and Labrador

1969

Joseph Smallwood	1,070			
John C. Crosbie	440			
Alec Hickman	187			
Randy Joyce	13			
Peter Cook	3			
Vince Spencer	2			

1972

Ed Roberts	564
Tom Burgess	82

1974

Ed Roberts	337	403
Joseph Smallwood	305	298
Steve Neary	57	—
Roger Simmons	24	—

1977

William Rowe	159	150	237	439
Ed Roberts	356	378	373	376
Steve Neary	238	220	215	—
Roger Simmons	115	100	—	—
Hugh Shea	2	—	—	—

1979

Don Jamieson acclaimed after William Rowe stepped down

1980

Len Stirling	666
Les Thoms	140

Edward Noseworthy	1
1984	
Leo Barry	517
Eugene Hiscock	51
Hugh Shea	24
1987	
Clyde Wells	564
Winston Baker	67

New Democratic Party of Newfoundland and Labrador

1970
John Connors   no records
1972
John Connors   no records
1974
Gerry Panting   no records
1977
John Green acclaimed
1980
Fonse Faour acclaimed
1981
Peter Fenwick acclaimed
1989

Cle Newhook	126
Gene Long	106

Progressive Conservative Party of Newfoundland and Labrador

1970

Frank Moores	425		
Hubert Kitchen	91		
Walter Carter	50		
John Carter	41		
Hugh Shea	2		
Joseph Noel	2		
Frank Howard-Rose	1		
1979			
Brian Peckford	200	272	331
William Doody	157	184	208

Walter Carter	87	83	—
Leo Barry	84	99	80
Jim Morgan	56	19	—
Ed Maynard	26	—	—
Tom Hickey	24	—	—
Ralph Trask	2	—	—
Kenneth Prouse	0	—	—
Dorothy Wyatt	0	—	(And her father was a delegate)

1989

Tom Rideout	313	363	403
Len Simms	262	318	377
Neil Windsor	109	64	—
Loyola Hearn	83	38	—
Hal Barrett	22	—	—

1991
Len Simms acclaimed

PRINCE EDWARD ISLAND
Liberal Party of Prince Edward Island

1978

Bennett Campbell	963
Gerard Mitchell	382

1981

Joe Ghiz	905
Gilbert Clements	482

The Island New Democrats

1969
David Hall   No records
1972
Aquinas Ryan   No records
1981
Doug Murray acclaimed
1983
Jim Mayne   Winner on 1st ballot   (results not made public)
David Burke
Maurice Darte

1991

Larry Duchesne	93	114
Mike LeClair	103	97
Judy Whittaker	49	—

Progressive Conservative Party of Prince Edward Island

1968

George A. Key, Jr.	691
Dr. Cyril Sinnott	474
Ivan Kerry	159

1973

Mel McQuaid acclaimed

1976

Hon. J. Angus MacLean	589
James Lee	437

1981

James Lee	581	665	737
Barry Clark	348	463	577
Fred Driscoll	282	261	—
Pat Binns	237	—	—

1988

Mel Gass	599
Andy Walker	572

1990

Pat Mella	473
Barry Clark	382
Roger Whittaker	32

NOVA SCOTIA
Liberal Party of Nova Scotia

1980

Sandy Cameron	340	412	558
Vince MacLean	244	327	356
Fraser Mooney	192	187	
Ken MacInnis	138		

1986

Vince MacLean	1,082
Jim Cowan	721

1992

John Savage	3,312	3,688
Don Downe	2,832	3,311
Ken MacInnis	755	
John Drish	60	
George Hawkins	39	

New Democratic Party of Nova Scotia

1968

Jeremy Akerman	80
Keith Jobson	76

1979

Jeremy Akerman unanimously re-elected

1980

Alexa McDonough	237
L.J. Arsenault	42
James McEachern	41

1983

Alexa McDonough acclaimed

Progressive Conservative Party of Nova Scotia

1967

G.I. Smith acclaimed

1971

John Buchanan	242	391
Gerald Doucet	282	346
Roland Thornhill	212	—

1991

Don Cameron	754	801	1,201
Roland Thornhill	736	775	1,058
Tom McInnis	680	762	—
Clair Callaghan	178	—	—

NEW BRUNSWICK
Liberal Party of New Brunswick

1971

Robert Higgins	737	986
John Bryden	575	683
Norbert Theriault	289	—

H.H. Williamson	89	—	
Maurice Harquail	21	—	
1978			
Joseph Daigle	700	1,042	1,363
John Bryden	647	775	899
Doug Young	432	565	—
Robert McCready	309	—	—
John Mooney	225	—	—
Herb Breau	100	—	—
1982			
Doug Young	1,324		
Joe Day	811		
Ray Frenette	306		
Alan Maher	160		
1985			
Frank McKenna	1,901		
Ray Frenette	854		

New Democratic Party of New Brunswick

1970
J. Albert Richardson acclaimed
1971
Pat Callaghan chosen by party provincial council (later overturned by NDP National Council)
1974
John LaBossiere   No records
1980
George Little   No records
1988

Elizabeth Weir	50
Mona Beaulieu	45

Progressive Conservative Party of New Brunswick

1969

Richard Hatfield	799
Charles Van Horne	554
Mathilda Blanchard	13

1989

Barbara Baird-Filliter	1,021

Hank Myers	348

1991

Dennis Cochrane	955
Bev Lawrence	116

QUEBEC
Parti Liberal du Québec

1970

Robert Bourassa	843
Claude Wagner	455
Pierre Laporte	288

1978

Claude Ryan	1,748
Raymond Garneau	807

1983

Robert Bourassa	2,138
Pierre Paradis	353
Daniel Johnson	343

Les Néo-Démocrates

1985

John Harney	1 ballot	No results announced
Pierre Bourgeois		
René Boulard		
Marie-Ange Gagnon-Sirois		

1987

Roland Morin	1 ballot	No results announced
Hélène Guay		

Parti Créditiste

1970

Camil Samson	1 ballot	1,035 total votes cast
Bernard Dumont		No results announced
René Lindsay		

1973

Yvon Dupuis	3,076	2,957
Camil Samson	1,621	1,809
Fabien Roy	1,178	949

Armand Bois	560	—

Union Nationale

1969

Jean-Jacques Bertrand	1,327		
Jean Guy Cardinal	938		
André Léveillé	22		

1971

Gabriel Loubier	529	568	607
Marcel Masse	482	544	584
Mario Beaulieu	178	99	—
Pierre Sévigny	26	—	—
André Léveillé	0	—	—

1976

Rodrigue Biron	764
Jacques Tetrault	270
M. Gerard Nepveu	123
Jean Guy Leboeuf	106
Bill Shaw	60

1981

Roch LaSalle acclaimed

Parti Québécois

1968

René Lévesque acclaimed

1985

Pierre-Marc Johnson	58.5%	Total of 97,389 votes cast
Pauline Marois	19.0%	in party-wide vote
Jean Garon	16.0%	
Francine Lalonde	less than 3%	
Guy Bertrand	less than 3%	
Luc Gagnon	less than 3%	

1988

Jacques Parizeau acclaimed

ONTARIO
Liberal Party of Ontario

1973

Robert Nixon	730	768	992

Norman Cafik	574	613	675		
Donald Deacon	402	316	—		
Michael Houlton	11	—	—		
1976					
Stuart Smith	629	742	998		
David Peterson	518	673	953		
Albert Roy	469	513	—		
Mark MacGuigan	308	—	—		
Larry Condon	37	—	—		
Michael Houlton	4	—	—		
1982					
David Peterson	966	1,136			
Sheila Copps	636	774			
Richard Thomas	234	148			
Jim Breithaupt	130	—			
John Sweeney	122	—			
1992					
Lyn McLeod	667	744	873	1,049	1,162
Murray Elston	740	767	865	988	1,153
Greg Sorbara	345	380	402	341	—
Charles Beer	247	307	289	—	—
Steve Mahoney	236	213	—	—	—
David Ramsay	216	—	—	—	—

Ontario New Democratic Party

1970		
Stephen Lewis	1,188	
Walter Pitman	642	
1978		
Michael Cassidy	675	980
Ian Deans	623	809
Mike Breaugh	499	—
1982		
Bob Rae	1,356	
Richard Johnston	512	
Jim Foulds	232	

Ontario Progressive Conservative Party

1971				
Bill Davis	548	595	669	812

Allan Lawrence	431	498	606	768
Darcy McKeough	273	288	346	—
Robert Welch	270	271	—	—
A.B.R. Lawrence	128	—	—	—
Robert Pharand	7	—	—	—
1985 (Jan.)				
Frank Miller	591	659	869	
Dennis Timbrell	421	508	—	
Larry Grossman	378	514	792	
Roy McMurtry	300	—	—	
1985 (Nov.)				
Larry Grossman	752	848		
Dennis Timbrell	661	829		
Alan Pope	271	—		
1990				
Mike Harris	7,175	(one person–one vote system)		
Diane Cunningham	5,825			

MANITOBA
Liberal Party of Manitoba

1969

Bobby Bend	877
Duncan Edmonds	483
Bernie Wolfe	142
Rev. Lloyd Henderson	16
1970	
I.H. Asper	720
Jack Nesbitt	329
1975	
Charles Huband	381
Rev. Lloyd Henderson	87
1981	
Douglas Lauchlan	493
Hugh Moran	300
1984	
Sharon Carstairs	307
Bill Ridgeway	238
Alan De Jardin	21
Stephen Zaretski	11

Manitoba New Democrats

1968

Russ Paulley	212		
Sid Green	168		

1969

Ed Schreyer	506		
Sid Green	177		

1979

Howard Pawley	467		
Muriel Smith	217		
Russell Doern	53		

1988

Gary Doer	631	744	835
Leonard Huraptak	543	622	814
Andy Anstett	317	290	—
Maureen Hemphill	167	—	—

Progressive Conservative Party of Manitoba

1967

Walter Weir	167	220	280
Sterling Lyon	141	170	183
Stewart E. McLean	87	73	—
Dr. George Johnson	71	—	—

1971

Sidney Spivak	261		
Harry Enns	215		

1975

Sterling Lyon	264		
Sidney Spivak	207		

1983

Gary Filmon	261	297	
Brian Ransom	217	251	
Clayton Manness	71	—	

SASKATCHEWAN
Liberal Party of Saskatchewan

1971

D.G. Steuart	404	535	

| C.P. Macdonald | 295 | 314 |
| George Leith | 171 | — |

1976

| Ted Malone | 563 |
| Tony Merchant | 496 |

1981
Ralph Goodale acclaimed

1989

Linda Haverstock	Landslide victory; margin not disclosed
June Blau[1]	
Neil Currie[1]	

Saskatchewan New Democratic Party

1970

Allan Blakeney	286	311	467
Roy Romanow	309	320	349
Don Mitchell	187	219	—
George Taylor	78	—	—

1987
Roy Romanow acclaimed

Progressive Conservative Party of Saskatchewan

1970

| Ed Nasserden | 250 votes cast; no results released |
| Martin Clary | |

1973

| Dick Collver | 453 votes cast; vote count not disclosed |
| Roy Bailey | |

1979

Grant Devine	418
Graham Taylor	201
Paul Rousseau	74

ALBERTA
Liberal Party of Alberta

1974

| Nick Taylor | 366 |

John Borger	293	
1988		
Laurence Decore	801	
Grant Mitchell	384	
Nick Taylor	259	

Alberta New Democrats

1968		
Grant Notley	143	
Gordon S.D. Wright	113	
Alan Bush	22	
1984		
Ray Martin acclaimed		

Progressive Conservative Party of Alberta

1985		
Don Getty	913	1,061
Julian Koziak	542	827
Ron Ghitter	428	—

Social Credit Party of Alberta

1968		
Harry Strom	814	915
G. Taylor	282	606
R. Reirson	255	—
Dr. W. Buck	184	147
E. Gerhard	137	—
1973		
Werner Schmidt	512	814
R. Clark	583	775
G. Taylor	406	—
J. Ludwig	71	—
1980		
Rod Sykes	538	
Julian Kinisky	292	

BRITISH COLUMBIA
Liberal Party of British Columbia

1968

Pat McGeer	686
Garde Gardom	316

1972

David Anderson	388
Bill Vander Zalm	171

1975

Gordon Gibson, Jr., acclaimed

1979

Jev Tothill	250
Hugh Chesley	27

1981

Shirley McLoughlin	195
Tom Finkelstein	146
Roland Bouwman	48

1984

Art Lee	319
Stanley Roberts	126
Will Pryhitkin	43
Ron Biggs	36

1987

Gordon Wilson acclaimed

New Democratic Party of British Columbia

1969

Tom Berger	364	411
Dave Barrett	249	375
Bob Williams	130	
John Conway	44	

1970

Dave Barrett acclaimed

1984

Robert Skelly	171	218	313	349	606
David Vickers	269	308	339	383	450
Bill King	240	263	292	333	—
David Stupich	132	147	114	—	—
Margaret Birrell	141	134	—	—	—

Graham Lea	101	—	—	—	—

1987
Michael Harcourt acclaimed

Progressive Conservative Party of British Columbia

1969

John de Wolfe	122	133		
Charles MacLean	111	128		
Don Paterson	24	—		

1971

Derril Warren	N/A	N/A	N/A	216

(Warren won on 4th ballot. Only partial results made public.)

John de Wolfe	N/A	N/A	N/A	146
Magus Verbrugge	N/A	N/A	89	—
John Green	N/A	48	—	—
Reg Grandison	28	—	—	—

1973
Scott Wallace acclaimed

1977

Vic Stephens	113
Larry Lewin	58
William Fairley	11

1980

Brian Westwood	219
Martin Dayton	105

1985
Peter Pollen acclaimed

1986
Jim McNeil elected unanimously by provincial executive

1989
Cal Lee named interim leader by provincial executive

1991
Peter Macdonald named leader by provincial executive

Social Credit Party of British Columbia

1973

Bill Bennett	883
Robert McClelland	269

Harvey Schroeder	204			
Jim Chabot	97			
Ed Smith	74			
James Mason	10			
1986				
Bill Vander Zalm	367	457	625	801
Grace McCarthy	244	280	305	—
Bud Smith	202	219	—	—
Brian Smith	196	255	342	454
Jim Nielsen	54	39	—	—
John Reynolds	54	30	—	—
Stephen Rogers	43	—	—	—
Bob Wenman	40	—	—	—
Cliff Michael	32	—	—	—
Bill Ritchie	28	—	—	—
Mel Couvelier	20	—	—	—
Kim Campbell	14	—	—	—
1991				
Rita Johnston	652	941		
Grace McCarthy	659	881		
Mel Couvelier	331	—		
Norm Jacobsen	169	—		
Duane Crandall	35	—		

FEDERAL LEADERSHIP CONVENTIONS (SINCE 1967)

Liberal Party of Canada

1968				
Pierre Trudeau	752	964	1,051	1,203
Robert Winters	293	473	621	954
John Turner	277	347	279	195
Paul Hellyer	330	465	377	—
J.J. Greene	169	104	29	—
Allan MacEachen	165	11	—	—
Paul Martin	277	—	—	—
Eric Kierans	103	—	—	—
Rev. Lloyd Henderson	0	—	—	— (his wife was a delegate)

1984

John Turner	1,593	1,862
Jean Chrétien	1,067	1,368
Donald Johnston	278	192
John Roberts	185	—
Mark MacGuigan	135	—
John Munro	93	—
Eugene Whelan	84	—

1990

Jean Chrétien	2,652
Paul Martin	1,176
Sheila Copps	499
Tom Wappel	267
John Nunziata	64

New Democratic Party of Canada

1971

David Lewis	661	715	742	1,046
James Laxer	378	407	508	612
John Harney	299	347	431	—
Ed Broadbent	236	223	—	—
Frank Howard	124	—	—	—

1975

Ed Broadbent	536	586	694	984
Rosemary Brown	413	397	494	658
Lorne Nystrom	345	342	413	—
John Harney	313	299	—	—
Douglas Campbell	11	—	—	—

1989

Audrey McLaughlin	646	829	1,072	1,316
Dave Barrett	566	780	947	1,072
Steve Langdon	351	519	393	—
Simon De Jong	315	289	—	—
Howard McCurdy	256	—	—	—
Ian Waddell	213	—	—	—
Roger Lagasse	53	—	—	—

Progressive Conservative Party of Canada

1967

Robert Stanfield	519	613	717	865	1,150

Duff Roblin	349	430	541	771	969
E. Davie Fulton	343	346	361	357	—
Alvin Hamilton	136	127	106	167	—
George Hees	395	299	277	—	—
John G. Diefenbaker	271	172	114	—	—
Donald M. Fleming	126	115	76	—	—
Wallace McCutcheon	137	76	—	—	—
Michael Starr	45	34	—	—	—
John P. Maclean	10	—	—	—	—
Mary Walker Sawka	2	—	—	—	—
1976					
Joe Clark	277	532	969	1,187	
Claude Wagner	531	667	1,003	1,112	
Brian Mulroney	357	419	369	—	
Jack Horner	235	286	—	—	
Flora MacDonald	214	239	—	—	
Paul Hellyer	231	118	—	—	
Patrick Nowlan	86	42	—	—	
John Fraser	127	34	—	—	
Sinclair Stevens	182	—	—	—	
James Gillies	87	—	—	—	
Heward Grafftey	33	—	—	—	
Dr. Richard Quittenton	0	—	—	—	
1983					
Brian Mulroney	874	1,021	1,036	1,584	
Joe Clark	1,091	1,085	1,058	1,325	
John Crosbie	639	781	858	—	
David Crombie	116	67	—	—	
Michael Wilson	144	—	—	—	
Peter Pocklington	102	—	—	—	
John Gamble	17	—	—	—	
Neil Fraser	5	—	—	—	

NOTES

CHAPTER ONE   The View from the Backroom

Most of the observations by politicians quoted in this chapter are from the authors' interviews with Nancy McLean, Gabor Apor, Patrick Lavelle, David MacNaughton, Larry Grossman, Tom MacMillan, Hershell Ezrin, Patrick Gossage, John Rae, Julie Davis, Senator Finlay MacDonald, Allan Gregg, and Keith Norton.

Goldwin Smith's observation about the nobility and vileness of politics is from his *Lectures on Modern History*, published in 1861 when he was Regius Professor of Modern History at Oxford. After settling permanently in Canada ten years later, he wrote extensively on Canadian and international affairs. The more he came to know Canada, the more he became convinced it was not viable as an independent nation. Smith became the leading proponent of his day of annexation with the United States.

1. For statistics on the underrepresentation of women, see *Reforming Electoral Democracy*, the report of the Royal Commission on Electoral Reform and Party Financing, Volume 1, Chapter 3.

CHAPTER TWO   Confessions of a Campaign Manager

Most of the stories and comments quoted in this chapter are from the authors' interviews with Errick (Skip) Willis, Ralph Lean, Jean Bazin, Douglas Bassett, Tom MacMillan, Boyd Simpson, David MacNaughton, Jean Pigott, Julie Davis, and John Latimer.

1. Ralph Lean chuckles at another memory of the quixotic Pocklington campaign: The candidate insisted that a floor pass to the convention be issued to the maître d'hôtel of his favorite Italian restaurant in Toronto.

2. That was about it for Pocklington, too. He placed sixth (of eight candidates) with 102 votes on the first ballot. He threw his support to Mulroney (taking 82 of his delegates with him). Mulroney won the leadership and became prime minister the following year. Pocklington never got close to the finance portfolio, however. The best he could get was an undertaking from Mulroney to look at the flat-

tax idea. Nothing ever came of it. And the Oilers lost to the Islanders in the 1983 Stanley Cup final.

3. Bud Smith cut his debt in half by organizing a business-outlook conference to which he invited two Toronto pollsters, Martin Goldfarb and Allan Gregg, to talk about the future of British Columbia under the new premier, Bill Vander Zalm. Both intrigued by and nervous about this strange fundamentalist with the simplistic right-wing views, businessmen uncomplainingly paid $1,000 apiece to attend. Because the conference was deemed to be a business expense, corporations were able to write it off against their income taxes, which they could not have done if Smith had simply asked the same corporations to donate the same amount to pay down his campaign deficit. Unlike individuals, corporations cannot claim tax credits for political contributions. The business-outlook conference netted Smith $115,000.

4. June Rowlands, the red and blue candidate, easily defeated Jack Layton, the green candidate, in November 1991 to become the first woman ever to be elected mayor of Toronto.

CHAPTER THREE Leaders and Lesser Mortals
In this chapter, the observations of backroom politicians about the leaders they serve are drawn in part from the authors' interviews with Robin Sears, Martin Goldfarb, Nancy McLean, Flora MacDonald, Patrick Gossage, David MacNaughton, Hugh Mackenzie, and Tom MacMillan.

John Naisbitt's comment on leadership is from *Megatrends.*

1. For a brief insider's account of this period, see Chapter 7, "The Phony War," of *Close to the Charisma: My Years Between the Press and Pierre Elliott Trudeau,* by Patrick Gossage, Trudeau's longtime press secretary.

2. See Senator Keith Davey's reminiscences in Chapter 13, "Powerless," of *The Rainmaker: A Passion for Politics.*

CHAPTER FOUR Where's the Pony?
Much of the material for this chapter is drawn from the authors' interviews with Michael Adams, Clare Westcott, Senator Keith Davey, Martin Goldfarb, Allan Gregg, Hershell Ezrin, and Bill Knight.

For a brief account of polling's early days in Canada, see Chapter 3,

"Coming of Age," of Claire Hoy's *Margin of Error: Pollsters and the Manipulation of Canadian Politics.*

1. Quoted in *Not Without Cause: David Peterson's Fall from Grace* by Georgette Gagnon and Dan Rath, p. 140.

2. Ibid., p. 141.

3. See Martin Goldfarb's introduction to *Marching to a Different Drummer: An Essay on the Liberals and Conservatives in Convention*, by Martin Goldfarb and Thomas Axworthy, p. xiii.

4. Keith Davey, *The Rainmaker: A Passion for Politics*, p. 45.

5. *Not Without Cause*, p. 160 [note].

6. Ibid., p. 120.

7. Ibid., p. 107.

CHAPTER FIVE The Ten Commandments

Much of the information in this chapter is drawn from the authors' interviews with Allan Gregg, Paul Curley, Nancy McLean, Michael Marzolini, Senator Keith Davey, Robin Sears, Hershell Ezrin, Larry Grossman, Julie Davis, Michael Adams, and Martin Goldfarb.

1. For a clear account of Allan Gregg's bomb-the-bridge strategy, see Chapter 12, "Bombing the Bridges," in Graham Fraser's *Playing for Keeps: The Making of the Prime Minister, 1988.*

2. Ibid., p. 322.

3. For an account of the strategies of the parties in the 1980 election, see Chapter 10, "The Right Question," in *Discipline of Power: The Conservative Interlude and the Liberal Restoration*, by Jeffrey Simpson.

4. Robin Sears knows whereof he speaks. As head of then NDP leader Ed Broadbent's palace guard in the 1988 federal election, he made certain the party's polling results were not shared beyond the inner circle, who absolutely had to know. When the campaign was over, with disappointing results for the NDP, disgruntled New Democrats made "Boy Stalin" (as Sears had come to be called) a

scapegoat in a post-mortem that was, as Sears says, "as vicious as any of them."

5. Careless as well as arrogant, Bud Smith, a married man, saw his political career devastated in 1990 when secretly recorded mobile-telephone conversations revealed his liaison with a woman television reporter. Smith resigned from the cabinet.

6. *Not Without Cause: David Peterson's Fall from Grace*, by Georgette Gagnon and Dan Rath, p. 144. For a discussion of the use of political focus groups, see also Chapter 8, "The Sultans of Spin."

7. See Chapter 14, "Poll Abuse," in Claire Hoy's *Margin of Error: Pollsters and the Manipulation of Canadian Politics*.

8. Edwin Goodman, *Life of the Party*, pp. 190–91.

9. Prince Charles to Joe Clark, Governor General's Dinner, Ottawa, June 20, 1983.

10. For an account of John Crosbie's leadership campaign, see Chapter 4, "Je suis canadien," in *Contenders: The Tory Quest for Power* by Patrick Martin, Allan Gregg, and George Perlin.

Crosbie's leadership ambitions self-destructed late in the campaign in Longueuil, Quebec. He was tired. He was irritable. And he had all he could take of questions about his inability to speak even the most rudimentary French. When reporters raised the language question again, his temper erupted. "There are 20 million of us who are unilingual English or French," he said. "I don't think that the 3.7 million who are bilingual should suddenly think themselves some kind of aristocracy and only leaders can come from their small group." When a reporter asked how he proposed to speak to the people of Quebec, Crosbie snapped: "I cannot talk to the Chinese people in their own language either. . . . I can't talk to the German people in their own language. Does that mean there should be no relationships between China and Canada or Canada and Germany, or whatever?" Crosbie had exposed the extent of his inability to come to grips with the concept of Canada as a country of two official, and equal, languages. As *Le Journal de Montréal* put it in a headline: "For Crosbie, French Is Not More Important Than Chinese or German."

11. The anti-Clark vote that might have gone to Lougheed and Davis went instead to Mulroney and Crosbie. Clark, with 1,091 of 2,988 votes cast, had the support of 37 per cent of the delegates, two points fewer than Robert Teeter had projected four months earlier.

CHAPTER SIX Meet the Machine

Material for this chapter is drawn in part from the authors' interviews with George Gibault, Tom MacMillan, Gabor Apor, Frank McMillan, Graham Murray, Hershell Ezrin, Paul Curley, Boyd Simpson, John Crosbie, Jane Crosbie, Ralph Lean, Bill Knight, Nancy McLean, and Robin Sears.

1. The intimidation tactics worked. Joey Smallwood beat back John Crosbie's challenge to retain his leadership in 1969, but the battle exposed his vulnerability. Two years later, the Smallwood government was toppled by the Conservatives, led by Frank Moores and supported by Crosbie.

2. Saskatoon *Star Phoenix*, June 22, 1989. Quoted by Preston Manning in *The New Canada*, pp. 127–29.

3. For Preston Manning's account of the Beaver River byelection and the Alberta Senate election, see Chapters 10 and 11 of *The New Canada*.

4. Jerry Bruno, *The Advance Man*, p. 52.

CHAPTER SEVEN Adventures in Videoland

Many of the observations in this chapter about the impact of television on the political process come from the authors' interviews with Hershell Ezrin, Gabor Apor, Ray Heard, Bill Knight, Barry McLoughlin, Jean Bazin, Boyd Simpson, Nancy McLean, Patrick Gossage, Eddie Goldenberg, Douglas Bassett, Clare Westcott, Robin Sears, and Doug Hurley.

Roger Simon's comment on choosing a president is from *Road Show*.

1. Lloyd Bentsen first tried the "killer line" during his debate rehearsals in a vacant bar in Austin, Texas. Ohio congressman Dennis Eckart, playing Quayle, made a Kennedy comparison, to which Bentsen replied: "You're no more like Jack Kennedy than George

Bush is like Ronald Reagan." The line got sharper with honing. For a good account of TV debates in the 1988 U.S. election, see Roger Simon's *Road Show*.

2. Quoted by journalist-author Graham Fraser in *Playing for Keeps: The Making of the Prime Minister' 1988*, p. 268. See Chapter 10, "The TV Debates," for a good account of the television debates in the 1988 election.

3. See *Reforming Electoral Democracy*, the report of the Royal Commission on Electoral Reform and Party Financing, Volume 1, Chapter 6, "Fairness in the Electoral Process."

4. Quoted by Fraser, *Playing for Keeps*, p. 187.

CHAPTER EIGHT Money Makes the (Political) World Go Round

Many of the observations quoted in this chapter are from the authors' interviews with retired senator John Godfrey, Robin Sears, Senator Finlay MacDonald, John Rae, Terry Yates, Jean-Marc Hamel, Wendy Walker, David MacNaughton, Eddie Goldenberg, and Paul Curley.

1. According to unofficial estimates, Joe Clark and Brian Mulroney may each have spent close to $3 million on his leadership campaign in 1983.

2. The advantage of incumbency is analysed by D. Keith Heintzman, a doctoral student at Carleton University, in a study for the Royal Commission on Electoral Reform and Party Financing. His paper, "Electoral Competition, Campaign Expenditure and Incumbency Advantage," appears in Volume 5 of the royal commission's research studies, published in 1992. Heintzman examined the success rate of incumbents in five U.S. House elections, from 1980 to 1988, inclusive, and in four Canadian general elections, from 1979 to 1988, inclusive.

3. See ibid.

4. Authors' study of results in thirty swing ridings in Ontario in the 1984 and 1988 elections. Spending figures as reported by candidates to the Chief Electoral Officer of Canada.

CHAPTER NINE   Bagmen and Other Heroes

Observations on political fund-raising in this chapter have been drawn from the authors' interviews with Paul Curley, retired senator John Godfrey, Senator Keith Davey, Jean-Marc Hamel, Bud Slattery, Bill Knight, Terry Yates, Robert Odell, Hugh Mackenzie, and Senator Finlay MacDonald.

1. As it turned out, the Conservatives stopped the Liberals but did not win a majority for themselves. They took 136 of the 282 seats, as there were then in the House of Commons. The Liberals won 114, the NDP 26, and Social Credit 6.

2. J.L. Granatstein prepared a study of Conservative party finances between 1939 and 1945 for the five-member federal Committee on Election Expenses, which reported in 1966.

3. Two years later, Ian Sinclair got even. He announced CP would no longer contribute to political parties and urged other companies to follow his example.

4. For a discussion of public participation in the financing of political parties, see *Reforming Electoral Democracy*, the report of the Royal Commission on Electoral Reform and Party Financing, Volume 1, Chapter 5, "Political Parties as Primary Political Organizations."

CHAPTER TEN   Can You Help Me Get Elected?

Some of the information in this chapter comes from the authors' interviews with John Rae, David MacNaughton, and Allan Gregg.

1. Betty Disero, a Liberal and a member of city council, was never a serious contender for the Toronto mayoralty in 1991. When she dropped out, her support went overwhelmingly to Rowlands. Susan Fish — a former city councillor, one-time Ontario cabinet minister, and a Red Tory — caused more concern. Initially, the Rowlands organizers, believing Fish was diverting votes from Jack Layton, encouraged her candidacy. Later, after Martin Goldfarb reported that, in fact, most Fish supporters favored June Rowlands as their second choice, prominent Rowlands backers pressured Fish to withdraw. She eventually did, although not soon enough to get her name off the November ballot. Fish's support went by a 2–1 margin

to Rowlands over Layton. Betty Disero, meanwhile, was re-elected as a councillor, only to have her election challenged in court on the ground that the money she had spent in her aborted mayoral bid pushed her over the spending limit allowed for a person running to be a councillor. The court later upheld her election.

2. Apparently uncomfortable with idea of having a professional organizer directing her mayoral campaign, Rowlands insisted on referring to Laschinger as her "general manager" rather than the customary "campaign manager." When the election was over, she sent him a note of thanks. It was a form letter addressed to "Dear Friend."

3. David MacDonald did win the Rosedale seat in 1988. He was not invited to join the cabinet.

CHAPTER ELEVEN So You Want To Be Leader
Observations on leadership candidates and campaigns in this chapter are drawn from a variety of sources, including the authors' interviews with Nancy McLean, John Rae, Senator Keith Davey, Paul Curley, John Crosbie, Larry Grossman, and Senator Finlay MacDonald.

1. John Sawatsky, *Mulroney: The Politics of Ambition*. See Chapter 16, "Aftermath."

2. Twenty-three leadership contests between 1967 and 1992 in Canada were decided by acclamation; twenty-two others drew only two candidates and were, therefore, decided by a single ballot.

CHAPTER TWELVE The Black Arts
Comments and observations in this chapter are drawn largely from the authors' interviews with Martin Goldfarb, Allan Gregg, Robin Sears, and Michael Adams.

1. Adams did not ask his computer to identify the one seat that the Conservatives would retain. It was in Quebec, however, and Adams suspects it was Charlevoix, held by Prime Minister Brian Mulroney.

2. Michael Adams anticipates that the vacuum created in the political system by the opting-out of men in the baby-boom generation

will be filled, in part, by women and candidates from ethnic groups. "We're going to move from men in their fifties to women and ethnic and racial minorities in their thirties and forties who are getting involved in public life," he says. "There's going to be . . . a demographic shift. We're going to see different colors of faces, different genders, different lifestyles, a very different group of people who are going to be the leaders in the future."

CHAPTER THIRTEEN   The Road to Reform

1. The Royal Commission on Electoral Reform and Party Financing outlines the history of direct democracy in Canada in its 1992 report, *Reforming Electoral Democracy*. See Volume 2, Chapter 9, "Direct Democracy in the Electoral Process."

2. Preston Manning, *The New Canada*, p. 326.

3. Ibid., pp. 325–26.

4. David Smith, quoted in the *Toronto Star*, April 8, 1992. Although the Liberals were the principal culprits in using ethnic voters to pack meetings in the 1988 election, they were not the only culprits. John Laschinger did not turn away the 150 Filipino-Canadians, few of whom spoke any English, who turned out to support his candidate, David MacDonald, for the Tory nomination in Toronto-Rosedale in 1988. It was never ascertained how many of these new Tories had heard of MacDonald before that evening.

5. See Lynda Erickson's paper, "Women and Candidacies for the House of Commons," published in *Women in Canadian Politics: Towards Equity in Representation*, ed. Kathy Megyery, Volume 6 of the research studies of the Royal Commission on Electoral Reform and Party Financing.

6. Since 1985, the Ontario Progressive Conservatives have operated what they call their WIN (for "Women in Nomination") program, which provides assistance, when funds are available, to women for brochures or other expenses in a nomination campaign. This assistance is typically in the $2,000-to-$4,000 range.

7. The royal commission explains its reasoning in Volume 1 of its

report, *Reforming Electoral Democracy*. See Chapter 5, "Political Parties as Primary Political Organizations."

8. For a fascinating account of the Mulroneys' adventures in home improvements, see Chapter 12, "Power Decorating," in Stevie Cameron's *Ottawa Inside Out.*

9. V.O. Key, *Public Opinion and American Democracy*, p. 8.

10. See Claire Hoy's *Margin of Error: Pollsters and the Manipulation of Canadian Politics*, Chapter 14, "Poll Abuse."

11. Theodore Roszak, *Where the Wasteland Ends: Politics and Transcendence in Post-Industrial Society*, p. 243.

CHAPTER FOURTEEN Back to the Future
Some of the thoughts in this chapter about the future of the Canadian political system came from the authors' interviews with Michael Adams, Gabor Apor, Julie Davis, Nancy McLean, Bill Knight, Hershell Ezrin, Allan Gregg, and Senator Finlay MacDonald.

1. Paul Saffo, quoted by Doug Underwood in "Reinventing the Media: The Newspapers' Identity Crisis," *Columbia Journalism Review*, March/April 1992, p. 25.

2. "Industry Image Study," by Walker Research & Analysis, Indianapolis, Indiana, 1990.

3. Jeffrey Abramson, "The New Media and the New Politics," in *The Aspen Institute Quarterly*, Spring 1990, p. 44.

4. John Naisbitt, *Megatrends: Ten New Directions Transforming Our Lives*, p. 53.

BIBLIOGRAPHY

Boyer, J. Patrick. *Money and Message: The Law Governing Election Financing, Advertising, Broadcasting and Campaigning in Canada.* Toronto: Butterworths, 1983.

Bruno, Jerry. *The Advance Man.* New York: William Morrow, 1971.

Cameron, Stevie. *Ottawa Inside Out: Power, Prestige and Scandal in the Nation's Capital.* Toronto: Key Porter Books, 1989.

Camp, Dalton. *Gentlemen, Players and Politicians.* Toronto: McClelland and Stewart, 1970.

Clarkson, Stephen, and Christina McCall. *Trudeau and Our Times: The Magnificent Obsession.* Toronto: McClelland and Stewart, 1990.

Davey, Keith. *The Rainmaker: A Passion for Politics.* Toronto: Stoddart, 1986.

Dobbin, Murray. *Preston Manning and the Reform Party.* Toronto: James Lorimer, 1991.

Fraser, Graham. *Playing for Keeps: The Making of the Prime Minister, 1988.* Toronto: McClelland and Stewart, 1989.

Gagnon, Georgette, and Dan Rath. *Not Without Cause: David Peterson's Fall from Grace.* Toronto: HarperCollins, 1991.

Goldfarb, Martin, and Thomas Axworthy. *Marching to a Different Drummer: An Essay on the Liberals and Conservatives in Convention.* Toronto: Stoddart, 1988.

Goodman, Eddie. *Life of the Party.* Toronto: Key Porter Books, 1988.

Gossage, Patrick. *Close to the Charisma: My Years Between the Press and Pierre Elliott Trudeau.* Toronto: McClelland and Stewart, 1986.

Hoy, Claire. *Margin of Error: Pollsters and the Manipulation of Canadian Politics.* Toronto: Key Porter Books, 1989.

Key, V.O. *Public Opinion and American Democracy.* New York: Knopf, 1965.

McCall-Newman, Christina. *Grits: An Intimate Portrait of the Liberal Party.* Toronto: Macmillan, 1982.

McGinniss, Joe. *The Selling of the President, 1968.* New York: Trident Press, 1969.

Manning, Preston. *The New Canada.* Toronto: Macmillan, 1992.

Martin, Patrick; Allan Gregg; and George Perlin. *Contenders: The Tory Quest for Power.* Toronto: Prentice-Hall, 1983.

Matthews, Christopher. *Hardball: How Politics Is Played — Told by One Who Knows the Game.* New York: Harper & Row, 1988.

Naisbitt, John. *Megatrends: Ten New Directions Transforming Our Lives.* New York: Warner Books, 1982.

Newman, Peter C. *Renegade in Power: The Diefenbaker Years.* Toronto: McClelland and Stewart, 1963.

Roszak, Theodore. *Where the Wasteland Ends: Politics and Transcendence in Post-Industrial Society.* New York: Doubleday, 1972.

Royal Commission on Electoral Reform and Party Financing. *Reforming Electoral Democracy,* 4 volumes. Ottawa: Minister of Supply and Services Canada, 1992.

Sawatsky, John. *Mulroney: The Politics of Ambition.* Toronto: Macfarlane Walter & Ross, 1991.

Sharpe, Sydney, and Don Braid. *Storming Babylon: Preston Manning and the Rise of the Reform Party.* Toronto: Key Porter Books, 1992.

Simon, Roger. *Road Show: In America, Anyone Can Become President. It's One of the Risks We Take.* New York: Farrar Straus Giroux, 1990.

Simpson, Jeffrey. *Discipline of Power: The Conservative Interlude and the Liberal Restoration.* Toronto: Personal Library, 1980.

Stevens, Geoffrey. *Stanfield.* Toronto: McClelland and Stewart, 1973.

Sullivan, Martin. *Mandate '68.* Toronto: Doubleday, 1968.

Wearing, Joseph. *The L-Shaped Party. The Liberal Party of Canada, 1958–1980.* Toronto: McGraw-Hill Ryerson, 1981.

INDEX